Making
Rocky Mountain
National Park

Making
Rocky Mountain
National Park

THE ENVIRONMENTAL HISTORY OF
AN AMERICAN TREASURE

Jerry J. Frank

 University Press of Kansas

Published by the University Press of Kansas (Lawrence, Kansas 66045), which was organized by the Kansas Board of Regents and is operated and funded by Emporia State University, Fort Hays State University, Kansas State University, Pittsburg State University, the University of Kansas, and Wichita State University

Library of Congress Cataloging-in-Publication Data

Frank, Jerry J.
Making Rocky Mountain National Park : the environmental history of an American treasure / Jerry J. Frank.
pages cm
ISBN 978-0-7006-1932-0 (hardback)
1. Rocky Mountain National Park (Colo.)—History. 2. Tourism—Environmental aspects—Colorado—Rocky Mountain National Park. 3. Nature—Effect of human beings on—Colorado—Rocky Mountain National Park. I. Title.
F782.R59F73 2013
978.8'69—dc23

2013021091

British Library Cataloguing in Publication Data is available.

Printed in the United States of America

10 9 8 7 6 5 4 3 2 1

For Jen and Ryan
My Everything

CONTENTS

ILLUSTRATIONS

Rifle. Rulison. Fruita. Cortez. Gustine. Grand Junction. Missoula. Moab. Colorado Springs. Gunnison. Ouray. Montrose. This is my American West—a list of the places that I have called home. Like everyone I know who has lived in the region—and many who have merely passed through it—the West is very much a part of who I am. This project has afforded me the opportunity to think about a remarkable western park and to understand it more thoroughly. The pages that follow represent my attempt to pass along some of what I have learned so that we all may understand Rocky Mountain National Park for what it is, what it is not, and what we have made it.

Millions of people visit Rocky Mountain every year. Despite the park's popularity and its rich past, historians have given it short shrift. In part, this book addresses that deficiency by offering a fresh look at how the park came to be and the complexities that make it such an engaging place.

More than a straightforward narrative of a single, albeit important, national park, I am interested in deeper questions that Rocky can answer about the modern American West. Thus, my primary focus is upon tourism and ecology—both powerful forces in the region—and how each has interacted with the nonhuman world in making and remaking Rocky Mountain National Park. We are often told that tourism provides western states an escape from the vagaries of extractive industry, just as we are often led to believe that the science of ecology is a force of restoration and regeneration. Both assumptions warrant much closer scrutiny than they have thus far received.

To gain a deeper understanding of national parks we must question other assumptions about them that have too long persisted. Parks are not, nor should we believe them to be, areas frozen in time and space. They are not slices of a perfect American past that the National Park Service has gallantly preserved, conserved, or protected. Rather, they are born of, and built upon, generations of dynamic environmental and cultural transformations. Parks are places the very existence of which begs constant interpretation and intervention. Viewing parks from this perspective enables us to understand—without pardoning—why the Park Service has managed them as it has, while also shining a ray of light on possible paths forward.

Understanding the past and future of Rocky Mountain National Park also requires that we integrate mountain lions, elk, deer, beaver, willow, trout, insects, as well as wind, soil erosion, and fire into our historical analysis. Knowing something about how fires burn, how seeds move, and how mountain pine beetles reproduce—and how humans have tried to make sense of it all—is central to coming to terms with the history of this place as well.

Like most historians, I am confined by the narrative form and bridled by the reader's willingness to read and a publisher's willingness to print. Thus, I have made several tough choices in how I framed and wrote this book. In that process, some things—even important things—have been left out. For example, there is no discussion of the Lawn Lake Flood, or the construction of the Alva B. Adams Tunnel. The omission of these and other topics should not be taken to mean that they are not worthy of time and consideration. They are. Perhaps other scholars will give them the coverage they deserve.

The reader may also find it odd—even disconcerting—that *Making Rocky Mountain National Park* contains not a single, solitary map. Like words, maps are powerful; they can and do reify those things that they depict. The act of mapping also often obscures more than the maps themselves reveal. How, for example, would one map a herd of elk, or mountain pine beetle outbreak, or a fire regime, all of which shift over short and long time scales? How would one map—without reinforcing all of the assumptions buried deep beneath the lines themselves—the park's outer boundary? Rather than compiling hundreds of pages of maps to honor the complexity of the historical and spatial processes at work, I will instead leave this important work to geographers.

Lastly, I hope that *Making Rocky Mountain National Park* will find its way into the backpacks and picnic baskets of park visitors. In a sense, this book is for and about them. All park visitors—past and present—are central characters in this history. What visitors see when they gaze upon this landscape, what they think they see, and what they want to see have all been powerful forces in creating Rocky Mountain National Park. It is a magnificent place made all the more beautiful if we understand the people, plants, animals, and ideas that have made it what it is.

Although my name appears on this book's cover, it is not mine alone. Over the past several years I have been humbled time and again by the gracious support of mentors, colleagues, friends, family, and complete strangers. I am honored to take this opportunity to offer my sincere gratitude to those who have made this book possible.

To begin, I could not have conjured a better mentor than Donald Worster. His work captured my imagination when I was in my early twenties, and I must admit that I am still under its spell. I have long marveled at his intellect, passion, ability to cut right to the heart of things, and his kind and generous soul. My work and my life are immeasurably richer for having worked so closely with him.

Byron Caminero-Santangelo, Karl Brooks, Gregory Cushman, Paul Kelton, and John Hausdoerffer all read versions of this manuscript and offered invaluable insights and advice. Timothy Silver and William Philpott served as anonymous reviewers, and I was struck by the time and attention that they gave to the project. The book is significantly better because of their insightful comments and cordial prodding. Maddalena Marinari, Shen Hou, Cheri Yost, Maple Taylor, Christy Briles, and Ann Leggett all reviewed various chapters of this book; I am grateful to them as well. I would also like to thank Dan Flores for introducing me to the study of parks and place, and for fostering my passion for both.

Museum curators Tim Burchett and Mariah Robertson patiently guided me through the archives at Rocky Mountain National Park. I also had the great good fortune of working the better part of a summer with Sybil Barnes, whose expertise in navigating the park's library was matched only by her kind spirit. Archives specialist Catherine Kisluk embodies the very best of the National Park Service, and I was continually impressed by her knowledge, professionalism, and generosity. Chris Kennedy, Junelle Pringle, Barbara James, Nate Williamson, and Kathryn Barth all shared with me portions of their private collections, and Paula and Edward Brown took time out of their busy schedules to collect research materials when I was not able to do it myself.

I was fortunate to receive financial support from the Rocky Mountain Nature Association, the National Park Service, and the Research Council at the University of Missouri. Their generosity makes projects like this possible, and we should support them every way we can.

My colleagues in the Department of History at the University of Missouri and our talented Melinda Lockwood have also offered steady support and counsel throughout this process. Likewise, Ranjit Arab, Fred Woodward, and the staff at the University Press of Kansas have been incredibly helpful, patient, and professional, and I owe them all a great deal for their work on my behalf.

Martin and DeEtta Frank, Paula and Edward Brown, and Maple Taylor have been steadfast supporters of my work all along. Last, no person has given more to me and this project than my amazing wife, Jennifer. She has patiently plowed every acre of this with me, and I could not have done it without her love, keen editorial eye, kindness, and friendship.

Jerry J. Frank
Columbia, Missouri, April 2013

*Making
Rocky Mountain
National Park*

INTRODUCTION

What exactly *are* national parks? The question is so obvious that it often goes unasked and unanswered. To the millions upon millions of people who visit them, parks float above time and culture, forever disconnected from the profane world that bustles beyond their borders. The language that we use to discuss them—*preservation, conservation, nature, wilderness*—reveals what we think parks are and what they should be. These words tell stories. They tell us that parks were not "built," at least not in the sense that a mine or a city is built. Rather, they deny any acts of construction at all. Parks simply exist.

We can all agree that parks entailed the building of roads, bridges, and visitor centers, but we assume that the rest of parks—their streams, forests, soils, animals, insects—have been protected in such a way that the rest of Yellowstone, or Yosemite, or Rocky Mountain is pretty much the way it has always been.[1] We do not think of parks as places imbued with culture and history but rather as timeless spaces that have been spared the heavy hand of change altogether. They are, in other words, natural. This is why we love them. This is why we seek them. This is why we fight for them.

But parks are more interesting, more complicated, and more contested than all of that. They are, in fact, some of the most culturally rich places in the world. Since the creation of our first national park in 1872, Americans have been engaged in a fascinating discourse about nature, change, history, and humans through the parks themselves. In incredible ways, national parks offer primary sources that reveal ever-shifting ideas about the natural world and the human place within it. As such, they can be "read" like George Washington's letters or the Pumpkin Papers. To read our national parks we must start by questioning nearly everything we see, everything we hear, and everything we smell as we pass through them. If we do this, a new and exciting understanding of the parks will emerge. No longer are they musty museums frozen in time and space; they come alive as we behold the history, the ideologies, the conflicts, and the ironies that make them dynamic and fascinating places.

Reading parks is not as easy as one might imagine. Generations of advertising and park management have conditioned many of us to expect to see nature in parks, and so we often see what we seek. But this raises still more questions. What *is* nature? To the National Park Service (NPS) and the majority of the traveling public, nature, wilderness, and parks all imply the absence of humans and human history.[2] Accordingly, most elements of parks that speak to human influence have been hidden, or softened, to the point where they are difficult to see. It has meant that parks had to be managed, sometimes intensively so, but in ways that often concealed the fact that any action was being taken at all lest the façade of the natural park be shattered. The razing of historic structures, the use of naturalized building materials along roads and trails, the removal of stumpage and dead and dying trees, and the furtive killing of thousands of elk all speak to this impulse.

The need to present the "natural" has brought about more significant, and less perceptible, changes as well. Although we would not know it by simply looking—which is, of course, the point—the trail that winds along a rushing stream, the trout that swim in that stream, and the stately trees that shade our campsites are also products of humans and our ideas interacting with the nonhuman world. Even more difficult to apprehend are those things that are no longer present. The predators that do not live in the park, the native fish that do not swim in its waters, the fires that have not burned its forests, the cabins and fences and sawmills and roads that have been erased from the landscape, and the aspen and willow that do not grow in its meadows are all connected to humans and our history, too.

The pages that follow offer insight into the very human history of Rocky Mountain National Park (RMNP). But it is not a history that has unfolded across a passive natural stage. In fact, the natural processes of this place are a crucial component of its history. At nearly every turn the NPS found itself face to face with a natural world that was difficult to anticipate and impossible to control. For more than a century elk, fish, mountain lions, beaver, aspen, lodgepole pine, fire, insects, soil, snow, and even wind have been powerful historical agents of change in Rocky Mountain National Park.

Within this broader natural context, two forces have been primarily responsible for giving shape to the park's history. In this regard the culture of tourism has been of central importance. As an industry, tourism is based upon the need to entice potential travelers. Easy access, pristine forests, majestic peaks, great fishing, ample wildlife, and wonderful skiing were part and parcel of promotional activities intended to do just this.[3]

In interesting ways, the promotional materials of local and regional boosters, businesses, corporations, and the NPS effectively created a Rocky Mountain National Park in the minds of travelers well before they even arrived.[4] When visitors' experiences met their expectations, they often wrote letters of thanks to the Park Service for a job well done. When their experiences did not meet expectations—when the roads were too rough, or when the fishing was poor, or when large charismatic animals were not readily visible from the roadside—visitors often wrote excoriating letters to their congressmen and others chiding the NPS for doing a poor job. To the Park Service, an agency that long sought to bolster its institutional power and stability, keeping visitors satisfied was a serious matter.[5]

The NPS has not acted alone in its efforts to attract visitors. Many cities, counties, and states have embraced tourism and recreation as sustainable alternatives to traditional extractive industries such as timber, mining, oil, and gas. And in the American West tourism and recreation have become very big business. In 2011 tourism generated $5.3 billion in economic activity in Colorado alone. If we add to those figures the $1.46 billion that recreation-related activities garnered, and the $1.4 billion spent by "day-trippers" in the state, the economic impact of such activities is stunning.[6] Contrary to popular belief, however, tourism and recreation are far from environmentally benign. Something as simple as watching wildlife, taking a stroll along a tree-lined trail, catching a beautiful trout, skiing down a snow-covered mountain, or going for an afternoon drive to marvel at the fall colors can unleash torrents of environmental change. If western states continue to fight for every tourist dollar—if they continue to sell the natural West to those who seek respite, relaxation, and entertainment in the out-of-doors—we would do well to know something more about the powerful forces that shape tourism, just as we would be well served to learn the manifold ways it changes anything it touches.

During the earliest history of the park, managing solely for the pleasure of tourists posed few problems. Over time, however, a competing vision of what the park was and what it should be challenged the culture of tourism that had so long reigned supreme. The science and culture of ecology came to Rocky in fits and starts, but they offered visitors and managers a new and different way of imagining the park that did not sit comfortably with a management paradigm so firmly rooted in recreation, aesthetics, and comfort.[7] Making matters all the more complicated, ecology arrived in Rocky well after the culture of tourism was entrenched and had reshaped so much of the park in ways that ecologists often saw as unnatural or damaging.[8] Like tourism, ecology has been dynamic and unpredictable. For decades, it has continually asked new questions, employed novel research techniques, and reached fresh conclusions, all of which manifest still newer ways of seeing this place. A good deal of the park's history can be understood as a contest between the fluid forces of tourism and ecology, each vying to re-create the park in its own likeness.

The parkscape bears witness to these competing ideas as Rocky became— like so much of America—subdivided.[9] Along the park's roads—the *front-country*—the culture of tourism that esteems breathtaking views, comfort, and convenience dominates. In the more distant reaches of the park—the *backcountry*—ecologically based values have come to rule. The tensions between tourism and ecology have also shaped aquatic and riparian areas as well as the park's hundreds of miles of trails. Thus, Rocky Mountain National Park is not one place, but many.

At first glance, tourism and ecology seem very different. In some ways they are. However, both spring from the human impulse to understand, explain, and imbue our surroundings with meaning. In this light, the promotional literature of the Union Pacific Railroad (UP) and the ecological studies of the park's flora and fauna represent attempts to create a culturally significant and intelligible place.[10] Both offered, and both continue to offer, lenses through which we view the park. They have also brought widespread change to Rocky, yet neither has cut the Gordian knot that binds human and natural history.

To understand how national parks have been created and re-created over time, to see the manifold ways they preserve and protect environmental ideologies just as they preserve trees and elk, we need a history that unites the dynamic cultures of tourism and ecology while anchoring each within a specific place. To accomplish this, the following begins with the rise of tourism in Colorado and the founding of its crown jewel, then focuses on driving, hiking, horseback riding, wildlife viewing, fishing, and skiing in Rocky Mountain National Park. Each of these activities has deep cultural roots that stretch far beyond the park; each has impacted the park's flora and fauna, often bringing widespread degradation; and each has been challenged by the rise of ecology and its unique way of understanding the world—all of which has brought still more change to Rocky.

Making Rocky Mountain National Park does not offer a tale of the fall of nature or an "unnatural" history of destruction and defilement.[11] The park's fauna, flora, water, and mountains are no less natural today than they were a century ago. They only appear to be so if we accept, at face value, definitions of "nature" and "parks" that exclude humans and human history. So much of Rocky Mountain National Park is a product of people imagining a space free from the human stain and then setting out to make that place a reality. The irony is difficult to escape. Making a *natural* park—one interlaced with roads and trails; one where fire and bark beetles were once banished but are now let in through the back door; one where the fisherman's whim has initiated an ongoing ecological revolution in which scientists themselves have been unwitting revolutionaries; one where massive elk herds are a great boon *and* a symbol of tragic mismanagement; one where unwanted aspects of the landscape such as old roads, cabins, and ski resorts that were once allowed have been literally erased—has very often pivoted on how the cultures of tourism and ecology see the park itself.

If, however, we grapple with the place of humans within nature—within *all* of nature—then we can no longer understand overgrazed meadows or soil erosion as immoral and unnatural aberrations. Yet we must still confront all of the ways that humans have impacted the park's ecosystems, some of which are in grave danger because of human beliefs and desires. But removing ourselves from the equation—seeing nature only in those places where we are not—makes this task impossible. This is one of America's greatest challenges in coming to terms with what national parks are and what they represent. Parks do not simply exist. Rather, they are in a constant state of creation and re-creation as our ideas, hopes, and dreams interact with dynamic and powerful environments.

Dedication of Rocky Mountain National Park, September 4, 1915. Courtesy of the National Archives, College Park, MD.

Making a National Park

It must have been a glorious day. Good cheer, good food, and plenty of congratulations for a job well done. On September 4, 1915, hundreds of Colorado residents and other honored guests gathered at the newly created Rocky Mountain National Park to offer thanks to its supporters and to enjoy the fruits of their labor. The day's events included coffee at noon followed promptly by the fine musical stylings of The Fort Collins Band. With bellies full of coffee and hearts filled with patriotic songs, luminaries including Enos Mills; Stephen T. Mather; Governor George Carlson; Mrs. John D. Sherman, president of the Conservation Department of the General Federation of Women's Clubs; and F. O. Stanley, inventor of the Stanley Steamer vehicles and a local hotel owner, gave brief speeches praising the new park.[1] A great day, indeed.

Like so many national parks, Rocky's history speaks to diverse interests that coalesced around a single idea at a single moment in time. Local naturalist Enos Mills spread the gospel of conservation and raised the profile of the Estes Park region, where he owned and operated an inn. The Colorado Mountain Club (CMC) also played a central role. Founded in 1912, the CMC was a staunch supporter of the national park idea, and its first president, James Grafton Rogers, deserves primary credit for crafting the parks bill that President Wilson eventually signed.

If we look deeper still, we see that the creation of RMNP was also a key element of a broader push to create the National Park Service itself. Between 1906 and 1913 Americans across the country joined

John Muir and the Sierra Club in the fight to prevent the Hetch-Hetchy Dam from being built in Yosemite National Park.[2] Debates about the potential national park in Colorado must be understood within this context. Time and again, influential men like landscape architect Mark Daniels and the president of the American Civic Association, J. Horace McFarland, lent their support to the creation of Rocky not because it held unique scenic wonders. Rather, these men saw the opportunity to build a broader constituency, which would bolster support for a national parks agency to better protect and manage America's growing constellation of parks.

Last, and perhaps most important, the elite businessmen of Denver were at the center of it all. Like McFarland and Daniels, businessmen agreed that a park nestled at the foot of Longs Peak was attractive because it held the promise of drawing tourists and generating revenue for the state and for Estes Park.[3] Tourism—and its ideologies, assumptions, and power to transform those places in which it predominates—was thus woven into the fabric of Rocky from its very earliest days.

Growing Denver

Settled as a series of isolated gold camps in the late 1850s, east-central Colorado was a rough place. By the late 1860s some twenty-seven freighting firms stretched across the Midwest, turning Denver into a sort of storage bin for westward-bound goods and eastward-bound natural resources. In 1870, the completion of the Denver Pacific Railroad and the Kansas Pacific Railroad linked Denver to Cheyenne, Kansas City, and St. Louis, thereby making it easier to move resources from Denver's hinterlands to the city itself, and then to faraway urban centers. These rails and roads facilitated the flow of people, information, and capital to and from eastern cities. The influx of capital, feeding off of and into the budding rail system, created an interconnected web of mines, smelters, and supporting industries, which brought alternating cycles of economic prosperity and desperation to the region.[4]

Over the course of a few decades, the flow of goods, money, and people drastically altered Colorado's leading city. From a population of about 4,000 in 1870, Denver grew to some 130,000 residents by 1900 and to more than 250,000 by 1920. Gone for good were the dusty mining shacks and musty canvas tents that once characterized the city. By 1920 Denver claimed about one-fourth of the state's total population and "was unchallenged in its urban dominance . . . across the interior of the American West." It had achieved the same sort of market gravitational pull[5] of Chicago, making it a natural location for "eastern capitalists and nearby mining magnates to locate their offices and investment." By the turn of the twentieth century it had become the unchallenged "business center of the state."[6]

Coinciding with Denver's demographic and economic growth were significant changes in its urban geography. The city grew more sophisticated as gas lamps and finely crafted buildings, such as the Tabor Opera House and Windsor Hotel, popped up around town. Key to the growth of Denver was a "close and profitable working relationship between the city's real estate developers and those who invested in and promoted the city's expanding street and cable car systems." Together, those interests altered the shape, size, and function of Denver, all while making tidy profits for themselves.[7]

Americans had long believed that the cleansing air, crisp blue skies, and sulfurous bubbling hot springs of the Rocky Mountains provided cures for a wide variety of physical ailments. By the 1880s, Colorado boosters hailed the state as a natural sanitarium for those suffering from lung disorders. Not only could a stint in the Rockies combat tuberculosis; it also promised to "'broaden the chest,'" foster a "'cheerfulness and contented frame of mind,'" and perhaps even ease the stress "'on the class of overworked brains, which, in the intensity of political, professional and business life is quite numerous nowadays.'"[8] Although Colorado Springs and Glenwood Springs surpassed Denver as Meccas for the unwell, the capital city nonetheless benefited mightily from the unhealthy multitudes seeking relief.

As towns and cities across Colorado sought to capitalize on their cool, clean air by luring the unhealthy from across the nation, they also actively attracted healthy and wealthy patrons. Gold, businessmen found, was often easier to dislodge from the tourist's pocket than from the stubborn quartz of the nearby hills. But the trip across the Great Plains in a Pullman Palace car was a pricey undertaking, out of reach for the commoner. This began changing, however, with the calamitous economic decline of 1893. Especially hard hit by the downturn were Colorado's silver mines and the railroads that fed them. Seeking to supplement their dwindling revenues, several railroads began offering reduced rates while ramping up advertising campaigns. The Denver & Rio Grande, for example, marketed an affordable four-day, thousand-mile tour through the most breathtaking portions of the Rockies for just $28.[9] Adding incentive for railroads to continue reduced rates were the increasing numbers of the middle class, who craved affordable travel and adventure in the American West.[10]

In time, the nascent middle class sought access to and through the West by way of automobile. As with rail travel, the automobile initially provided transport only for the wealthy. In 1908, however, the Ford Motor Company introduced its $850 Model T. Over the next couple of years Ford continued to streamline production techniques, and by 1914 the company could produce one car every ninety minutes and sold more than 250,000 in that year alone.[11] Eager to attract and accommodate the growing number of automobile tourists, citizens of Denver founded the Colorado Automobile Club in 1902, the Rocky Mountain Highway Association in 1908, and the Colorado Highway Commission in 1909, all of which pushed for more and better roads in the state.[12] Commercial interests in the area also actively sought to bolster the city's appeal by building a system of roads and parks to better serve and attract the driving public.

Such was the character of Colorado and its leading city on the eve of the creation of Rocky Mountain National Park. This park, as we shall see, required more than any single devoted and impassioned individual; it required a city with deep pockets and political clout, the very name of which had the power to conjure evocative images in the minds of American tourists. Indeed, this park required city folk with money to spend and a desire to spend it in the wilds of Colorado.

Muir of the Rockies

In 1884, the state of Colorado not yet a decade old, fourteen-year-old Enos Mills of Linn County, Kansas, journeyed westward. Upon arriving at Estes Park, a hamlet of only 150 residents, the plucky young man worked for two years building a "little log cabin on the slope of Longs Peak," where he lived much of his adult life. Often, when the weather turned cold or work became scarce, the untethered Mills packed his scant belongings and tramped about the West, where he "spent great days with the old prospector, the trapper, the capable cowboy and the Indian."[13] More often than not, Mills worked at least part of the year as a miner in Butte, Montana, or in Cripple Creek or

Ward, Colorado.[14] His mining experiences, which were "full of red blood, excitement and real characters from every mining region of the earth," also led to a chance meeting with the naturalist John Muir.[15]

After underground fires at Butte's Anaconda Mine halted production in the fall of 1889, the nineteen-year-old Mills set out for San Francisco.[16] By Mills's recollection, he was walking aimlessly across a San Francisco beach in December 1889 when he saw an older man surrounded by an interested crowd. As he drew near, the young Mills realized that "the small gray bearded little man," John Muir, was intensely describing the inner workings of the plant and animal world. Fascinated as much by the speaker as the message, Mills stuck around and eventually introduced himself to Muir. The two then embarked upon a lengthy walk through the Golden Gate Park.[17] Mills had met his idol.

The chance meeting between Mills and the Apostle of Nature seems to have been a life-changing event for the young man. In Muir he found a father figure, a mentor, and an example of how to gain and sharpen his own public image later in life. Muir apparently urged Mills to learn as much about the natural world as possible while honing his literary skills. Following that advice, Mills spent a semester at Heald's Business College in San Francisco, then set out to see "some of the wilder sections of America," including Yosemite, Kings Canyon, and portions of Alaska.[18]

After his contact with Muir, Mills continued working in mines across the West while endeavoring to learn more about the natural world. By 1902 he had traveled across much of Europe, gaining a new appreciation for the potential of tourism, all while saving enough money to purchase Longs Peak House from his mother's brother, Carlyle Lamb. After changing its name to Longs Peak Inn in 1904, Mills intensified his efforts to refine his skills as a nature guide, writer, and speaker—all of which served nicely to draw guests to his rustic wayside inn.[19]

Through a combination of self-promotion, determination, and persistence, Mills had made himself familiar to many important people by 1907. Among those acquainted with his reputation as a public speaker and nature writer were Chief Forester Gifford Pinchot and President Theodore Roosevelt. Seeing in Mills a man who might work well to publicize conservation efforts, Pinchot offered, and Mills accepted, appointment as an official lecturer for the United States Forest Service (USFS) in 1907.

For nearly two years the relationship between Mills, Pinchot, and the Forest Service benefited all parties. Mills received a steady wage, the opportunity to promote the ideals of the Forest Service, and notoriety, all the while dropping hints to audiences that the Longs Peak region offered almost unparalleled opportunities to hear the call of the wild.[20] For their part, Pinchot and the Forest Service found a tireless and effective speaker willing to travel untold miles to spread the gospel of conservation. Speaking to his passion and drive, Mills conducted perhaps 200 presentations between October 1908 and May 1909 as he traveled to dozens of states. His message, varying somewhat according to the audience, emphasized the importance of science, education, and government regulation in maintaining healthy forests for future generations.[21]

By April 1909, Pinchot and the Forest Service no longer required Mills's services. He had broadcast Pinchot's brand of conservation across the nation, giving a friendly, weather-worn face to the Chief Forester's environmental policy. In his last lecture for the Forest Service, which he delivered on April 28, 1909, Mills said nothing derogatory about either Pinchot or the Forest Service. Both of them, however, he would later venomously attack.[22]

Backbone of the Country

In September 1909, the Estes Park Improvement Association was searching for ways to bolster tourism in its area. To aid in the investigation, it called upon U.S. Forester Herbert N. Wheeler of the Forest Service to offer an opinion. Wheeler proposed the creation of a game preserve, which would improve and increase wildlife in the area and thereby, he thought, strengthen Estes Park's appeal to cash-laden tourists. The Estes Park Improvement Association thought Wheeler's idea was a good one, and a few days later Mills broadened Wheeler's plan by calling instead for the creation of Estes National Park. Agreeing that a national park would better serve to make the Estes Park region more popular and profitable, the association quickly threw its support behind Mills's idea.[23]

With a national park plan stirring in his heart and mind Mills worked to muster as much public support as possible. In this endeavor, his relationship with J. Horace McFarland, president of the American Civic Association and devoted preservationist, was of crucial importance. From 1910 to 1915 McFarland proved to be a steadfast and loyal supporter, more than willing to use his strong public voice and deep political connections to help ensure creation of the park. Although the relationship with Mills later soured, McFarland wrote Mills often, offering moral and political support while attempting to stay Mills's frequent public and private tirades against all those who showed even the slightest disagreement with his vision.

McFarland was clearly interested in protecting worthy "pleasure grounds" for future generations of Americans. He wrote of nature's ability to revive the spirit and purify the mind, but he was also well aware of the broader import of a park at Estes. In a letter to Secretary of the Interior Richard Ballinger in 1910, for example, McFarland anticipated a crucial chord in the movement's eventual success: "Having gone directly from Estes Park to Yellowstone National Park," he stated, "I am in a position to say that while it in no sense compares with the Yellowstone in respect of natural wonders, it does compare most favorable [sic] in respect of its availability as a great accessible and beneficent pleasure ground." At the time there was "no available national park in the large sense east of the Yellowstone," and Estes Park already had a reputation as a summer resort within easy reach of Denver.[24] By McFarland's reckoning, a national park near Estes was needed not because of its inherent wilderness or aesthetic values but rather because of its prime location and potential as a resort for traveling Americans. We must remember, however, that even as McFarland was midwifing the creation of RMNP, he was actively involved in protecting Hetch-Hetchy and Niagara Falls, as well as creating an independent National Park Service.[25] Viewed in this context, Rocky Mountain National Park takes on broader significance.

Mills and McFarland were not alone in recognizing the potential of a park in the region. In December 1910, the Denver Chamber of Commerce gave its wholehearted endorsement to the plan and formed a national park committee to champion the cause.[26] Led by Frederick Ross, a local real estate mogul, the Denver Chamber was key to the final passage of the bill. Shortly after the formation of the Chamber's national park committee, another wing of the same group threw its support behind the plan. Representing "some two hundred . . . retail firms of the City of Denver," the Retail Association of the Denver Chamber "emphatically urge[d] that Estes Park be thus set aside" as a national park.[27] To these men, a park at Estes "would be of incalculable benefit to the business interests of the city and state, besides assuring the control and preservation of one of the most beautiful spots in the world."[28] Not to be left out, the Denver Real Estate Exchange also heartily endorsed the idea.[29]

As details of the proponents' plan crystallized, so did opposition. Initially, Boulder County and Grand County—both of which stood to lose a large section of territory if the initial proposal went through—opposed the plan. At the core of their opposition was the belief that a park threatened "many thousands of acres of undeveloped agricultural land" and several active mining projects, including the "finest grade of Gilsonite known." Furthermore, county commissioners in Grand County "confidently believed" that "every one familiar with this territory" knew "that it is liable at any time to become one of the greatest mining Districts yet known."[30] Echoing similar concerns, the Boulder County Metal Mining Association objected to taking "119 square miles of the 440 square miles of our mountain and mineral bearing area . . . and making a play-ground . . . out of what we believe will become one of our most highly productive mineral sections in the near future."[31]

By the summer of 1911, several concerned citizens had banded together under the auspices of the Front Range Settlers' League (FRSL) to oppose the creation of the park. Comprising citizens of Estes Park as well as neighbors, relatives, former employees of Mills, among others, the FRSL fought tooth and nail, writing sheaves of opposition letters to state and federal politicians, Department of Interior administrators, and two sitting presidents. Although the reasons for this opposition were many, a few chief complaints surfaced time and again. Mills, they charged, was not only a man of questionable character (they claimed that he had earlier been convicted of assault and perjury); worse, he was "not sincere in his pretended love of nature." According to the FRSL, Mills was interested in little more than "making a nature faking shrine out of his summer hotel." It also claimed that many of his "hair-raising personal reminiscences" were written while "destroying, pioneer fashion, the scenic beauty about him by cutting the finest trees and otherwise using the best of everything in the public domain."[32] Lastly, members of the FRSL believed the land in question to be "imperishable" and thought that the U.S. Forest Service was best suited to manage the area.[33]

The complaints from this organization are significant for many reasons. In addition to raising questions about the Muir of the Rockies himself—insight we often do not see in the historical record—the FRSL's complaints reveal the friction generated as the economic base of the Estes Park area moved more firmly toward tourism and recreation. As the FRSL often pointed out, a national park at Estes did not mean the end of economic development. Rather, they feared that such a shift would come at the expense of traditional resource extraction. On that count, they were right.

The last two months of 1911 were crucial for the national park. After writing numerous cordial but insistent letters, the Denver Chamber of Commerce and the Denver Real Estate Exchange were finally reaching and convincing the right people in Washington.[34] Central to their message was the claim that all they needed to make the park a success was "the proper sort of publicity, coming from reliable sources to attract the tourist."[35] Soon, the Department of the Interior awakened to their case, concluding that "apparently there will be a strong effort made by the people interested in this proposed park to have it created during the coming session of Congress, and we had probably just as well prepare therefore." Accordingly, Commissioner of the General Land Office George A. Ward requested that a map of the area be prepared.[36] The following day, the commissioner's order was forwarded to the General Land Office, along with a letter from the Denver Chamber claiming that "all of the best and most influential citizens of our state are heartily in favor of the park."[37] It is worth pointing out that the Department of the Interior and the General Land Office eventually sent Chief Geographer Robert Marshall to prepare the crucial map because they heard, understood, and agreed with the economic argument of Denver's business class and McFarland's broader political appeal.[38]

As word got out that Marshall would soon visit the area, those opposing the plan redoubled their efforts. Senator Simon Guggenheim, Republican of Colorado, cautioned Secretary of the Interior Walter Fisher about the park proposal. Guggenheim had "received a number of letters and telegrams from Colorado protesting against the establishment of Estes Park as a National Park." He also believed that much "of the land said to be included in the contemplated change is mineral land" upon which "extensive mining operations have been conducted in the territory for many years." Speaking on behalf of Grand County and Boulder County, the Metal Mining Association, and many members of the FRSL, Guggenheim also "feared that such a proclamation or order would work irreparable injury to the mining industry, as well as to the agricultural settlement of the country."[39]

Much to the chagrin of those laboring to stem the tide of park support, the formation of the Colorado Mountain Club in April 1912 heralded yet another major victory for park supporters. The organization, whose founding members dedicated themselves to raising local awareness and support for a park in Colorado's Rocky Mountains, also played an important part in the political process of its creation. Almost immediately, the club began an active publicity campaign.

Perhaps just as important as the club's community activism was the fact that it boasted some well-connected members, including "a young lawyer named Morrison Shafroth whose father [John] was a leading Democratic senator in the Wilson administration and who was ready to travel to Washington with boxes of lantern slides and portfolios of photographs" to sell the park idea.[40] Early leadership of the organization fell to James Grafton Rogers, a handsome young attorney whose legal and political acumen was of incalculable benefit to the cause of park creation. Not only would Rogers craft and redraft numerous iterations of park proposals, but he also understood the value of working with—not against—interested parties.

As Chief Geographer Marshall's visit drew nearer, the Denver Chamber, Enos Mills, and the Front Range Settler's League each insisted that he meet, stay, and tour the area with them. Realizing the potential volatility of accepting one offer over any other, especially prior to completing his surveys, Marshall wisely demurred.[41] As park supporters had hoped, Marshall's visit was a boon to their efforts. After making the surveys, Marshall listened, in turn, to the concerns of the FRSL, Mills, Colorado Senator John Shafroth, Governor-elect Elias Ammons, Frederick Ross, and former Colorado Senator Thomas M. Patterson. To Marshall, the crux of the opposition's argument lay less with the creation of the park and more with concerns over its size. In an early effort to quiet the opposition, he proposed boundaries that encompassed far less land compared to some initial suggestions, omitting as many private landholdings as possible without violating the integrity of the park.

Park supporters later read with delight Marshall's official report, which claimed that, although there were no "commanding natural feature[s]" as was the case in other national parks, the "region as a whole is as beautiful as any to be found in the United States, or, indeed in the world." And even though Marshall highlighted the area's beauty, he found it of secondary importance to what was "perhaps the most attractive feature of the plan to create this park . . . from both the National and State standpoints," which was the "accessibility of the area." Apparently won over by the Denver Chamber of Commerce and J. Horace McFarland, Marshall echoed their refrain that "Estes Park can be reached from Chicago in about 30 hours and from Denver by automobile in about 3 hours." Moreover, the effusive Marshall believed that because Denver was "the center of practically all the railroad systems west of the Mississippi River, the number of visitors that may be expected annually in the proposed park will add enormous revenues to the State of Colorado and will make this one of its most productive sections."[42] Making the park idea even more palatable was the paucity of other marketable commodities in the area. Although there were sweeping vistas "spread[ing] before the eye a gorgeous assemblage of wonderful mountain sculpture[s]," the proposed park contained "little merchantable timber" and "no well-developed mines." Thus, the arguments that the park would forever "sew up" valuable resources were less than persuasive.[43]

From a purely business standpoint the Estes Park region had many things going for it. These included a solid reputation as a vacation destination, a potentially profitable location mere hours from the Queen City of the Plains, and relatively few usable natural resources. Still, the entire proposal lacked something. Where, actually, was Estes Park? Did "Estes National Park" have the same cachet as, say, the Grand Canyon or the Grand Tetons, which sent the mind along fantastic journeys to faraway places? Realizing this deficiency, Marshall proposed changing the park's name to something more evocative and marketable. By his reckoning, this national park "should bear a name of broader significance. This striking section of the Rocky Mountains—the backbone of the country," should be named Rocky Mountain National Park.[44] And so it would be.

On the heels of Marshall's visit, and upon his recommendation, the Denver Chamber of Commerce sought someone to draft the designating legislation. To Marshall and the Denver Chamber, the CMC's president, James Grafton Rogers, seemed the perfect candidate. This young attorney, a Yale graduate in private practice in Denver, was not only enthusiastic, but also a skilled negotiator and well connected. Rogers was willing to provide services and began collecting and synthesizing the legal details required to craft the bill.[45] Over the next three years, he patiently shaped a bill with language that satisfied the varying demands of most parties.

Rogers's first bill was introduced in the 62nd Congress in February 1913 as "An Act to Establish Rocky Mountain National Park" (Senate Bill 8403 and House Resolution 28649). Much to his dismay, it made little progress. Undeterred, he sought to isolate and to negotiate with those who opposed it. Much of the debate lay with Section 2, which protected private inholdings, reserved water rights to the State of Colorado, and preserved limited opportunity for mineral exploration within the proposed park. There was concern in Washington and in the Centennial State, however, that such provisions might not meet the standard of protection required for a national park.[46] In his defense, Rogers explained that he hoped that the section would "still local opposition in Colorado" and that it was "not really of very much importance." Candidly, Rogers admitted that he "desired to get a bill through, even if it contain[ed] some awkward minor clauses. When the wedge is once started," he added, "no one will be readier than I to urge the most complete restrictions in the park."[47]

By October 1913, after conferences with the Denver Chamber of Commerce, Denver Real Estate Exchange, Governor Ammons, Senator Patterson, and the joint committee of the Denver Chamber of Commerce[48] as well as local mining, grazing, and timber interests, Rogers had a revision in hand that he hoped addressed the most pressing points of contention.[49] His hard work began to pay dividends in the summer of 1914 when Colorado Senator Charles Thomas introduced S 6007 and U.S. Representative Edward Taylor of Colorado introduced HR 17614. As passage of a bill seemed within reach, opposition—from both familiar and surprising corners—emerged.

Although he had never marshaled any evidence to support his claim that the USFS opposed the park outright, and though he received several letters stating USFS support, Mills was deeply suspicious of the Forest Service and most of its champions. And much to Mills's chagrin, Rogers had been holding conferences with the Forest Service to work out an equitable (and passable) proposal. By 1914 Mills began suspecting that Rogers's intentions were also less than pure. In a personal letter to Rogers, Mills fumed that he could no "longer remain silent while the President of the Colorado Mountain Club exhibits the Forest Service on one shoulder and the Park on the other." Although Mills rightly claimed that the "overwhelming majority of the Colorado Mountain Club desire to see the Rocky Mountain National Park established," he contended that Rogers had not "given adequate expression to this opinion." Mills went on to demand that Rogers cease "further conniving with the Forest Service in this connection." Mills closed by stating that his letter represented "a last effort to arouse you with the hope that you will see your way clear to frankly cooperate with us in securing the Rocky Mountain National Park."[50]

Although Mills's tirade doubtless set Rogers on his heels, the last-ditch effort of the Front Range Settlers' League to scuttle the bill came as no surprise at all. Grasping at straws, the FRSL claimed that a new park would cost the federal government twice as much to administer as the Forest Service was currently spending there. Moreover, the park would be only a "great advertisement," drawing tens of thousands of visitors from places far and near at taxpayers' expense. To them, the proposed park was little more than a "selfish scheme concocted for the benefit of certain parties, in which it is proposed that Uncle Sam shall act as an advertising and press agent."[51]

Whereas the FRSL cast the bill as an economic burden to federal government, officials within the Department of Interior saw things otherwise. Mark Daniels, who was Interior's general superintendent of Yosemite National Park and landscape engineer for the NPS, found in the pleas of the FRSL "not a single good argument." Moreover, Daniels contended that Rocky Mountain National Park need not in any way create an extra charge upon the federal government. If the parks were "administered along the lines now being outlined," he argued, "they will produce revenue rather than be a charge upon the Government."[52] At a time when many people—both within and without the Department of Interior—were working to create a separate and self-sustaining National Park Service, Rocky Mountain National Park took on new significance. What better way to bolster the campaign to create the National Park Service than with a park that had the potential to draw 100,000 or more tourists annually?[53]

As the cold winter winds swirled briskly around the nation's capital in January 1915, passage was at hand. Representative Edward Taylor of Colorado, standing proudly before Congress on January 18, 1915, proclaimed that it was through the good works of himself, Senator Thomas, Frederick Ross of the Denver Chamber of Commerce, the Denver Real Estate Exchange, and a handful of other interested politicians that Rocky Mountain National Park had congressional approval. Taylor was quick to point out the physical beauty of the area: more than sixty peaks above 12,000 feet, a "thousand varieties of wildflowers," and countless other interesting life-forms. It was true, he admitted, that Estes Park region already attracted some 10,000 automobiles annually from outside the state, but if a national park were created there it could, he imagined, pull in more than 125,000. Believing that "the American people have never yet capitalized our scenery and climate, as we should," he felt the time was ripe to "cultivate the 'See America First' movement." Providing well-publicized, easily accessed parks would compel Americans, now largely unable to tour Europe due to World War I, to spend their hundreds of millions of dollars not in Switzerland, but here at home.[54] In the end, that economic argument carried the day, and President Woodrow Wilson signed into existence Rocky Mountain National Park on January 26, 1915.

Conclusion

The creation of Rocky Mountain National Park tells us a great deal about Colorado and the rise of tourism in the American West. The fact that Denver was, by the turn of the twentieth century, a well-connected, well-known health resort in a nation itching and able to travel was crucial to the park's creation. In this regard, Rocky Mountain National Park was partially a product of greater urbanization in the United States. At a time when city life often dehumanized, rationalized, and sterilized the human experience, this park held the promise of peace, solitude, and rapture that so many urban Americans craved.

Enos Mills, J. Horace McFarland, James Grafton Rogers, Robert Marshall, and several politicians and government employees all experienced and responded to this sentiment. Although their personalities and professions varied widely, all agreed upon one simple fact: this park had the potential to draw a crowd—and that was a very good thing. Rocky Mountain National Park would bring money for city coffers, generate wealth for local and regional businessmen, and provide a place of play for Colorado's outdoor elite, all while adding breadth and depth to the national campaign for a parks agency. In the end, they all got what they wanted.

But what exactly had they created? The park now had an evocative name and precise lines on a map demarking a world inside and one outside. It had rules and laws that were to govern and protect the sanctuary itself. But the work of park advocates was far from finished. In many ways, the moment

President Wilson affixed his signature to the final bill marks the moment that Rocky's creation began in earnest. For the generations that have followed, tourists, elected officials, business people, and scientists have gazed into this giant looking glass and imagined divergent futures there. And what they have all seen, it turns out, has mattered a great deal.

2

A Vast Moving Caravan

There is something primal about commanding an automobile. Most of us, whether we are willing to admit it or not, are different people once we sit behind that wheel. We shed our decorous selves and quickly become honking, flipping, yelling masters relentlessly whipping our hulking steel beasts. And so much of the built world has been made solely to cater to us and our mechanical minions. Suburbs. Drive-through windows. Parking lots. Strip malls. Gas stations. Bridges. Interstates. Although we have little trouble pointing to those ways that automobiles and roads impact our daily experience, we often do not consider the ways in which the human-auto relationship has also shaped how we conceive of—and relate to—the natural world.

Most of us imagine Rocky Mountain National Park as a great natural preserve, which it is. We often fail to appreciate, however, the tight and complicated connections it shares with automobiles. In obvious ways, automobiles in RMNP provide the catalyst for nearly all other change that has taken place within the park itself. High visitation required extensive and elaborate trails, well-stocked lakes, fire suppression, roadside game management, ski resorts, and other elements of outdoor recreation.

Automobiles and roads are significant for more subtle reasons, too. Similar to a local strip mall, Rocky was built with automobiles very much in mind. More than a means to simply *get* to the park, automobiles have provided the most common way to *experience* and *understand* the park. Automobiles shape where we can and cannot go, just as they provide a moving panorama of the park itself. Behind the wheel of a vehicle, one can escape the confines of paintings and photographs and see the park in motion. The NPS has long been aware of this very important fact and developed strategies to shape exactly what drivers see—and do not see—through this powerful prism.

When you drive through Rocky you are not, despite what most of your senses are telling you, seeing a "pristine" landscape. Rather, you are imbibing images that reflect ideas about what is beautiful and natural. Often unwilling to reveal the human and profane history of the park, the NPS has dedicated significant resources to reforesting old roads, dismantling historic cabins and lodges, conducting roadside cleanup, and cutting trees to open vistas along park roads.

Tens of millions have entered RMNP over the past century. For many, perhaps even most, RMNP is primarily a sensory experience had from the seat of an automobile—truly a "windshield wilderness."[1] The deep connections between RMNP and driving, however, are not the product of historical accident. Rather, they are the result of specific and direct efforts by individuals and organizations seeking to make it so. In this sense, linking driving to the park experience was a complete success. With each passing year park superintendents witnessed a strong correlation between road-building and rising annual visitation.

But carried to its ultimate extreme, the mass popularity and accessibility of RMNP has posed considerable challenges. Traffic, noise, pollution, and the destruction of important park features were consequences of this management tack. The downward crush of automobiles in Rocky became so great, in fact, that by midcentury it effectively split the park from a single entity into two parks. Those portions of the park that lay closest to roads—the frontcountry—would support certain behaviors and management practices, whereas those areas that lay distant from roads—the backcountry—would see other ideologies and management paradigms come to dominate.[2]

The Logic of Good Roads

Since its creation in 1916, the NPS has striven to demonstrate to the American public and Congress that parks matter. The desire to do so, however, was more than a bureaucratic self-pat on the back. In fact, forging tight

Intrepid auto tourists in Estes Park, circa 1915. Courtesy of the National Archives, College Park, MD.

connections between the NPS and the broader American public held the keys to the very existence of the NPS, not to mention any hopes of future expansion it harbored. NPS directors and individual park staff have worked diligently to demonstrate that Americans value their "living museums" by facilitating the highest visitation possible and by publicizing high visitation in annual reports, local and national newspapers, and official Park Service publications.

As part of its strategy to grow a broad constituency, the NPS used roads and ease of access to promote parks, thereby initiating the institutional practice of connecting roads to the national park experience.[3] In this sense, the early policy of the NPS showed great foresight. Standing on the cusp of what would become an automobile revolution, early NPS directors like Horace Albright, Stephen T. Mather, and others rightly gauged that the NPS's institutional success and longevity would increase if they could link parks and automobiles in patrons' minds. Of course, diverting a rising tide of humanity to Rocky Mountain required higher and more regular budget appropriations as well as more and better roads. To a nation first enamored with the automobile—and later beholden to it—roads meant a stronger, more stable bureaucracy. For these and many other reasons, the NPS has understood roads as essential to its mission statement and existence.[4]

Corporate entities like the Union Pacific Railroad saw a network of smooth and interconnected roads to and through the park as a prime opportunity to generate revenue. Although Rocky Mountain National Park never received a railroad terminus, the neighboring communities of Lyons and Fort Collins did. From these depots, especially in the earliest years of the park, tens of thousands of tourists stacked their grips in rented cars and headed toward Estes Park. Without smooth and reliable roads to the park, and without good roads throughout, the Union Pacific faced a difficult task in convincing tourists to use its rails to visit the region.

Local businessmen, as much as the NPS and Union Pacific, saw a good road system as essential to future prosperity. Although some visitors did not mind riding bumpy roads or a lathering horse to reach the Fall River Lodge or Stead's Guest Ranch, many did. To local businessmen, better roads meant more people. More people meant more business. The history of park roads and the exponential increases in park visitation since 1915 attest to their foresight.

Building great roads, however, would not be enough to draw robust crowds. The public needed to associate Rocky Mountain National Park with freedom, excitement, and the convenience of open roads. The coevolution of a "driving park" and the rise of the automobile nation is no coincidence. The two are bound together in complex ways. Building a bridge between them—linking America's love affair with driving to the natural world—required advertising, and lots of it.

Selling Good Roads

Even prior to the park's creation in 1915, the Union Pacific relied upon accessibility and good roads to entice travelers to use its rails. Take, for example, a UP brochure published in 1911 titled "Colorado: For the Tourist." Under the heading "COLORADO IS THE PLAYGROUND OF AMERICA," UP claimed that Colorado was "awakening to her possibilities as a tourist state" and that the "great city of Denver" was "building fine roads to make the glorious mountains, with their natural parks and their unmatched hunting and camping grounds, still more easily reached." The railroad wanted to make it clear that it was moving more than freight to distant markets. Railroads were also being built "to places from which points most attractive to the tourist can be found with least trouble," the best example of which was the "Union Pacific from Denver to Fort Collins." From there, the UP boasted, it was "but a 30 mile ride into the heart of Estes Park, acknowledged to be the most rugged region of the Rocky Mountains."[5]

In addition to the purple prose used to drive home the region's ease of access, the Union Pacific also peppered its brochure with alluring photos to achieve the same end. Of the fifty-three photos of nonurban areas that appear in the pamphlet, twenty contain one or more roads. The pervasiveness of roads in this brochure is curious. Perhaps the UP was doing its part to balance the depiction of the West as a wild place of gunfighters and "savages" against a playground with modern amenities. The UP attempted to walk a razor-thin line. The exciting West of yesteryear, a place of wild women and rough-hewn men, lacked modern contrivances. Rail lines, roads, and all they bring with them, however, threatened the very existence of the romantic West that drew millions to the region to begin with. The dilemma the UP faced in balancing the wild with the modern was little different from that the NPS later faced in creating a parkscape where the human imprint was nearly imperceptible, but where tens of millions would tread.

The UP was not alone in recognizing and amplifying the "motoring opportunities" in and around Estes Park. The *Estes Park Trail* newspaper, a steadfast booster of the region, carried articles that also looked to automobile tourism as the future: "A vacation trip in an automobile is no longer a fad," they proclaimed, "but everything considered, is a cheap and enjoyable way of taking the whole family and having a good time. Year by year this way of seeing the country is growing, and once a successful trip has been made, never again the stuffy Pullman for the man who owns a machine."[6] It was true that Colorado had long been known as a state containing vast natural resources, but according to the *Trail*, "its greatest asset, the one thing that will yearly add to it [*sic*] permanent wealth, is good roads."[7] To promote the region and draw the driving public to the park, the Estes Park Business Association published 10,000 copies of a "very attractive booklet," which were distributed across the United States.[8]

Focusing upon the availability of good roads in and around RMNP was no fleeting phenomenon. In a 1925 *New York Times* article titled "Curtain Rises on Nation's Park Show," columnist William Du Puy rightly stated that some significant changes were afoot in national parks. In the heady 1920s, penned Du Puy, America's natural wonders had become accessible to "a vast moving caravan." The seemingly endless line of autos heading to and through national parks was indeed "something new under the sun" and of vast importance to the future of parks. No longer forced to choose between lengthy and expensive railroad vacations or no vacation at all, more people were touring national parks in automobiles. According to Du Puy, total national park visitation jumped from 100,000 in 1910 to 1.1 million by 1924. In Rocky Mountain alone, more than 250,000 entered its gates in 1924, up from an estimated 31,000 during its first year of operation.[9] "The automobile," concluded Du Puy, "having brought so many parks to the door of the citizen, now goes in search of offerings for its devotees."[10]

One organization seeking devotees for its offerings was the Rocky Mountain Transportation Company (RMTC). Whereas the businessmen of Estes Park and the Union Pacific Railroad viewed motoring opportunities in and around the park as a means to supplement their income, the Rocky Mountain Transportation Company's entire business derived from shuffling curious onlookers from point to point around Estes Park. Roe Emery, who had operated a successful touring company in Glacier National Park since 1914, consolidated the Stanley and Osborn transportation lines in 1916 with his own and began offering service to and through Rocky Mountain National Park.[11] By 1918, Emery operated one of three official companies moving people to the park. His competition included Denver Herdic Transportation and Boulder Transportation. During 1918 alone, the three companies delivered more than 600 carloads of tourists to RMNP. Of the three, however, the RMTC was by far the most successful, driving more than 400 tours through the park.[12] In addition to experience and capital, Emery also enjoyed close connections to Director Stephen Mather and key railroads, which served several stops in Denver and across the Front Range.[13]

By the summer of 1919 the RMTC was well positioned to receive exclusive franchise rights to bring tourists to the park. In a move that shocked and appalled many locals (including the ever-vocal Enos Mills), Rocky Mountain National Park offered the transportation franchise to Emery's company in May 1919, thereby excluding all others from taking paying customers by automobile through the park.[14] The partnership between the RMTC and the park benefited both parties. From the park's perspective, having a relationship with a reliable business dedicated to bringing as many visitors to the park as possible meant only good things. The skeleton crew at the park could not offer such services; yet through the RMTC thousands of Americans could visit the park, contact its personnel, and come to understand the importance of the nascent agency. For its part, the RMTC was permitted to operate a monopoly—a mere dream for most entrepreneurs—and was allowed to advertise its services within official national park publications.

The National Park Service itself had a vested interest in drawing connections between driving and the park. Through its brochure *Rocky Mountain National Park, Colorado*, for example, the NPS sought to inform prospective visitors of the park's rules and regulations (that was the official intent of the 47-page document) and to entice them with the great variety of activities that the park offered. After a brief primer on the region's natural history, the booklet again echoed the chorus of the park's founders under a section titled "ACCESSIBILITY." Here, claimed the NPS, "one of the most striking features of the Rocky Mountain National Park is the easy accessibility of these mountaintops." Not only was it a mere 30 hours from Chicago and St. Louis, but upon arriving one could "motor" from one side of the Continental Divide to the other in just four hours.[15]

Through their efforts, the NPS and others were promoting more than roads. They were constructing expectations about how best to interact with the natural world within the park. Using photographs, maps, and detailed descriptions, they all made it clear that driving was not just possible but preferred.[16] These expectations, in turn, brought further pressure to bear upon park management to build and maintain a system of first-class roads.

Road Work

Bear Lake Road is one of the most heavily used roads in Rocky Mountain National Park. Winding its way from the Beaver Meadows entrance on the eastern side, the road now skirts Moraine Park and then meanders along the picturesque Glacier Creek before reaching its terminus. Along the way motorists might glimpse grazing elk, a roiling brook, and a towering crescent of majestic peaks. Today, the road is wide, smooth, and efficient, delivering visitors to destinations including Sprague Lake, the Glacier Gorge Trailhead, and Bierstadt Lake Trailhead. Traffic during summer months can be intense as bikes, cars, and the park's many shuttle buses pulse toward Bear Lake. Although park managers and visitors have long appreciated the physical beauty of the little lake, delivering oneself to its shores was not always as effortless as it is today.

Upon the park's creation in 1915, no reliable road existed to deliver visitors to Bear Lake. Instead, there stood a patchwork of privately constructed roads and trails, which under the best of circumstances could deliver one to within a mile of its shores but not in the comfort of an automobile. Abner Sprague likely built the first leg of the road, which ran parallel to Glacier Creek for 1.5 miles and brought patrons to his "summer resort." West of Sprague's Lodge, a rudimentary "road" climbed an additional two miles toward the lake.[17]

Park Superintendent Claude L. Way, realizing the importance of Bear Lake to the park experience, reported to the Washington, D.C., NPS office that Bear Lake Road was "destined to be one of the most traveled roads in the National Park" and directed crews to dedicate the bulk of their efforts to placing it in a passable condition for the 1920 season.[18] Adding to the road's popularity was the construction of a makeshift wagon road from Glacier Basin to within a half-mile of Bear Lake. Although the road was not intended for automobile use, many brazen drivers nervously perched atop their machines as they reached the "heart of some of the wildest and most beautiful country in the Park."[19] The arrival of the first automobiles at Bear Lake stands as a watershed in the history of RMNP. For the first time since the mountains thrust themselves skyward, humans would come to dominate the landscape and reshape many of its natural processes. A continual program of road improvement was central to this process.

Roger Toll, who took over the superintendency from Way in 1921, also recognized the importance of good roads. Astutely realizing that the automobile was changing how visitors experienced the park, Toll commented that a "certain proportion of visitors seem to be interested primarily in the opportunities for automobiling," and their "stay in this park is usually brief." To Toll, the shift toward more cars heading to and through the park was troubling, especially considering Rocky contained limited motoring opportunities, all of which were in close proximity to Estes Park.[20] To meet the growing desire and expectations of the driving public, the NPS would have to dedicate more resources to building and maintaining roads.

By 1926 Congress was becoming increasingly aware of the rising popularity of national parks and allocated more money to support them. In that year, Congress allotted Rocky Mountain National Park a three-year sum of $445,000 to improve its roads. Toll, who had long harbored the desire to bring Bear Lake Road up to the highest of standards, used much of the 1926 appropriation for the Bear Lake project.[21] Hoping to make it one of the premier destinations in the park, RMNP quickly advertised for construction bids, and by the fall the firm of Shields & Flat had earned the $122,000 contract to rebuild and relocate 6.9 miles of the road, primarily between Sprague's resort and the lake.[22]

As the Shields & Flat steam shovel rent the earth and churned its way toward Bear Lake, park staff witnessed a sharp increase in the number of cars chugging up toward the lake. With construction nearing completion in 1928, for example, an estimated 21,593 visitors made their way to the Glacier Gorge campground alone.[23] In the first full season of use the road delivered more than 37,000 people to Bear Lake in more than 10,000 automobiles.[24] Although visitation to Bear Lake would never again be so low, it is important to note that only nine years had passed since the first automobile had made the journey. Through greater and more reliable appropriations, the NPS was able to build itself a premier destination. In doing so, however, it began to face the management consequences of that decision.

Higher annual visitation demanded more upkeep and the expansion of facilities to handle the crowds. Primary to the care and maintenance of the new road was managing the contrails of dust produced by the churning wheels of thousands of automobiles. To treat the problem and to ensure the smoothest possible roads for the summer season, the NPS initiated a program of regular road maintenance in 1929, which included applying an estimated .3 gallons of oil per square yard to the road's surface. Given that the width of the road was contracted at 18 feet, and that the portion treated was seven miles in length, the NPS spread more than 20,000 gallons of oil atop Bear Lake Road alone each time crews oiled it.[25]

Through the application of money, technology, and sweat, the NPS transformed Bear Lake Road from a dusty trail into "decidedly the best road in the park," but in doing so it created yet another problem: more people—and more cars—demanded more parking. To further accommodate the driving public, the NPS built parking areas at Glacier Gorge and Bear Lake to accommodate 100 and 350 automobiles, respectively.[26] As early as 1929, then,

Truck oiling Bear Lake Road, 1930. Courtesy of Rocky Mountain National Park, ROMO MSF NEG 820.

the staff at RMNP began to witness and experience a recurrent management theme. Better facilities brought more people, but more people required more resources and placed a greater demand on the park's infrastructure. For the better part of the twentieth century the park staff would implement a variety of management strategies to deal with this conundrum in nearly all of its management arenas, often with little or no success. By 1932 visitation to the lake had surpassed 80,000, with no end in sight.[27]

As RMNP poured money into the construction and refinement of Bear Lake Road, it launched a more public, and in some ways more important, road-building campaign. Unlike Bear Lake Road, which was built to deliver drivers to a primary destination, Trail Ridge Road was conceived, designed, and built to bring drivers to a variety of destinations as they motored *through* the park. The appeal of the road has always been its breathtaking views, the variety of ecosystems it made accessible, and the sheer novelty of commanding an automobile to elevations in excess of 12,000 feet.

Grand County and Larimer County first responded to this desire in 1913 with the start of construction of Fall River Road. Although this road eventually offered motorists the opportunity to stand where the nation's waters

Bear Lake parking lot, 1931. Courtesy of Rocky Mountain National Park, ROMO MSF NEG 1720.

divide east and west, it suffered from a variety of shortcomings. In general, the road was not designed with the same sensitivity to "vistas" that the National Park Service would later find so important. Instead, as one climbs Fall River Road, lodgepole pine and spruce often obstruct the view, and most of the trip is spent traversing the north side of Fall River Canyon. Although the drive offers striking views of the south side of the canyon, opportunities to behold the mountain majesty of RMNP are limited primarily to the portion of the road near the Continental Divide itself. Given that park managers have always placed a great deal of emphasis on making the park visually appealing, Fall River Road left much to be desired.

The road suffered in other regards as well. Its engineers built many sections too steep, and several of its switchback corners required maneuvering to and fro to make the turns. This, coupled with steep grades and often precipitous drop-offs, provided too much stimulation for many drivers. To address the problem of drivers too frightened to continue, the NPS posted a permanent patrol on the road to assist the overwhelmed to lower ground. In addition to Fall River's lack of "great vistas" and its rugged construction, it suffered perennial landslides and avalanches, which required great effort and expenditure to remedy. In short, after several years of management experience, the staff of RMNP knew well the deficiencies of the road by the mid-1920s.

Hoping to enhance its ability to build good and appealing roads, the NPS partnered with the Bureau of Public Roads in 1926. Through this cooperative agreement the NPS undertook construction of some of its most famous roads. For its part, the Bureau of Public Roads provided technical and engineering advice while the National Park Service and its many landscape architects concerned themselves primarily with the aesthetic aspects of road construction.[28]

More than simply building roads, the NPS labored to construct roads that amplified, illuminated, and made accessible spectacular natural scenery. Employing techniques that originated in a tradition of landscape architecture and gardening stretching back into the nineteenth century, the NPS relied upon rigorous theory and years of practical experience to build the most spectacular roads possible.[29] Blue Ridge Parkway, Going to the Sun Highway, and Trail Ridge Road all reflect its ability to do so. In 1927, NPS Director Stephen T. Mather established a new regional headquarters in San Francisco to advise the agency on matters of "engineering, landscape architecture, education, forestry, and sanitary engineering." Henceforth, the NPS devoted increasing resources to building parks that were especially appealing to the eye. Central to these efforts were the talents and ambitions of Thomas Vint.[30]

Vint, who was trained in a variety of fields including landscape architecture, took control of the landscape division at the new field office in 1927 and earned the official title of chief landscape architect in October 1928.[31] Beyond assembling a talented and energetic staff, Vint helped craft construction standards and practices to minimize disruption and damage to natural areas adjacent to roads. The new standards, for example, stated that all "holes left by the removal of stumps and roots were to be backfilled. Borrow pits were to be located in areas not visible from the completed road." Further, contractors were not allowed to use longstanding blasting practices that marred the landscape.[32]

Building roads, in other words, was more than a simple matter of blazing a smooth path across the mountains. It required careful planning and thoughtful hands ever conscious of the danger of revealing the human efforts behind such magnificent creations. To the extent possible, roads had to be naturalized. Suppressing—even hiding—the human role in the road's creation reflected and deepened the assumption that humans and nature were separate. Following Vint's lead and employing his new road construction standards, the NPS and the Bureau of Public Roads turned their attention to Trail Ridge Road.

Mindful not to repeat the mistakes of the Fall River Road, the new Trail Ridge Road would wind its way from Deer Ridge to the Continental Divide along a new route that broke frequently upon incredible views of the park's mountains and valleys. Along the way the motorist would not face grades in excess of 7 percent or be forced to seesaw around dangerous hairpins. The new road would be wider and smoother, allowing for faster automobile travel.

Landscape architect Charles W. Eliot II had even higher hopes for this road. In his well-trained hands, park roads, he believed, could help the visitor "understand and enjoy a crescendo of carefully composed pictures." Properly constructed roads enhanced the driving experience by allowing the viewer to evaluate the natural features "in relation to each other" and revealed them "as parts of larger compositions to preserve and enhance the relative scale of near and distant objects." More than quotidian components of engineering grades, bar ditches, and culverts, these were "matters involving knowledge of human psychology, of natural history, and appreciation of harmony, sequence, line, and color."[33] After months of striving to lay out a road that offered the "proper" panoramas to drivers, the NPS was poised to initiate construction of its iconic Trail Ridge Road in 1926.

Surveying Trail Ridge Road, 1930. Courtesy of Rocky Mountain National Park, ROMO MSF NEG 4659.

Upon the road's completion in 1932, the *Estes Park Trail* hailed the achievement as a "culmination of almost three years of hard work performed under adverse conditions." Ebullient, the paper stated that "at no point is there a steeper grade than 7 percent and many cars make the trip from the village to the 'top' without changing gears." Hoping to allay fears that the new road would present narrow passages and hairpin corners such as those that characterized Fall River Road, the paper proclaimed that Trail Ridge Road was "amply wide for four lanes of traffic." In addition to a speedy ascent into the heavens, the new road offered views of "range after range of the high, rugged peaks of the Rockies," which are "spread in wonderful panorama before the driver."

The *Trail* also reveled in the skills of Vint, Eliot, and the builders of Trail Ridge Road, commenting that "everything possible has been done to preserve the beauty of the terrain through which the road leads. After each blast of dynamite, workmen have cleaned up all 'country rock' thrown over the landscape so that there would be no unsightly white rock among the lichen

Automobile caravan at Iceberg Lake on Trail Ridge Road, 1937. Courtesy of Rocky Mountain National Park, ROMO 10239.

covered boulders that contribute to the scenery."[34] It is telling that the road itself, a massive tattoo stamped across the spine of the Rockies, was not an eyesore, but the rocks that had been strewn over the alpine tundra to build it were. The road, in other words, was becoming naturalized.

Throughout the remainder of the 1930s, the Civilian Conservation Corps (CCC) and others continued refining the park's roads and building spurs and connections, but never again would Rocky Mountain National Park witness the expansion of roads it did during its first 18 years. The work was largely complete. Between 1915 and 1933 the National Park Service, Union Pacific Railroad, Rocky Mountain Transportation Company, and local business interests had succeeded in connecting the national park experience with driving. By the end of the 1930s, with the nation's economy still very much on uneven ground, more than 650,000 people found their way to RMNP in more than 200,000 cars. Both numbers are all the more impressive when compared to the 31,000 people who came to the park in 1915.

Working Roads

More than building fine roads and expanding parking facilities to accommodate drivers, RMNP officials dedicated significant time, effort, and financial resources to shaping the roadside into a specific visual experience. Although the reasons for such projects were many, at the heart lay the desire to fashion the parkscape into something that mirrored the NPS's understanding of what constituted "natural" and "beautiful." In the hands of properly trained landscape architects and conscientious rangers, roads enabled the NPS to act as artists of the natural.

As early as 1918, for example, rangers began placing salt blocks along the roadside near Sheep Lake. Doing so, argued Superintendent Way, kept the bighorn sheep in the lower reaches of the park all year, where visitors could easily admire them. As the sheep came to depend upon the roadside handout, they became "wonderfully tame," and bands numbering as many as fifty-seven could be counted at one time. Having lost their "fear of automobiles" and "persons on foot," the sheep were "almost surrounded by automobiles" with throngs of tourists eagerly pointing their Kodaks at them.[35]

The Park Service manipulated more than sheep in its efforts to enhance the roadside view. In 1921, for example, crews worked to erase older portions of the Bear Lake Road no longer in use. Thickly planting those portions where the old road left "unsightly . . . open swaths" did much, thought the NPS, to improve the park's visual appeal.[36] As would later be the case along Trail Ridge Road, efforts directed at replanting old roads reveal a certain aesthetic. For the millions who have traveled through the park, casting a gaze upon a "pristine" nature is of primary importance. Visible remnants of old roads raise obvious questions about just how pristine the landscape actually was.

During the summer and fall of 1930, the NPS dedicated more resources to roadside beautification as a crew of some twenty men conducted "roadside cleanup" along the park's most popular roads.[37] By season's end, these efforts produced what Superintendent Rogers called a "very desirable effect in the appearance" of the roads.[38] Tidying the bosky roadside no doubt provided park officials with a tool to reduce available fire fuels. In addition to safety, however, park managers were keenly interested in making the roadside more aesthetically pleasing. Following an especially successful season of roadside cleanup in 1933, Superintendent Rogers candidly admitted that the "limits of the cleanup is more or less determined by visibility" of the detritus.[39] If fire-fuel management provided the sole logic for roadside cleanup, the "visibility" of debris would be of little or no concern.

As crews continued with fine grading and other finish work on the west

Revegetation project along Trail Ridge Road, circa 1935. Courtesy of Rocky Mountain National Park, ROMO 10487.

side of Trail Ridge Road in 1933, the NPS redoubled its efforts to manufacture a first-class roadside view. For instance, twelve men working under the supervision of a landscape architect began "vista work" to open views of Horseshoe Park from Trail Ridge Road. This vista enhancement, which was part of the original construction plan for the road, consisted mainly of selectively thinning trees that obstructed the panoramic views. By July, the crew was done with its work and created "a good view of Horseshoe Park."[40]

To landscape architect Charles W. Eliot II, opening views of serene mountain meadows was of primary importance to shaping the "proper" parkscape. "Valleys are enormously important to the scenic and recreational values of the area," claimed Eliot, as "they constitute the ideal foil to the mountains and therefore constitute the ideal foreground for mountain views." If a trained and loving human hand was needed to reveal such beauty, so be it.[41] Here again, it is important to bear in mind that the sweeping vistas one experiences along Trail Ridge Road have to some degree been manufactured. Certainly the valleys, mountains, and streams one sees on a drive up Trail Ridge are natural in the popular sense, but most drivers are not aware of the degree to which NPS officials shaped the experience with their own hands.

As the work of shaping the view from the road continued, the NPS turned its attention to another matter that had long concerned park managers. Since the creation of RMNP in 1915, the park's superintendents had grown increasingly concerned over the patchwork of privately owned land (so-called inholdings) that dotted the landscape. Beginning with Roger Toll in the 1920s, RMNP initiated a decades-long program of purchasing such inholdings. This program, which provided a means to unify, rationalize, and simplify park management, also reveals a substantial bias toward fashioning a park that obscured the region's human history and amplified its "pristine" qualities.

In 1932, for example, after the NPS acquired a number of properties within the park, crews "immediately" set about "obliterating" all evidence of "development on private property purchased during the past year," which included the removal of all buildings and barbed wire. "After the buildings have been wrecked and fences removed," recounted Superintendent Toll, the "region certainly present[ed] a different picture (one we have all been wishing for)."[42] Toll's language is insightful. Here crews were "immediately" directed toward the work and their efforts rectified a situation that had been an obvious bother to park management. A similar scenario played out in 1933, as park crews again set about "wrecking several of the old buildings" that the park purchased in 1931 as part of the Moraine Lodge property. Superintendent Rogers was confident that "when complete this obliteration will greatly improve the lower Moraine Park Valley."[43] Demolition of any and all signs of a permanent human presence in the park marked, as Rogers put it, an "improvement."

Luring animals roadside, selective thinning of trees, the removal of dead and dying trees, and the demolition of human settlements all speak to the efforts to present the park in a manner that matched well what both the NPS and the American public defined as "natural" and "beautiful." The construction of the roads themselves—perhaps the most obvious indication of human presence—presented managers with a host of decisions about how and where roads should be built and maintained. Employing the skills of landscape architects and knowledgeable rangers, the NPS demonstrated that it had the capacity and desire to blend the constructed *into* the natural. More than that, they also revealed a belief that roads, if harnessed as a medium for generating certain emotions, could actually enhance the natural appeal of any park.

Roadside cleanup in Hidden Valley, 1933. Courtesy of Rocky Mountain National Park, ROMO 4008, MSF NEG 2931.

"See the U-S-A in Your Chev-ro-let"

In many ways the Depression stands as a high point in the history of RMNP. Though a difficult time for millions of Americans, the economic calamity delivered to the federal government the power, courage, and public support to expand government agencies. RMNP benefited greatly from four CCC camps and the hundreds they employed. These workers, paid largely through emergency funds, built additional campgrounds, expanded and refined its utility area, planted tens of thousands of bushes and trees, conducted roadside cleanups, fought wildfires, and treated thousands of trees for insect infestation. As the 1930s came to a close and an aggressive Germany pushed its way across Europe, however, dark days loomed on the horizon for RMNP.

After the bombing of Pearl Harbor and the full engagement of the military and industrial forces of the United States, RMNP began losing resources on a regular basis. In addition to loss of rangers, clerks, and others to the draft, the park was also forced to close its CCC camps during the summer of 1942.[44] Reflecting the difficult times was the drop in the number of Americans willing and able to travel to the region for pleasure. Whereas 663,819 people in 194,581 automobiles motored through the park in 1941, only 392,565 people in

109,191 cars did so in 1942.[45] The park was also forced to relinquish its Snogo snowplow in 1943, which was crucial to keeping open roads in winter, to an airbase in Rapid City, South Dakota. The park suffered still more as various branches of the military and civilian agencies stripped its CCC camps of all usable equipment.[46] More than siphoning off men and machinery, World War II also had a negative impact on budgets. Between 1941 and 1943 alone, RMNP saw its operating budget cut from $196,095 to $105,665—a reduction of more than 45 percent.[47] Although the cuts in manpower, machinery, and money greatly circumscribed RMNP's ability to meet its management directives, far more difficult times lay ahead.

It is no secret that following World War II the United States became once again a nation of consumers. During the war years, largely due to the simultaneity of rationing, high employment, and relatively high wages, Americans managed to save billions of dollars. The end of the war unleashed more than a decade of pent-up consumer demand, and in relatively short order Americans bought millions of washing machines, television sets, automobiles, houses, and other goods.[48] Concomitant with this spending spree Americans increasingly looked to tourism as an exercise in consumption.[49]

Collectively, the return of American economic prosperity, the increasing popularity of the automobile-centered family vacation, and the desire on the part of millions of Americans to visit national parks put enormous stress on the National Park Service and the lands it administered. A brief look at the visitation record is instructive. In 1935, 7,676,000 Americans visited a national park or monument. By 1950, however, that number had surged to 33,250,000, and by 1955 park visitation exceeded 56,573,000.[50]

By 1951 a record 1.33 million people made the trip to RMNP, nearly double any previous year's number.[51] The confluence of widespread economic prosperity, the rise in consumption of goods and services, and lagging appropriations created a serious public-relations issue for the NPS. Not only was firewood scant and roads in poor condition, but the volume of visitors traveling daily through the park put public toilets and campgrounds in a wretched state. Year by year the staff at Rocky Mountain received an increasing flow of letters complaining about various aspects of the park.

Longtime park supporter and historian Bernard Devoto wrote a sort of exposé on national parks for *Harper's Magazine* in October 1953 titled "Let's Close the National Parks." To Devoto, there were two options: either give the

NPS the money needed to meet current demands, or close the parks. Outraged, Devoto went so far as to characterize some parks—like Yellowstone and Rocky Mountain—as "true slum districts." It was clear to many that national parks were in great peril.[52]

Letters from visitors also spoke to the poor conditions in RMNP. Mrs. Veit of Corpus Christi, Texas, for example, wrote a passionate letter to Senator Lyndon B. Johnson regarding her family's vacation to RMNP in 1957:

> None of these areas have showers which to me seems very primitive for our progressive America. Many, many thousands of persons from every state in the Union visit these campgrounds every summer and it is time some improvements should be made to better the conditions for these thousands of middle class American's hard-earned vacations. The revenue taken in by the Parks comes from us Middleclass vacationers and in my opinion should not be turned over to the Treasury for various and sundry uses (especially overseas improvements) but belongs to the Parks Department to be used for the benefit of those vacationing and spending their money there.[53]

In a single handwritten letter, Veit captures much of the complexity and tensions that characterized the National Park Service and RMNP itself in the years following World War II. Parks *were* in serious danger of collapsing under the strain of postwar demand. Visitors from across the nation urged the NPS to build wider roads, to increase the number and modernity of restrooms, and to construct more comfortable camping facilities. Furthermore, in RMNP at least, the growing popularity of the summer vacation would force difficult decisions regarding how the NPS presented the park to the public.

As evinced by letters from park visitors, reports issued by the National Park Service generally, and the management of Rocky Mountain National Park specifically, postwar Americans increasingly traded lengthy traditional park vacations—once characterized by hikes and in-depth educational tours—for breezy "day trips." By the end of the 1940s and increasingly throughout the 1950s, millions of Americans demanded that parks become places where they could sit comfortably behind the wheel of an automobile and glide across the landscape—a behavior that the Park Service had promoted and facilitated in RMNP since its founding. Many Americans strongly implored the NPS to take action and redesign parks in a way that better conformed to the needs and desires of a growing middle class. Under the leadership of Conrad Wirth, this is exactly what the National Park Service attempted to do through a 10-year development program known as Mission 66.[54]

Mission 66

Facing a daunting task, National Park Service director Conrad Wirth envisioned, planned, and initiated the most ambitious building program in NPS history with the hope of protecting the parks from the depredations of hordes of eager tourists. Presenting Mission 66 only as a response to postwar tourist demands, however, fails to capture the complexity and, one might even argue, the historical value of the program. It was a massive construction project reflective of the ambition and optimism of postwar America. But the story is more complicated. Mission 66 also reveals rising tensions surrounding what constituted proper behavior in (and thereby the deeper meaning of) our national parks. To perhaps a majority of Americans—and a powerful cadre of NPS officials—park development and widespread use were seen in the late 1940s and 1950s as not only acceptable but also *necessary* for the future of the national park system. This progressive ideology, best embodied in the person of Director Wirth (and revealed in the letter from Mrs. Veit), played a central role in formulating Mission 66.

By Wirth's reasoning, the Bureau of Reclamation, Army Corps of Engineers, and other of the NPS's institutional cousins generally had much better luck in the appropriations game than did the beleaguered Park Service. Though the reasons were many, Wirth understood that part of it was attributable to the fact that the other agencies often proposed multiyear, multilayered programs, which appealed to a wider range of members of Congress and thus were less likely to get trimmed from the budget.[55] Drawing on his most trusted and experienced employees, Wirth put together a steering committee and gave them just seven months, until September 1955, to draft a comprehensive, forward-looking plan to save the national parks.[56]

Over the next seven months the steering committee collected and compiled information from many of the 181 NPS-administered lands, and it worked diligently to flesh out general trends and needs. By September 1955, the NPS had a solid proposal and coined a catchy slogan to help sell the idea to the public: Mission 66. According to Wirth, the "Mission" reflected the sense of duty that NPS employees felt regarding the rebuilding of the parks;

the "66" represented the endpoint of the program, intelligently selected to coincide with the fiftieth anniversary of the National Park Service. On a more personal level, it seems clear that Wirth wanted America to know that it was he who had saved the National Park System. And there was no better way to chisel his name into NPS history than to have a grand celebration that connected the history of the NPS to the reign of Conrad Wirth.

At the heart of the proposal lay fourteen key points that outlined the NPS philosophy and posed solutions to the current crisis. The most important and strikingly ideological of the fourteen stated: "Substantial and appropriate use of the National Park System is the best means by which its basic purpose is realized and is the best guarantee of perpetuating the System."[57] In short, the key to saving the "system" lay not in curtailing visitation but in facilitating more of it. Under Wirth's confident leadership, this federal agency was going to organize and present itself to Congress and the American people as the most important purveyor of modern tourism in the nation.

Amid this reform, Wirth ordered the superintendent of Rocky Mountain National Park, James Lloyd, to draft a prospectus outlining the Mission 66 program for his park. Drawing upon decades of NPS experience, Lloyd began the planning phase by asking the staff of RMNP for their insights. Collectively, they raised three significant areas of concern: roads and trails; interpretation and education; and land acquisition.

During the months that followed, the staff at Rocky Mountain drafted a prospectus that they hoped would adequately address the challenges RMNP faced. At the core of the plan lay the basic assumption that the park was "truly an outdoor museum with unsurpassed accessibility for the full enjoyment by the public." The park was unsurpassed in its accessibility (and would become more so through Mission 66) and park management had come to believe that "the visitor need not penetrate far into the mountain vastness of the Park until the feeling of remote, primeval conditions becomes distinctly apparent." The conclusion that "a visitor to the Park may have a truly significant and enjoyable visit in the space of one day" had replaced nearly a half-decade of the NPS urging the public to explore in some detail the hidden natural wealth and spiritual rejuvenating forces of this park. Based on the above two assumptions, Lloyd and his team labored to recast RMNP primarily as a "day use" area.[58]

Superintendent Lloyd had witnessed firsthand the changing character of

*Rocky Mountain National Park Superintendent James Lloyd with Director of the
National Park Service Conrad Wirth at Hidden Valley Lodge, 1958. Courtesy of Rocky
Mountain National Park, ROMO MSF NEG 4374.*

travel through the park after World War II. Commenting on the phenomenon, he stated that more people were "making use of their private vehicles
and less use of their legs." As a whole, Americans were making more "hur-
ried trips," as the "American family continues to boast of how many miles
they traveled and how many National Parks they entered on their vacation
trip."[59] Hoping to gain a better understanding of how exactly postwar Americans interacted with the park, RMNP conducted a brief study at the park's
ever popular Bear Lake. Through a multiday traffic study, park staff collected
information on the number of cars entering the lot, the number of riders
per car, and the duration of their stay. The study supported the conclusions
Lloyd reached the previous year. More people were making quick tours of
the park compared to those who partook in more in-depth investigations
beyond their automobiles. According to the study, an average of 66 percent

of visitors spent less than 30 minutes at the Bear Lake parking lot, while only 33.5 percent stayed longer than thirty minutes.[60] Given such information, rebuilding the park's roads in a manner that better facilitated a smooth and rapid flow of traffic became one of the central components of Mission 66 in RMNP.

In autumn 1957, landscape architects and engineers began the process of laying out plans for a new and improved Trail Ridge Road and for more efficient entrance stations. Keeping with Mission 66's emphasis on maximizing visitation, RMNP managers called for the construction of new parking areas at Forest Canyon Overlook, Lower Tundra Curves, Little Rock Cut, Rock Cabins, and Horseshoe Park.[61] By July 1959, these parking lots were nearly complete, as was the work of rebuilding, reshaping, and realigning portions of Fall River Road. Two additional parking areas were built in Phantom Valley during the 1957 season, and further parking was created at Aspenglen Campground. The NPS also improved the High Drive entrance road, refashioned the Beaver Meadows entrance station, build new comfort stations at Glacier Basin Campground and Stillwater Creek Campground, and installed new water and sewer systems at the Aspenglen Campground.[62]

By 1963, with the bulk of the Mission 66 improvements completed, RMNP managers and staff must have viewed their accomplishments with a sense of pride. In addition to adding two new miles of roadway and reconstructing three more, they added 594 additional parking spaces, upgraded and reconstructed five miles of roads within campgrounds, and built an additional 2.5 miles of trails. To accommodate more overnight visitors, the NPS added 410 campsites and built two new campfire circles/amphitheaters, capable of seating a total of 600 persons at a time. The newly fashioned RMNP now boasted a total of seven campfire circles and amphitheaters, with a combined seating capacity of more than 1,700.[63]

Reinterpreting Nature

Revamping the park's infrastructure to better accommodate larger crowds meant that the NPS would have to make difficult decisions regarding other aspects of park management. One area that increasing visitation had significantly impacted was RMNP's interpretive and educational apparatus. "Interpretation" had always been near the heart of the National Park Service mission. NPS directors, superintendents, and general staff all realized that nothing was more effective in endearing the NPS to Americans than a strong and personal interpretive program.

By the mid-1950s, however, the park found itself increasingly unable to make such strong, personal connections with the public. There were too few park employees to regularly take visitors on guided day hikes and fewer and fewer people were interested in such activities, choosing instead not to wander far from parking lots and Packards.[64] Although the raw percentage of "interpretive contacts" had risen from just 7.7 percent in 1934 to 13.8 percent in 1955, the number of travelers who had no contact whatsoever with staff had jumped from 337,363 to 1,250,806 during the same period. In short, too many people were moving through the park without being exposed to the NPS "message."[65] To an agency historically self-conscious about its image— and always striving to make clear to the public the importance of its role in safeguarding America's natural treasures—something had to be done.

To the management at RMNP, the solution seemed clear: revise the interpretive program to better meet the needs of those traveling through the park in their cars. Accomplishing this meant reducing the number of staff dedicated to personally guided tours, planting a large number of interpretive signs and information stations across the park, and making a more concerted effort to "contact" travelers at entrances. Through each of the above, the function and character of RMNP was transformed from a personal landscape where travelers came to know park staff and learned directly from other human beings, to a less personal one that lent itself more easily to the demands of commercial tourism.

In 1955 Superintendent James Lloyd decided to cut drastically the number of guided tours and hikes that RMNP offered. Given their popularity, it comes as no surprise that the reduction upset a great many visitors, including Bill Ladd of the (Louisville) *Courier-Journal.* Ladd had been a longtime patron of RMNP and had always appreciated and enjoyed the personal and extensive contact with rangers and naturalists. While visiting the park in the summer of 1956, however, Ladd was shocked to find that park officials had curtailed guided nature hikes. Ladd was so upset, in fact, that he traveled to park headquarters to discuss the matter with Superintendent Lloyd. During their discussion, Lloyd informed Ladd that "the former interpretive program was unrealistic in that it was tailored to the long-term visitor while the average visit was a day and a half and a huge percentage of visitors simply drive through the park and had no contact with the interpretive program at all." Lloyd observed that "while a ranger-naturalist was taking 75 people on a day hike on the Fern-Odessa trail, 1,000 visitors were going through the park with no contact with the interpretive service."

After hearing Lloyd out, Ladd conceded that the superintendent had a point but wanted to make clear that the park management was making a big mistake. As Ladd saw it, the "hiking party led by a ranger-naturalist is made up of the people who are most valuable to the park system and the park service. These are the people already fired with a desire to learn something about the park, its animals, flowers, trees, geology and place in the natural picture."[66] These were the people, Ladd argued, who would become future conservationists and "battle" for the NPS in the "crises which are always coming in the park service program." Most regrettable to Ladd was plopping down highly trained and capable scientists at "information stations" for the "gang of stampeding tourists who eat breakfast at Loveland, throw their lunch papers off the Rock Cut and have an early dinner at Hot Sulphur Springs."[67] To Ladd, the park was best served not by having such personnel hand out flyers at the gates, but rather by employing them to lead educational tours through the park.

Revealing the progressive optimism of Mission 66, its bias toward vehicle-based tourism, and the consequences such shifts entailed, Rocky Mountain National Park also embraced new technology to animate the park's landscape. According to researchers Maren Thompson Bzdek and Janet Ore, the park installed the "latest audiovisual technology to deliver automated messages at wayside interpretive points, auditoriums, and outdoor amphitheaters." Meanwhile, New York City–based Comprehensive Communications developed an "auto tape tour" for Trail Ridge Road, which they sold near the park. In addition to pacing the car so that the tape "coincide[d] with the timed description of features encountered along the road," the auto tape tour also included sound effects to enhance the drive. For some, experiencing the park in an automobile—an activity that separated visitors from the park with panes of glass, sheets of steel, and a rumbling engine—necessitated taped sound effects to enrich the experience and make it more evocative.[68]

Perhaps the most visible NPS effort to increase "interpretive contacts" was the construction of three new visitor centers. According to Conrad

Wirth, the older museum-like structures that parks like Rocky Mountain had used were no longer serving the needs of the NPS. To stimulate more interest and use, the NPS endeavored to replace the outmoded museums with modern visitor centers wherein tourists could find clean restrooms, interpretive exhibits, rest areas, curio shops, and food services.[69] RMNP eventually planned and built three new visitor centers—one located near the Beaver Meadows entrance, one at the Grand Lake entrance, and one near the top of Trail Ridge Road.[70]

Challenging Tradition

Upon the conclusion of Mission 66, few could claim that it did not bring significant change to Rocky Mountain National Park. Through the program, the NPS built and rebuilt roads and expanded parking facilities to welcome more tourists into the park system. In this basic sense, Mission 66 was a total success. Headed by bureaucrats like Conrad Wirth, the NPS obtained an incredible amount of capital to bolster its infrastructure, meet current visitation demands, and promote future growth. Although the program did much to improve the sagging physical infrastructure of the park, its architects failed to anticipate the consequences of the program's success.

Facilitating visitation via the construction and maintenance of an automobile-centered parkscape only brought more tourists, and within less than fifteen years the NPS again faced a situation similar in kind, if not in scale, to that which they had encountered immediately following World War II. The second problem, which stemmed in part from the development of the first, was widespread and significant environmental changes brought about within the park by the construction and presence of roads, and the cars and humans they delivered, throughout the park.

Although various scientific studies of the park had been conducted as early as the 1930s, they were relatively few and far between. Moreover, none addressed specifically the impacts of visitors. Beatrice Willard, who specialized in alpine plant ecology, earned a contract with the NPS to study the ecological impacts people had upon the places they trod. Her final report, "Effects of Visitors on Natural Ecosystems in Rocky Mountain National Park," comprises more than 400 pages of data and analysis and offers a wonderful window into the park just past midcentury. Making Willard's report even more valuable is the fact that she was able to witness many of the environmental consequences of Mission 66, as several of her study areas coincided with locations recently expanded and enhanced through the rebuilding effort.

Willard carefully selected a range of study plots, including locations along Trail Ridge Road at Rock Cut, Little Rock Cut, Forest Canyon Overlook, and Iceberg Lake, in addition to Bear Lake and the system of trails that connected it to Nymph Lake and Dream Lake. She then set about compiling quantitative data on the various plants found at each.[71] She also examined historic park photos, as well as those she took while in the field, to ascertain degrees and types of environmental changes over both long- and short-term intervals.[72]

In harsh environments like those found along much of Trail Ridge Road, deep snow, ice, bracing winds, intense sun, and a short growing season combine to make plant life precarious. Over thousands of years, however, natural processes produced a rich layer of humus and duff (top-level detritus) to the point where plant life could grow. In time, plant communities extended over much of the tundra, forming a thin plate of armor over it. When the system operates as it should, the plants are generally able to hold fast to the soil below and protect it against the erosional forces of wind and water.

When the top layer of life is disturbed and a chink in the armor develops, however, erosion and deterioration of the ecosystem often result. The removal of cushion plants, for example, could initiate soil erosion almost immediately. In relatively short order, the duff layer (essentially decomposed or decomposing organic material) begins to erode. As the duff washes and blows away, so does the soil's humus layer, further impairing its ability to support plant life. "Therefore," concluded Willard, the "loss of any portion of the duff and humus from the ecosystem alters environment factors of vital importance to the major vegetation components of the plants."[73] Over time, as the soil's ability to retain moisture declines, its average seasonal temperature increases, and a "favorable environment for colonization by other plants" is created.[74]

Spanning her five-year study, Willard found time and again that the most significant and lasting visitor-caused changes were tied directly to upsetting the plant and soil dynamics described above. For example, if an area received enough foot traffic, especially during spring runoff when the plants of the tundra are most vulnerable, plants could be trampled to the point of death.

Over a short period of time, dead plants could allow erosional forces and ecological transformation to begin. The removal of rocks, either unintentionally by kicking or intentionally by rock "collectors," had the same effect. Once a rock was moved or removed, water, wind, and heaving frost could quickly carve its way through the tundra's topsoil. "Thus," concluded Willard, "trampling and other visitor activities, together with natural environmental forces interact to bring about the continued erosion of areas laid bare by removal of rocks."[75]

Revealing the irony of roads in perceived natural places, Willard concluded that the "tundra adjacent to places where visitors stop is showing considerable alteration and semi-permanent damage. . . . Therefore, most of the tundra which visitors see close up cannot be considered natural and undisturbed by man."[76] Hundreds of thousands of tourists had driven up and down Trail Ridge Road to see amazing natural scenes. To those who lacked ecological understanding, tundra was tundra. To Willard, however, who was deeply interested in how ecosystems function as opposed to how places appear, much of the park's valuable tundra was no longer natural.

The work of Beatrice Willard is remarkable in many regards. The fact that Rocky Mountain National Park agreed to fund a meaningful long-term ecological study reflects a degree of institutional self-reflection not generally present during the earlier years of the park. Willard's study also demonstrates shifts in environmental thought following World War II. Well before the first Earth Day in 1970, she and many of her colleagues were challenging how millions of Americans understood the natural world and humans' place within it.[77] Although visitor satisfaction continued to play a significant role in shaping policy in RMNP, the decision-making process was increasingly up for debate as concerns over environmental health and sustainability entered the management dynamic. A new and competing way of looking at the park's roads and roadsides had thus arrived.

Beyond Mission 66

Amid this growing division over roads and their place in parks, a team of scholars from Colorado State University authored "A Study to Develop Criteria for Determining the Carrying Capacity of Areas within the National Park System."[78] In the broadest sense, this report was an early attempt to

balance the economic, social, biological, and ecological aspects of park man
agement. Throughout, the language and ideologies of ecology such as "equilibrium" and "carrying capacity" were deployed to better understand and
define human uses.

Finding any level of equilibrium—especially between visitor use and park
health—was not easy. The management problem lay across a spectrum. At
one end was total ecological integrity and zero visitation and at the opposite
end was complete visitor use and the literal consumption of the park's natural
resources. The National Park Service, reasoned the authors, had a mandate to
establish a rational *and* practical balance between these two positions.

Further complicating matters was the fact that different visitors chose different methods for experiencing the park. Although the vast majority reported
sightseeing as their primary objective, the way in which visitors chose to see the
sights varied widely. In managing a landscape for its visual-emotional appeal,
the rate of speed, depth and field of vision, and general setting were all determining factors, of which landscape architects had long been aware. "While all
may be moving much of the time," found the Colorado State researchers, "it is
one thing to see the park through the windshield of a vehicle moving at a rate
of 35 miles per hour and seeing it along the identical route from a bicycle or on
foot at a much slower rate of movement." The differences in how one experienced the park, in turn, meant that "the same user is likely to demand a higher
standard of landscape and environmental quality when he is hiking than when
he is riding through a natural area in an automobile."[79]

After reasoning through the complex set of variables involved in determining carrying capacity, including social, economic, aesthetic, and ecological components, the team recommended that park managers craft a definition of "carrying capacity" as "the capacity of an area in terms of man-days
(or man hours per day) of recreation use that can be tolerated without irreversible deterioration of the physical environment," and that they then
manage just shy of that point.[80] Doing so, they contended, would protect the
park's natural systems from irreversible harm while maximizing visitor use.

The Colorado State study may not sound radical today, but placed in historical context its findings mark a significant shift in how RMNP was conceptualizing its mission. Just three years following the completion of Mission 66—a program that overwhelmingly valued visitor use over anything
approaching sustainable environmental practices—the NPS began to recog-

nize that previous management solutions to longstanding problems were no longer tenable or even desirable. The study also reflects how ecology and concepts like carrying capacity were challenging the culture of tourism that had, since the beginning, dominated.

With park popularity soaring, the question of how millions of visitors could be best accommodated remained a pressing issue. Between 1967 and 1978 visitation rose from an estimated 2 million to more than 3 million, an increase of more than half. By the middle of the 1970s NPS officials estimated that an astonishing 4,200 vehicles *per day* traveled the Bear Lake road during the peak of the season.[81] If a visitor stood roadside between the hours of 7 A.M. and 7 P.M. and watched every car that passed en route to and from Bear Lake, a car would have rumbled by every five seconds. Reeling, RMNP initiated a shuttle system to deliver visitors to Bear Lake in 1978.[82] By 1980 the new shuttle route, which made stops at the Moraine Park and Glacier Basin campgrounds before arriving at Bear Lake, moved more than 154,000 people. An additional 5,015 people rode the shuttle between Moraine Campground and Fern Lake Trailhead.[83]

Although the shuttle brought about a marked decrease in the overall number of automobiles in the park, the system was far from perfect. Perhaps the most vexing problem was that the new system, focused as it was upon Bear Lake, brought about even more intensive use of the popular destination. Hoping to find a more effective system that reduced the strain there, the NPS hired a Denver outfit in 1979 to investigate alternatives.[84] At the first public meeting on the issue, the study team put forth three management possibilities, including no action, dispersed visitor use, and concentrated visitor use.

Under the dispersed visitor alternative "visitors to the Park would be channeled away from the popular use areas of Bear and Sprague Lakes and encouraged to explore the less-populated areas of Glacier Creek Basin." It also called for an expanded shuttle system that "would originate with a primary staging area of the west side of Estes Park and connect with secondary shuttle staging areas within park boundaries." The new bus system would also operate in such a way that passengers were better dispersed along the Bear Lake corridor. A less popular alternative called for funneling visitors toward Bear Lake and Sprague Lake—effectively sacrificing these areas in the hopes of lessening the burden on other locales across the park.[85]

After further study, the NPS decided upon a mixed approach to solve congestion along the Bear Lake corridor. Rather than limiting the total number of visitors per day, as some advocated, the NPS sought to "design areas to withstand large numbers of visitors" and to encourage use at areas that were less popular. Accordingly, the final plan called for a shuttle to make stops at Park Headquarters, Moraine Park Visitor Center, Tuxedo Park, Hallowell Park, the Glacier Basin Shuttle area, and three other stops along Bear Lake Road before ending at Bear Lake. In all, the new, expanded transportation system was to cost more than $3.5 million, including $552,000 for the construction of a staging area at the Beaver Meadows entrance, plus shelters and benches along the route.

The NPS also proposed construction of 500 additional parking spaces at the primary shuttle area, an expansion from 5 to 30 spaces near Tuxedo Park, 45 to 100 spaces at Sprague Lake, and 10 to 20 spots at the Bierstadt trailhead. Meanwhile, parking at Bear Lake was reduced from 200 to 150 spaces, and the number of turnouts between Moraine Park and Bear Lake was reduced from 133 to 100. Although the plan represented a massive 540 net gain in parking spaces, the vast majority of spaces was at the margins of the park. Inside the park, and revealing the thrust of the dispersed use plan, the park essentially reallocated parking away from Bear Lake toward less popular destinations and reduced the number of turnouts along the corridor by about 25 percent.[86]

Although not a perfect solution to overcrowding, congested roads, and taxed ecosystems, expanding public transportation reduced the number of automobiles traveling the Bear Lake corridor. Between 1987 and 2006, for example, a total of 3,661,942 people rode the Bear Lake Loop, while 342,233 rode the Moraine Park Loop.

Although the NPS has taken more steps since 1978 to address traffic and congestion, scientific study continues to indicate that roads and automobiles are active and significant agents of environmental change. During the 2003 and 2004 seasons, Barbara Keller and Louis Bender, two researchers from the New Mexico Cooperative Fish and Wildlife Research Unit, studied the impact of traffic on RMNP's iconic bighorn sheep. The park is home to four bands of bighorn sheep, one of which lives in the area around the mineral lick at Sheep Lake. Hoping to "interpret relations among bighorn sheep crossing behavior and the degree of disturbance at Sheep lakes," the team conducted traffic counts and gathered statistical data on how many times bighorn sheep tried and failed to cross the road to access the mineral lick.[87]

The location of the study was important for two reasons.[88] First, the mineral lick at Sheep Lake is segregated from the bighorn's preferred habitat by Fall River Road, which "receives heavy recreational traffic use during the summer months." Sheep Lake and its mineral lick are also significant because "Rocky Mountain bighorn sheep, especially pregnant or lactating ewes, seek out mineral licks from early to late summer to help balance the metabolic costs associated with lactation and/or replenish bone mineral reserves." In other words, bighorns have a physiological need for what Sheep Lake provides, but they must cross a busy park road to access it.

Complicating matters is the fact that bighorn sheep are "particularly sensitive to disturbance" and often avoid areas of high human activity. The researchers were concerned that road-induced stress could initiate unhealthy physiological and behavioral responses from the animals. Faster "heart rate, depleted energy reserves, adrenal gland enlargement, and increased susceptibility to disease," were all likely outcomes of the commingling of cars and bighorn sheep at the site. In the end, the team concluded "that human and road-related disturbance at Sheep Lakes is negatively affecting bighorn sheep use of the mineral site," which they believed would have a detrimental impact on the animals' overall health and productivity.[89]

Drivers had long relished the opportunity to see such beautiful animals from the comfort of their automobiles. Admiring the sheep from behind the wheel gave visitors the impression of peace and abundance. Through the eyes of ecologists, however, the stressed and struggling roadside sheep were symbols of a natural world out of whack.

Conclusion

The roads of Rocky Mountain National Park are as fascinating as they are significant. For more than a century, individuals and institutions sought to connect the park to the act of driving. Although this connection worked just as some had hoped, roads are far more than a means to get from Point A to Point B. To millions of park visitors, roads provide a powerful means to experience and understand parklands.

As long as the culture of tourism remained unchallenged, feeding wild animals, felling trees, removing historic structures, conducting roadside clean-ups, and expanding parking lots were all intended to create an experience that mirrored ideas about what constituted nature and beauty. Those who viewed Rocky Mountain through the lens of ecology, however, saw a very different place. Whereas many Sunday drivers beheld breathtaking views of alpine tundra, ecologists witnessed destruction, change, and the loss of na-ture. Where some visitors marveled at bighorn sheep gathering roadside to enjoy a bit of salt, ecologists saw disruption and degradation of the natural world. Both were culturally and historically important ways of seeing the same place at the same time. Both shared the belief that humans were not a part of nature. The proponents of tourism sought to hide the human hands that had shaped the park to maintain a façade of the pristine; the ecologists sought to still those very same hands.

More than 3 million people visited the park in 2000 alone, and overall park visitation is expected to increase by as much as 45 percent by 2020. In raw numbers, this equates to 4.9 million annual visitors.[90] Although RMNP has undertaken several expensive projects to ameliorate the impact of high traffic volume, visitors and their automobiles pose significant—and grow-ing—management problems. If the above predictions hold true, the time may soon come when we will all need to leave our steel steeds at the gate and find a new way to pass through this enchanted place.

3

Happy Trails

If archeologists of the future happened upon the trails that stretch across Rocky like cracks in a broken windshield, what would they conclude about the paths and the people who trod them? No resource extraction; no apparent agriculture; no permanent settlements; but ample evidence that hundreds of millions of human beings traveled well-worn paths from parking lots to a slew of high mountain destinations. A great mystery, indeed.

The reasons that people hike, climb, and ride across the trails of Rocky are as varied as the millions who do so every year. For some, a stroll around Bear Lake provides the family a welcome break from the tedium of hours in the car and respite from squabbles about who touched whom last. For others, creaking saddle leather and the company of gentle horses provide glimpses of a West long since passed. For a few, hefting a pack filled with carefully assembled gear onto one's back and setting out for a week in the rapturous solitude of the backcountry is reason enough to endure the other 51 weeks of the year.

For the majority of the millions who visit RMNP, the park's network of trails provides a crucial means to experience and engage the area. But trails turn out to be complicated—even contested—spaces. They allow for more than the movement of humans and pack animals; trails also facilitate the movement of soil, invasive plant species, and ideas. For nearly a century, use conflicts along Rocky's many trail corridors have shaped the visitor experience and the ecology of the park. Initially, the steady growth in visitation necessitated more trails and the separation of horses and automobiles. When building and maintaining more trails was no longer an economically, politically, or environmentally feasible solution to congested and overworn trails, the NPS began managing the park in innovative ways. In part shaped by evolving social and legal definitions of wilderness, and by the philosophy and aims of Mission 66, the park was transformed from a single entity into various units cleaved generally into either frontcountry or backcountry. Within each category, certain behaviors were encouraged, discouraged, and sometimes prohibited. Generally, wilderness values including solitude and ecological integrity came to dominate activities and management of the backcountry. Meanwhile, more traditional tourist demands for recreation, beauty, and convenience continue to dominate the frontcountry. Often knitting the two together are the park's hundreds of miles of trails.

Dude Ranching

The prospect of hiking, riding, and climbing in and around Estes Park has long been a powerful draw to the region. Intrepid traveler and outdoor writer Isabella Bird, for example, spent time in Estes Park and played an important role in promoting the region as early as the 1870s. Bird, an Englishwoman who began traveling the world with the hopes of improving her health, wrote rapturously about the Rockies and Estes Park. Her travel letters, which she later published as *A Lady's Life in the Rocky Mountains*, invigorated a broad audience.

In the 1870s simply arriving in Estes Park, as Bird discovered, was an adventure. A woman who never flinched at a challenge, Bird made two attempts to find the settlement. Her first trip, which was foiled by her incompetent braggart of a guide, did not dissuade her. Soon after the failed attempt, more reliable guides brought Bird to her destination. Peering at Estes Park from above, Bird wrote that the valley was "lighted up by the bright waters of the rushing Thompson" and "guarded by sentinel mountains of fantastic shape and monstrous size, with Long's Peak rising above them all in unapproachable grandeur." Seeing glorious peaks thrusting skyward all around, she was gripped by "mountain fever" and pushed her horse to a "delirious speed" toward the valley below.[1]

Although her accommodations in Estes Park were modest at best, Bird paid no mind. Instead, she seemed to revel in the simple hospitality of Griff Evans's ranch, where she "gamely assisted with the chores" and "tend[ed] cattle when asked to help out."[2] Once she was settled into her quarters, the area so enchanted Bird that she became "almost angry with Nature for her close imitation of art." Here, "grandeur and sublimity, not softness, are the features of Estes Park." Nestled high in the Rockies, she found that "the glades which begin so softly are soon lost in the dark primeval forests, with their peaks of rosy granite, and their stretches of granite blocks piled and poised by nature in some mood of fury."[3] But Bird wanted more than to simply admire the mountain's gloom and glory.[4] She imagined testing her will and strength as she climbed skyward on those very same "granite blocks" that nature had so furiously arrayed.

Longs Peak, which was "one of the noblest of mountains," seemed to tease and torment Bird from the moment she arrived.[5] With the help of "Rocky Mountain" Jim—a shady figure who formed a quick and strong bond with the Englishwoman—and two other male companions, Bird set off to climb it. Like many early adventurers, the four traveled first by horseback as far as timberline, where they camped beneath the crisp mountain sky. The next day, Rocky Mountain Jim tethered himself to Bird, and the foursome picked their way toward the peak. Pulling, hefting, and heaving, Rocky Mountain Jim made good on his promise and delivered the exhausted Bird safely to "the storm-rent crown of this lonely sentinel of the Rocky Range." Once atop "one of the mightiest of the vertebrae of the backbone of the North American continent," Bird stood in awe as she cast her gaze upon the very place where the "waters start for both oceans." By the conclusion of her trip, Bird proclaimed that Estes Park was hers "by right of love, appropriation, and appreciation; by the seizure of its peerless sunrises and sunsets, its glorious afterglow." To so many who would follow the Englishwoman to Estes Park and later Rocky Mountain National Park, the trails, peaks, and valleys of the region promised sublimity and awe.[6]

Bird's visit to Estes Park marked important shifts in the region's economy. After all, she found accommodations at Griff Evans's ranch, where she paid "$8 a week" for a "small cabin." Evans was not alone in realizing that money could be made playing host to out-of-town guests. Subsequent to their homestead claim of 1875, for example, Reverend Elkanah Lamb and his son Carlyle built Longs Peak House in the shadow of the great mountain and "began guiding people up Longs Peak for five dollars a trip."[7] Lord Dunraven (Windham Thomas Wyndam-Quin, the fourth Earl of Dunraven), meanwhile, used his considerable resources to commission Albert Bierstadt to paint the area in 1876 and opened the Estes Park Hotel the next year.[8] Meanwhile, other homesteaders of the region such as Abner Sprague also offered lodging, food, and guide services to travelers. Before long, the hunting, mining, and cattle-raising that characterized so much of the economic activity of the region would be supplemented, and later supplanted, by tourism and outdoor adventure.

The early homesteads and hunting camps of Estes Park provided a crucial bridge between the extractive industries of the past and the emerging tourist economy. Almost from the start, the Lambs, Evanses, Spragues, and others were selling more than rooms and food. They were offering an experience unique to the myth and mystique of the West. When Isabella Bird helped Griff Evans with the cattle and other chores, she was effectively entering into a new sort of relationship with the proprietor. No longer was she a passive patron; instead she became—if only for a brief while—integral to the operation of a working western ranch. She was, in other words, one of the earliest dudes of Estes Park.

To contemporaries, a dude was "someone from another area who came to the West and paid for food, lodging, riding, and/or guiding services."[9] A dude ranch was essentially a cattle operation that opened its doors to paying customers. As business owners, dude ranchers sought to promote their facilities and the natural world as core western experiences. In this way, the "economic effects of dude ranching percolated through the entire economy as dude ranchers helped make the Rocky Mountain West well known throughout the rest of the country."[10]

By promoting the scenery of the West as well as its hunting, fishing, and riding opportunities, dude ranches drew adventurous urban Americans and "remittance men" from England who were "especially eager to experience western life and ranching activities" around Estes Park.[11] In time, more dude ranches developed across Colorado and the western states. "Squeaky" Bob Wheeler, for example, set up the Hotel de Hardscrabble to cater to trout fishermen and hunters at what would later become the Phantom Valley Ranch.[12]

While the dude ranches of Colorado were linking the mountains of the

West to wildlife, scenery, hiking, and horseback riding in the minds of travelers, other establishments, like the Elkhorn Lodge, were doing the same. In its turn-of-the-century brochure, for example, the Elkhorn Lodge claimed that Estes Park, "nestl[ed] under the shadow of Long's Peak," offered the "sublime and the awful," which were "presented in strong contrast."[13] The pamphlet included descriptions of horse rides to Black Canyon, Hallet Glacier, Flattop Mountain, Gem Lake, and Wind River, among others. "For those who delight in mountain climbing," extolled the pamphlet, the area "affords ample opportunity." It should come as no surprise that Longs Peak, which at the time required a guide to ascend, was listed as a rewarding challenge. Whereas the Union Pacific Railroad and others were touting the roads and convenience of the Estes Park region, the Evanses, Spragues, and others were making a living by offering access to a romantic and rugged West.

Building Trails

The founding of Rocky Mountain National Park brought still more attention to hiking, climbing, and riding in the region. Upon its creation, the park inherited more than 128 miles of trails. Some of the trails had long been in use, like Grand Lake Trail via Flattop Mountain, which connected Estes Park and Grand Lake. Other trails, like the one stretching from Glacier Creek to Bierstadt Lake and Storm Pass Trail, were built as recently as 1914 by the U.S. Forest Service. Still others, such as Loch Vale Trail, had been built by the Estes Park Improvement Association to attract and please tourists.[14] Like all management during the early years of the park, however, the NPS was not yet sufficiently influential to garner large appropriations for trails. Thus, it early struggled with annual appropriations of less than $500, barely enough to keep the most popular trails in passable condition.[15]

Hoping to attract visitors, however, the NPS used the power of the press to trumpet its trail-related activities. On foot, claimed an early NPS brochure, hikers could take "tramps and picnics" to various mountaintops just as they could hike across the Continental Divide to Grand Lake. The park also offered "the horseback rider . . . an infinite variety of valley roads, trails, and cross-country courses, or he may strike up the mountain trails into the rocky fastnesses [sic]."[16] Furthermore, horses were available for rent at "many of the hotels," and camping gear, clothing, and food were also available.[17] Although the NPS touted automobile tours through the park, trails also received ample attention in promotional materials.[18]

Building and maintaining a network of trails that delivered visitors to desirable destinations was a complicated matter. The more the NPS sought to increase visitation through the construction and promotion of roads, the more it increased the need for diverse, reliable, and well-marked trails. The more the park was able to funnel hikers, riders, and climbers beyond the comfortable confines of the roadside, however, the more it effectively put visitors farther and farther from predictable environments. Although it is true that automobile accidents became a common—though not frequent—occurrence in the park, hiking, climbing, and riding incidents were far more common. Increased trail traffic also raised the likelihood of conflicts between users, just as it amplified the environmental impacts of heavy trail use itself.

Eager to enhance the park's trail system, a five-man detail used a portion of the $2,000 trail appropriation for 1922 to improve signage along the popular Longs Peak Trail. Although the lower section was easy enough to follow, beyond the "Keyhole," which is a massive rock fin where climbers effectively pass from one side of the towering peak to the other, the trail was "often difficult to find or follow." Here, the peak towers high above the left shoulder of hikers and a dizzying array of sheer cliffs plummet some 2,000 feet just beyond the hiker's right foot. A clear, safe, and well-marked trail through the debris-strewn labyrinth was much needed. Making the matter still more pressing was the fact that as early as 1922 more than 1,000 people were making the climb every year. Carrying paint buckets and brushes, park rangers set out to paint dots on the rocks to mark the trail between the Keyhole and the summit. Still today, hikers use the system of painted dots to find their way to the top.[19] Despite such early and somewhat primitive efforts, not all hikers and climbers were willing to follow the rangers' breadcrumb trail.

In the winter of 1925 Agnes Wolcott Vaille set out with Swiss alpinist Walter Kiener to climb Longs Peak's challenging East Face. Vaille, an educated woman who served as the secretary of the Denver Chamber of Commerce, had previously led several successful group ascents of Longs Peak. But this climb was more grueling than either she or Kiener expected and by the time the two reached the frozen summit Vaille was exhausted. Perhaps not thinking clearly, the two picked their way off the mountain along the North Face route, and Vaille lost her footing and fell. Remarkably, she was not injured, but she did not have the strength to carry on and Kiener quickly set off for help. By the time the ordeal was over, Vaille had died of hypothermia and one of her would-be rescuers, Herbert Sortland, had died as well.[20]

This tragedy, argues historian Ruth Alexander, put Superintendent Roger Toll in the position to more actively manage popular and perilous areas like Longs Peak. In part hoping to offer inexperienced climbers an alternate route to the summit that bypassed the somewhat harrowing journey and hard-to-follow trail beyond the Keyhole, the NPS installed nearly 200 feet of cable up the popular North Face of Longs Peak in 1925. Once in place, the cable provided climbers with a sort of handle as they pulled themselves up the mountain.[21] The NPS also planned to install a telephone line between Hewes-Kirkwood Inn and the new Boulderfield Shelter cabin to facilitate communication during rescues.[22]

The park's rising popularity posed more challenges yet. Horses and horse-drawn wagons, both of which had dominated early road use, were losing popularity as visitors increasingly chose the comfort of automobiles, which NPS encouraged. The completion of Fall River Road in 1920, for example, necessitated destruction of the old horse trail that passed through the canyon en route to the Continental Divide. There were more subtle indications of the ascendancy of automobiles in the park as well. Early park regulations, for example, required that automobile horns "be sounded on approaching curves on stretches of road concealed for any considerable distance."[23] This policy, intended to enhance communication and awareness among drivers, did not lend itself to horse travel along the park's expanding network of roads. Instead, this regulation reveals important shifts taking place within the park's human, equestrian, and automobile geography. With more than 3 million people visiting the park in 2011 alone, one can only imagine the cacophony that would be heard if this regulation were in effect today.

Still, park managers understood that horses and hikers needed the opportunity to access the Divide. To replace the horse trail sacrificed at Fall River, the NPS built a new one in 1923 that passed through Hidden Valley to the top of Trail Ridge.[24] Once finished, the new trail made "it possible for horseback parties to cross the range to the northwestern portion of the park, without having to ride over the Fall River road, which [could not] safely be used by both automobiles and horses."[25] The destruction of the horse trail up Fall River Canyon and the building of trails up Hidden Valley demonstrate that, as early as 1922, the NPS was employing use-based segregation as a management tool in the park—a trend that would intensify over time.

Throughout the remainder of the 1920s the NPS spent considerable time and effort building, rebuilding, and marking trails through the park.[26] By 1931 they had completed the system of trails that connected Bear Lake with the Nymph Lake, Dream Lake, Loch Vale, North Longs Peak, and Storm Pass trails. In addition to linking a series of popular destinations to major parking areas, this work also "remove[d] all horse travel from the upper three miles of the Bear Lake Road." Expanding trail access across the park was a pressing concern, as trail counts in 1932 showed that some 7,000 pedestrians and 3,000 horses used the trails around Bear Lake alone.[27] Although pushing horses off of park roads onto trails resolved one set of problems, it generated more pressure, and opportunity for conflict, along the park's expanding trail system.

Just as more hikers and riders used the trails around Bear Lake and other popular destinations, Longs Peak continued to see greater use and therefore concerns about safety and communication. In July 1936 Arthur Draper of the *New York Times* attempted to reach the summit of the 14,259-foot peak. Although the distance from the trailhead to the Boulderfield posed no difficulties for Draper, when he arrived at the Boulderfield at the base of the peak the self-admitted climbing novice felt as though he was in "serious danger." Draper was unprepared for the challenges that lay ahead, in part because a park ranger had earlier informed him that "all one needed for the hike and climb from Bear Lake" to the summit "was common sense and a lot of endurance." Beyond the Boulderfield, however, Draper "could not discover, except for two rather general and vague signs, anything that was of much directional value." Pressing ahead, he followed another party until "a short distance below the top" he found himself "stymied," not possessing "the equipment, experience, or nerve to go farther." At some point during his failed attempt, the frazzled Draper concluded that it was "decidedly foolish to allow such inexperienced persons as" himself to "attempt such a climb without better preparation or more adequate warning than is at present given." In a letter that he later penned to RMNP Superintendent Thomas Allen, Draper recommended that the NPS plant better signs, station a ranger at the Boulderfield, print more reliable literature on the nature of the climb, or prohibit unguided and inexperienced visitors from attempting the climb.[28]

Bear Lake Odessa Trail, 1932. Courtesy of the National Archives, College Park, MD.

Superintendent Allen, like those who served before and after him, was in a difficult position. He was well aware of the challenges that the popular mountain posed to his agency, and he admitted that it would "always be a problem." At various times, the NPS had considered limiting access to only qualified climbers, but it lacked the resources to implement a screening process. A shelter cabin had offered meals and protection to hikers and climbers, but the structure was eventually deemed unsafe and closed. Even if the park had the resources to mark every landmark along the trail and to station rangers along it, such measures would, concluded Allen, "utterly destroy the atmosphere" of the peak.[29]

Allen and his staff were walking a thin line. They certainly needed to maintain visitor safety and security, but such measures could be pushed only so far before the very reason that hikers and climbers ascended the peak—solitude, danger, excitement, and a desire to test one's steel and resolve—would be compromised. When possible, park staff took measures that enhanced safety yet took a limited toll on the freedom and thrill of mountain climbing. The installation and maintenance of phone lines up the mountain illustrate the point. Although often less than reliable, the phone lines provided important communication between rescue teams and visitors in trouble without visibly intruding upon the mountaineering experience.

The park took other preemptive measures as well. In 1940, for example, it purchased four metal chests and filled each with "climbing ropes, pitons, carabineers, piton hammers, ice axes, crampons, headlamps, signal flares, emergency rations, wool blankets, complete sets of woolen clothing, chemical heating pads, pack sacks, thermos bottles, mess kits, first aid kits, canteens, miner helmets and rappelling hooks." The chests were then stashed in strategic locations, including along Longs Peak Trail and at Bear Lake, where hikers and climbers often found themselves in trouble.[30] Unless the gear was needed, however, its presence would not impinge upon the "atmosphere" of thrilling destinations such as Longs Peak.

Although rescue caches, phones, cables, and better signage were all part of NPS efforts to enhance visitor safety without degrading the mountain experience, education was perhaps the most powerful and cost-effective weapon. Reckoning that climbers would not take kindly to the strict bridling of their pursuits, the NPS instead relied upon education to gently shape climbing in the park. In this regard, RMNP had an advantage. Since Rocky's creation, various rangers and superintendents had been members of the Colorado Mountain Club. Employing rangers who were avid and respected mountaineers made it easier for the NPS to shape the behavior of the climbing community.[31] Ranger Ernest K. Field, for example, was both a respected park employee and experienced climber. As the park sought avenues to better control climbing activities in the park, Field and others served as important bridges between the NPS and the broader climbing community.

Together, Field and CMC members hosted a "Climbing Training Course" for park staff and hoped that the day would come when such courses were as pervasive as the firefighting training academies held in the park. Field and the CMC had also been working on an "informative poster for mountain climbers," which was eventually posted at key areas around the park. The park also encouraged all climbing questions to be routed through the chief ranger's office, which enabled trained experts to check the climbers' equipment, give them detailed information on the climb, and answer any questions they might have. Ranger Field also wrote an article for the "Vacation Edition" of the *Estes Park Trail* to promote a "better understanding of mountain climbing, its techniques and safety features."[32]

Postwar Problems

The postwar flood of visitors washing across America's national parks, as recounted in Chapter 2, presented new and demanding challenges that would forever shape Rocky Mountain National Park. Between the founding of the park in 1915 and 1948, more than 40,000 people found their way to the summit of its highest peak. In 1948, with demand for park resources surging, a record 1,800 ascents of Longs Peak occurred that year alone. To further ensure hiker and climber safety, the NPS stretched additional phone lines to the shelter cabin at Chasm Lake, posted twelve new safety signs, hosted a six-hour "mountain climbing training school" at the park, and participated in the first "Service-wide mountain climbing and rescue school" at Mt. Rainier, Washington. These efforts, combined with a bit of good fortune, resulted in no fatalities and only minor climbing and hiking injuries that year.[33] The rising importance of managing for the safety and well-being of climbers is reflected in the fact that in 1949 "mountain climbing" earned itself its own category in the superintendent's annual report, and for good reason.

As more visitors sought the outdoor adventure that Longs Peak promised, more tourists were also subjecting themselves to afternoon lightning storms, rock slides, falls, and falling rocks. Responding to the dynamic situation, the staff at Rocky began holding "intensive in-service climbing school[s]" as the number of requests for information about the peak surged.[34]

The resurgence of automobile travel and the urbanization of the United States brought still more challenges to trail management in Rocky. Not only were more people visiting the park but more and more people were coming from cities where horses were scarce and knowledge of techniques of mountain climbing and outdoor experience limited. Mid-century studies showed, in fact, that a majority of those visiting the park were college-educated, middle-class urbanites.[35] Like the Isabella Birds of previous generations, many of those who came to Rocky from Kansas City, St. Louis, Chicago, Dallas, and the like were coming to experience an authentic, natural West. But such urbanites often had little experience with the vicissitudes of mountain adventure.

In July 1945, for example, Chicagoan Albert Furch was riding a rented horse on the beautiful Loch Vale Trail. As Furch and his horse rode alongside a steep drop-off, a thunderclap spooked his horse and a second one sent the man plummeting to his death.[36] The records do not speak to Furch's skill as a horseman, and it is impossible to know even if a skilled rider might have averted disaster. Much like the tragic death of Agnes Vaille on Longs Peak, however, Furch's death and the public outcry it generated put the NPS in the position to more firmly regulate horse use in the park. Before 1945, the NPS did not have the need or the desire to regulate saddle and pack horse liveries that were located outside the park. After World War II, and following Furch's death, the NPS began the gradual process of regulating horses in the park. The first step in this process involved issuing permits to the owner of each livery as a means of at least tracking how many horses were in the park at any one time.[37]

The trails of Rocky presented other challenges as well. By the early 1950s, visitor complaints were becoming more common as trails became crowded and interaction between hikers and riders more frequent.[38] In the summer of 1953, for example, Robert Kahn of Houston, Texas, was hiking from Bear Lake to Nymph Lake. After enjoying the scenery at Nymph Lake, Kahn, his wife, and three children (ages 5, 6, and 11) headed back toward the Bear Lake parking lot. On their way down they met a string of horses guided by Dutch Wooley of Bear Lake Livery. Even though park regulations merely required hikers to stand quietly as horses passed, Kahn and his family yielded the trail to the horses as best they could on the narrow path. Wooley was apparently not satisfied with the berth the family had given, and he "*forced his horse to shy and sidestep and lift its front feet toward* [Kahn's] *wife and five year old girl as tho to push them off the steep edge.*" Wooley's "bullying" behavior led to a heated exchange between the Kahns and the ill-tempered guide and an eventual rebuke of the insolent guide by park rangers.[39]

To address the growing conflicts between users and to "prevent damage to particularly fragile high altitude meadows," the NPS began prohibiting horses in those areas where conflicts were most common and threats to fragile scenery most acute. From 1963 forward, the very popular "Bear Lake nature trail, Bear Lake to Emerald Lake, Dream Lake to Haiyahs [referring to Lake Haiyaha], and Chasm Lake trail from its junction with the Longs Peak trail to Chasm Lake," were all closed to horses. Although the *Estes Park Trail* and park staff were quick to point out that "only 5.2 miles of the 303.1 miles of Park trails" were impacted by the closures, the trails listed above were among Rocky's most popular.

Turf Wars

In 1964 Superintendent Granville Liles called together his staff to discuss backcountry management. After the meeting, Liles formed a committee of engineers, wildlife experts, landscape architects, and park rangers to further investigate the issue. Using "A Back Country Management Plan for Sequoia and Kings Canyon National Parks" as a template, the men set out to better understand the unique management challenges that were emerging with a shifting appreciation of wilderness.

The committee's work marks a watershed in the history of the park. At no time before had the staff at RMNP acknowledged so clearly that the "back country [was] used by those people who desire to escape the confines of more formal civilization in order to relax or simulate the exaltation that so inspired their forefathers." Neither had their predecessors so clearly understood that backcountry and frontcountry users often had little in common. Although frontcountry users did not mind the "urban type compaction of people," backcountry users often sought to get away from such crowds and to escape "hectic everyday environments." For a long time, the committee proclaimed, the park had been "providing the visitor a clean, well kept, and supervised experience in the front country—now they *must* provide the same consideration for the back country users."[40] The language of the report is instructive. Just a few decades before, park staff and superintendents spoke of the "atmosphere" of places like Longs Peak. By the 1960s, concepts like frontcountry, backcountry, and wilderness had supplanted such vague signifiers with a new way of envisioning the park. Modern wilderness had arrived.

Drawing from the research and recommendations of Beatrice Willard's five-year study on the impacts of tourism in Rocky, the committee advocated breaking the park into four distinct management categories, ranging from remote wilderness sites to historic backcountry sites. The committee found that 63 percent of trail users in the park were hikers and that horseback riders—the majority of whom rented horses—constituted some 30 percent of all trail users riding an estimated 40,000 horses annually. They also found that "about 70 percent of all horse use in the park is in the 'front' of the backcountry, never getting very far into the Park." Considering that the vast majority of riding took place during the summer season, and that it was concentrated near the frontcountry, it is not difficult to imagine that on any given summer day hundreds of rented horses trod across the park's most popular trails. Overnight backcountry campers represented a third set of users, amounting to about 4 percent of all trail use, and climbers contributed some 3 percent to trail use. In all, nearly 140,000 visitors used the park's backcountry in 1964, as compared to some 1.5 million frontcountry users.[41]

As it turns out, Mission 66 posed significant challenges for backcountry management. The "increased numbers of vehicles in the Park, additional campgrounds, greater burden at entrance stations," and "increased demand at information stations" meant that backcountry patrols were "almost nonexistent." Without sufficient patrols, the backcountry had become a sort of lawless area where littering and environmental degradation were common. Backcountry camping had increased an incredible 70 percent in just the previous four years. Clearly, more intensive efforts were needed to manage human and horse waste, pick up trash, protect trampled vegetation, and attend to a host of other problems that were becoming all too common in the backcountry.[42]

Unlike the philosophy that guided so much of Mission 66, the committee

Impact of excessive horse use on trail, 1972. Courtesy of Rocky Mountain National Park, ROMO MSF NEG 5710.

concluded that the limited ranger staff and the fragile nature of backcountry resources meant that new regulations must be put in place to *limit* backcountry use. Based on the ecological concept of carrying capacity, the committee recommended that the park more strictly manage fire permits, limit or prevent the gathering of firewood, place properly constructed privies at strategic locations, and install hitching posts for horses. Furthermore, the committee recommended that all new trails and/or relocation of old trails only be undertaken after "ecological reconnaissance [was] made" and the area "determined to be capable of tolerating use."[43]

One of the most complicated and contentious management issues in the backcountry was the question of horse use. Although the committee recognized the cultural and economic significance of horse use in Rocky, it also understood that horses had a "serious impact upon the trail system . . . and natural features of the park," of which park staff had been aware since the early 1930s. Making matters worse was the fact that a significant portion of guided rides focused on a few popular and easy-to-reach trails, which meant that such areas were "over worn," exhibited severe erosion, and were increasingly expensive to repair and maintain.

With the above in mind, the committee recommended placing a two-hour minimum on rides in the park (to further disperse riders and to lessen site-specific impacts), "establish a numerical ceiling on the number of horses per livery" that enter the park every day, close all livery operations within the park itself, and close some trails to horses altogether. To emphasize the need for reform and regulation, the committee included photographs of horses and trails in the park. In one photo, a string of at least forty-seven horses and riders are making their way through Moraine Park, while another photo demonstrated the formation of informal parallel horse trails.[44]

Influenced by scientists like Beatrice Willard who demonstrated the ecological harm that was occurring in parks, the committee spoke often about wilderness and wilderness values. At the forefront of the wilderness movement was a deep-running antidevelopment bent. Historian Paul Sutter, for example, argues that the wilderness movement was born first and foremost in response to the proliferation of roads and automobiles in natural places. Certainly the rise in automobile travel through Rocky and the rising tides of visitors, trash, and waste put the committee members and others in a position to see development, trails, and backcountry in new and distinct ways.

As the committee's report reveals, an increasing number of Americans valued the existence of vast expanses of territory where human impacts were imperceptible. The Wilderness Act, and the wilderness ideas and ideals that gave it shape and political momentum, was signed into law the same year (1964) the committee in Rocky began their work. At the heart of the Wilderness Act was a deep concern about modernity and its impact upon humans. As such, in all lands classified as wilderness cars and roads were strictly forbidden, as were other modern contrivances. Although the legislation did not deal specifically with national parks, the director of the NPS called upon national parks to conduct studies to determine how much, if any, land within the system was suitable for wilderness designation.

Following the orders of the NPS director, Rocky Mountain National Park Superintendent Roger Contor and his staff eventually "identified five units totaling 238,000 acres, or approximately 91 percent of the Park as suitable for inclusion in the National Wilderness Preservation System." The five areas

String of guided horses in Moraine Park, 1965. Photo from "A Report to the Superintendent for a Back Country Management Plan in Rocky Mountain National Park," 1965. U.S. Department of the Interior, Rocky Mountain National Park Library, i–iii.

included 83,700 acres of the Mummy Range, 9,500 acres on the eastern slope of the Never Summer Range, 4,300 acres between Fall River and Trail Ridge Road, 138,000 acres south of Trail Ridge, and 2,200 acres in the southwest corner of the park. Although Mission 66 further tightened the connections between automobiles and the frontcountry, the resonance of the wilderness movement and its anti-road, anti-crowd sentiments were beginning to assert control over the park's backcountry.[45]

Evolving ideas about wilderness also challenged decades of behavior on Longs Peak.[46] As was the case across the park, use of Longs Peak had surged in the postwar era, thereby increasing the likelihood of accidents and environmental degradation. By the late 1960s RMNP began investigating the history of accidents on its high-profile peak. The research found that the cable route, which was initially installed to offer a safer and faster way to the summit, had become quite dangerous. In fact, all six of the nontechnical route fatalities that occurred on the mountain took place on the cable route. Icy conditions, crowding, dangers from falling rocks, fatigue, and lightning all made the popular route an all-too-harrowing experience for many.

But park rangers were alive to more than growing safety concerns. Before wilderness achieved its more modern incarnation, connected as it came to be to ecological integrity and seclusion, the cable route provided many a shorter—if not more dangerous—way to the summit. As wilderness values evolved, however, the cable became an affront to those values, and as early as 1968 park rangers began considering removing the cable. Although, as historian Ruth Alexander points out, their initial concerns were primarily aesthetic, broader environmental concerns soon infused the debate surrounding removal of the cable. At the core of the objections regarding the cable's presence on the North Face of Longs Peak in the early 1970s was the "growing consensus among members of the park staff that the cables were antithetical to wilderness values" that were supposed to provide the management paradigm for so much of the park's territory.[47]

In 1973 park rangers removed the cables from Longs Peak. Hoping to allay public outcry, Superintendent Contor argued that removing the cables was needed "to manage [national parks] in as near their natural condition as possible." Further, only by taking the cables off of the mountain could the area be considered for inclusion in the nation's wilderness system. Although removal of the cables did keep unskilled climbers from the dangers of that route, nontechnical ascents continued to increase as hikers simply chose the longer—and still thrilling—Keyhole route instead.[48]

The increasing popularity of the area meant that human waste was also a mounting problem. Especially during peak seasonal use, the simple privies located at the Boulderfield and at other popular backcountry sites could not keep up with demand, and the overflowing facilities became an affront to wilderness and ecological sensibilities, not to mention visitors' senses. During peak summer use, for example, the four toilets located along the Longs Peak trail accumulated an impressive 8,000 pounds of human waste.[49]

In response to the situation, the NPS launched an innovative pilot program in 1972. At ten locations across the park, including the toilets at the Boulderfield on the Longs Peak trail, park staff dug a pit and installed a liner, which was then fitted with a large fiberglass vault. Then, a privy was built atop the pit, liner, and vault. The vaults, which look like giant buckets with steel cables attached, were flown out by helicopter once they reached capacity and dumped into an awaiting septic truck. During the busiest time of the year, the vaults at the Boulderfield would need to be flown away every two to three weeks. Here, the NPS was attempting to maintain open access to popular locations while managing for wilderness values—not an easy task.

Although the vault system worked well at removing human waste from pristine reaches of the park, it did so at the expense of helicopters buzzing popular destinations every couple of weeks, which posed a different sort of threat to wilderness values.[50] Helicopter waste removal was also expensive and dangerous, as indicated in one instance where one of the full "honey buckets" was lost during flight. Eventually, "the crash of a helicopter on the peak prompted the abandonment of aerial removal" of human waste. The park experimented with other solutions, including incineration, but the "smoke and odor" proved to be too much. Finally, park staff installed solar toilets in 1983 that dehydrated the majority of the human waste, the remainder of which pack animals could then carry out.[51]

As park officials worked to solve this and other problems, the debate on whether to seek wilderness designation continued. In 1974, RMNP hosted public hearings on wilderness designation within the park. Some citizens and groups interested in park management in terms of ecological health and diversity supported wilderness designation, while others more closely aligned with the tourist industry tended to oppose it. The initial wilderness proposal, and the impassioned hearings that followed, reveal a sort of ideological turf war playing out between various factions of park patrons. The final settlement of the dispute would further subdivide the park.

The Estes Park Chamber of Commerce (EPCC), which had a direct economic stake in the day-to-day operation of RMNP, represented well the opinions and attitudes of those opposed to wilderness designation. Speaking on behalf of the chamber group, Ron Railand stated bluntly,

The fact that the Park has the authority to maintain, protect, and preserve the land within the perimeters of the Park, and the fact that the past Park Administrations have both preserved and actually improved upon the natural scenic beauties therein has caused many to wonder if we need to include 91 percent of Rocky Mountain National Park in the Wilderness Preservation System. There are presently fewer horses and concessionaires in Rocky Mountain National Park now than at any time in its history.

In the estimation of the EPCC, the NPS had done enough to protect the ecological integrity of the park; little else needed to be done. Furthermore, continued Railand, "by Park statistics, a very small percentage of those using Rocky actually use present wilderness land . . . therefore, the Chamber whole-heartedly endorses a reduction in the lands being proposed as wilderness."[52] The local chamber's opposition to wilderness designation stemmed not from an ideological opposition to what wilderness areas were but rather from a fear that the good of the many who use the park's roads and built environment was being subverted for the pleasure of a small contingent of patrons.

William Van Horn from High Country Stables also opposed wilderness designation, but for more specific economic reasons. According to Van Horn, wilderness designation violated RMNP's organic act because wilder-ness would limit use of and recreational opportunity within the park. "In fact," he concluded, "putting 91 percent of the park into wilderness would prohibit the Park Service from providing the needs of the public for which it was established." At the heart of the horseman's concern was the fear that designating so much of RMNP as wilderness would curtail his ability to make a living running livery operations in and around the park.[53]

Van Horn had reason to worry. Over the preceding decades, complaints about horse use in the park were on the rise and the park had begun mov-ing toward tighter regulation of horses, a process heightened by the ascen-dancy of wilderness ideologies and the rise of ecology. Clearly, complaints from visitors like Thomas Bulat of Davenport, Iowa, were striking a chord with park staff. Although Bulat and his family enjoyed their time in Rocky in the summer of 1970, they were "surprised to find that horses were allowed on major trails." The Fern-Odessa trail, which Bulat thought was "one of the most beautiful mountain trails in the world . . . was a solid carpet of horse manure." The stench of the manure was "continuously oppressive and the flies were massive." In closing his letter, Bulat argued that such horse use was not in keeping with the "natural ecology of the area" and that horses "should be kept off the regular nature trails."[54] In his reply to Bulat, Superintendent Theodore Thompson admitted that "horse-hiker conflict" was a problem and that "restricting certain additional portions of the existing trail system to each use may be the most feasible alternative" to solving this management issue.[55]

Whereas Van Horn, Railand, and others vehemently opposed wilderness designation, there were many present at the wilderness hearing who supported the plan. For example, Raoul Bates of the National Parks and Conservation Association moved well beyond the NPS's proposals. To Bates, the best course of action included the closure of Fall River Road to all but mass transit and the obliteration of the road through Moraine Park. In calling for the removal of roads and the implementation of mass transit in the park, Bates's testimony embodied much of what the EPCC and others found objectionable about wilderness designation. If the NPS and its supporters had their way, massive tracts of the park would henceforth be closed to roads and driving. To those with a direct economic stake in Rocky Mountain National Park and its reputation as a "driving park," wilderness designation represented a dangerous first step in challenging that tradition.[56]

As the debate over wilderness in RMNP wore on, the NPS put forth its Final Master Plan in 1976, which marked an important victory for backcountry advocates. Based on the belief that the "land resource and man's experience are endangered" in the park through the crowding of the postwar era, and the fact that not all park visitors wanted the same experience, park staff advocated zoning the park along the same rough contours as laid out in the 1965 report. In all, the park would be managed in three zones, including the "scenic viewing or drive-through zone, the day-use zone, and the primitive or backcountry zone."[57]

Drawing directly from language in the Wilderness Act, park staff echoed the sentiment that wilderness was "'an area where the earth and its community of life are untrammeled by man, where man himself is a visitor who does not remain.'" Management for wilderness values did not constitute a "prohibition of use," as Van Horn and others argued, but was "rather a higher order of use."[58] But the rising demand for a "wilderness experience" in Rocky posed an interesting challenge for park staff. On one hand, managers increasingly envisioned the vast majority of the park as a wilderness area, and so accommodating the growing demand for a wilderness experience meshed well with the overall aims and philosophy of the park. On the other, however, rising demand for wilderness experiences meant higher traffic in, and greater demand for, an experience based primarily upon solitude and freedom. In the frontcountry, rising demand had necessitated the building of more roads, the enlargement of those roads, and eventually the implementation of voluntary mass transit. At no point in Rocky's history did management attempt to curtail frontcountry access.

Allowing throngs of wilderness-seekers to simply break across the quiet corners of the park, however, would undermine the very experience such people sought and further imperil ecosystems they esteemed. In response to this conundrum, park staff had sought to control access to the park's backcountry through implementation of a free—but mandatory—backcountry reservation system in 1972.[59] The 1976 Final Master Plan formalized the practice in park operations, concluding that the policy was needed to mitigate backcountry impacts.[60] It is interesting that the park required wilderness-seekers to partake in a premeditated act of claiming a reservation before they could enjoy the primeval, pristine solitude and freedom of the backcountry. Although implementing a mandatory reservation system would help ensure a measure of solitude in the backcountry, it did so at the expense of campers' freedom to stay where, when, and as long as they wanted.[61]

Although park patrons had, by the 1970s, more than 300 miles of trails to choose from, backcountry use was increasing more rapidly than all other park uses, and with it came potential conflict and environmental degradation.[62] During the summer of 1976 alone, park staff estimated that 350,000 day-users accessed Rocky's backcountry, with approximately 600,000 visitors in the backcountry for the entire year.[63] Between 1965 and 1975, backcountry use in RMNP increased by an incredible 700 percent.[64] To better understand the dynamics of trail use in RMNP, Richard Trahan, a professor of sociology at the University of Northern Colorado, spent the summer of 1977 polling users along several park trails that prohibited horse use. The results of his survey demonstrated that there was a correlation between the users of specific trails and their opinions about horse use in the park. For example, more than 30 percent of hikers at Glacier Gorge "strongly" opposed commercial horse use in the park, while more than 60 percent of hikers along Longs Peak Trail opposed it. Trahan also interviewed people at the in-park liveries, as well as hikers on multiuse trails. Here, he found that 90 percent of all riders in the park had never been on a horse and that most riders would have enjoyed themselves equally as well on Forest Service land adjacent to the park.[65] To those interested in pushing horses out of the park, Trahan's research provided valuable ammunition.

With tens of thousands of park visitors patronizing more than a dozen liveries, however, horseback riders and regional liveries were a powerful interest group that would not go quietly. When park staff began urging closure of the stables located within Rocky by the early 1980s, they discovered just how powerful such interests were. Although the NPS had been receiving complaints about hiker-rider conflicts for decades, Rex Walker, owner of High Country Stables, which owned the horse concession permits for Rocky, contended that hiker-rider conflicts did not "really exist," and he argued instead that "great pressure [was] being brought upon the Park from environmental and conservation groups" who were going through the "hierarchy" of the NPS to push horses completely out of the NPS system. Claiming that "20 to 25 percent of the trails in Rocky Mountain National Park have already been closed to horses," Walker accused backpackers of wanting the "entire Park for their exclusive use."[66] The efforts of Van Horn, Walker, and others were successful when, in March 1981, the NPS announced that it would keep the two in-park stables open for another five years, at which time they would again revisit the issue.[67]

In a sense, Walker had a point. For generations the NPS knew that horses were responsible for excessive trail wear in the park; that horse use often led to conflicts with hikers; that long strings of horses fouled popular stretches of trails with manure and urine; and that heavy trail use was directly responsible for erosion on many of the park's trails. But emerging scientific research also indicated a troubling connection between trails and exotic and invasive plant species. Trails, as it turns out, are just as efficient at moving foreign plant species through parks like Rocky as they are at moving people and horses. Through an analysis of plant distribution and composition along selected trails in RMNP, researcher Mary Benniger found that horses acted as significant mechanisms of plant dispersion through the park. Specifically, analysis of horse scat in the park showed that "fifteen species [of plants] were found growing from seeds in horse scat, eight of which were identified as exotics."[68] Trails, argued Benniger, represent areas of soil and plant disturbance. Constant traffic ensures that plants do not take root on the trails themselves but that they colonize the "corridor edge habitat" adjacent to trails. Horses can and do play a major role in this process, both as agents of soil disruption on trails and through the dispersal of manure containing nonnative seeds along those trails.[69] As the NPS became more attuned to the consequences of invasive plant species in places like Rocky, widespread horse use became even more troubling.

By 1994 park staff admitted that efforts to address the problems of horse management had failed and that there were now "significant problems" in the park.[70] Although the total miles of trails open to horses had declined to 260 miles of the park's 316 miles of trails, horse use continued as a powerful agent of environmental change. Park staff also pointed to recent research that showed a hardening of environmental attitudes held by many backcountry users regarding equines. Specifically, researchers had found that "hikers who disapprove of horse use also have stronger relationships with wilderness, placing more value on solitude opportunities than those who do not express a dislike for horses." Meanwhile, other investigations found that "conflict over wilderness uses partially results from differing conceptions of wilderness as a sacred place; a shifting conceptual definition of wilderness, which now emphasizes ecological preservation." With the above in mind, the NPS used its 1994 Horse Management Plan to set a ceiling of 41,600 horse-trips annually through the park, which had been the average over the previous 18 years.[71] Moreover, the plan set up a "voluntary contribution system to take additional payments from the commercial horse users to help fund maintenance on the trails they impact"; it also mandated the use of "certified weed-free forage" for horses.[72]

Current debates over trails, wilderness, and horse use in the park demonstrate the fluid and varied environmental ideas that continue to require subdivision of the parkscape according to use and environmental ideologies. A study of wilderness values conducted in the park in 2004, for example, showed that "beauty and scenic integrity" were key to wilderness enjoyment of the park. Likewise, the power of the remote reaches of the park to provide an escape from "urban dwellings" was central to backcountry visitor satisfaction. The survey also revealed that a variety of intrusions, ranging from "unnatural" sounds to visitors acting inappropriately in the park by littering or feeding the animals, threatened to diminish the wilderness experience of the park. The "two main issues that emerged out of the overall analysis" of possible threats to enjoyment of a wilderness setting, however, "were horse use and the presence of cell phones in wilderness areas." To many visitors interested in a wilderness experience, "horses and horse droppings are viewed as environmentally degrading," and cell phones shattered the calm and quiet solitude so many sought in wilderness areas.[73]

In 2009, backcountry advocates finally won out as Rocky Mountain National Park received the official wilderness designation it had been seeking since 1974. In certain reaches of the park—the frontcountry—driving and other modern contrivances are allowed and encouraged. In other spaces, however, cars are banished while horseback riding—and all that comes with it—is allowed. In still other places, only those willing and able to travel by foot are allowed. The emergence of cell phones raises interesting questions about the future management of the park. In time, will the NPS further subdivide Rocky into places that ban the ringing, buzzing, and vibrating devices and places that do not? The history of trails in RMNP tells us one thing for certain: social and environmental changes are ongoing elements of the management of our national parks.

Conclusion

When Isabella Bird first rode into Estes Park in the 1870s, horses were a central—even requisite—element of the experience. She and others relied upon horses to get to remote areas like Estes Park, just as they relied upon them to access many of the area's high-mountain destinations. And horses seemed quintessentially western. In time, however, the equestrian geography of the region began to change. The rise of automobile tourism, early championed by the NPS, necessitated the removal of horses from the park's growing network of roads. But the NPS, then as now, recognized horseback riding as an important means of experiencing the park. Accordingly, horses were gradually pushed onto the park's trails. As long as visitation remained low, and as long as visitors did not conceive of horses as agents of environmental destruction, all was well.

In the postwar era, however, visitation surged, and more and more visitors began associating horses and their byproducts as antithetical to parks and an evolving appreciation of wilderness. The NPS, which had to pay for trail maintenance and respond to the growing piles of complaint letters related to user conflicts, addressed the issue by segregating certain uses within the park. The entrenchment of wilderness values, combined with a deepening understanding of the ecological destructiveness of horses, intensified the need to limit horse access to the park and to further segregate horses from hikers.

Increasing visitation and demand for backcountry wilderness experiences had other consequences for the park as well. Popular destinations like Longs

Peak became more dangerous and crowded. In such places, the NPS limited backcountry camping through a reservation system, installed phone lines, and stashed rescue gear, all in an effort to balance visitor safety against a satisfactory wilderness experience. In the end, something so personal as a privy or something so mundane as a cable stretched toward a mountain peak has the power to tell us much more about places like Rocky than we might have expected. Viewed from far above, the landscape of Rocky reveals, often in very subtle ways, the attitudes of visitors and those charged with managing this environmentally and socially dynamic place.

Our Friends the Trees

Lounging beneath a quaking aspen as a breeze rattles through the fall foliage is one of life's great pleasures. With a hat drawn down tight to your brow and wrapped in your favorite flannel shirt it is easy to imagine that this is how the forest should be. And it's easy to believe that this is how it has always been. The forests of the Rocky Mountain West are beguiling. We all know intuitively that trees sprout, age, and die, but their longevity—measured not in years or decades but often in centuries—makes it all too easy to forget that they belong to dynamic and active communities.

If you close your eyes and adopt an Olympian view, one that embraces a longer time scale and broader geographic scope, Rocky's forests are a symphony of change. Spanning thousands of years, climate change pushes Engelmann spruce up and down mountainsides. Fires ravage stands of Douglas fir, and lodgepole pines emerge in their place. Over time, the Douglas fir may once again gain the upper hand. Hungry hordes of insects chew away vast stands of limber and ponderosa pine. Taking advantage of the sun that now reaches the forest floor, still other trees erupt in their stead. Providing the tempo to this amazing symphony is the four-count rhythm of the seasons. Annually, cones form and fall, a yellow mist of pollen fills the summer air, and a crescendo of autumnal aspen provides the most vibrant array of oranges, golds, and reds that the mind's eye can imagine. Stands of trees sprout, compete, thrive, and die amid a seemingly endless range of environmental variables. Trees and their communities are simply amazing.

In this symphony of change humans have come to play a lead role. By the time RMNP was founded in 1915 a complicated social stew—including elements from nineteenth-century landscape painting, the urban park movement, as well as an aesthetic that equated living trees with healthful environments—all shaped forestry in Rocky Mountain National Park. Although only a few of Rocky's visitors likely came explicitly to see the trees, many nonetheless expected ponderosa pine, aspen, and Engelmann spruce to infuse their park experience. Protecting living trees and maintaining healthy-looking forests, however, brought nearly a century of management conundrums and ecological ramifications, all of which continue to shape the park.

The emergence of ecology and its impact upon fire sciences complicated matters following World War II. As revealed in previous chapters, ecology held a new way of viewing the natural world and new concepts of what constituted natural. Through the eyes of a twentieth-century ecologist, fire-scarred landscapes and dead and dying trees were not reflections of a dead and dying landscape. Rather, they often stood as sentinels of life itself. In the postwar era, ecological appreciation for the role of fire and insects in maintaining healthy ecosystems existed in rising tension with older attitudes about natural beauty. Scientists, inside and outside the NPS, increasingly called for park management based on ecological principles. A good portion of the traveling public, however, continued to demand parks whose beauty was visual and based predominantly upon aesthetics developed over the preceding century and a half. The National Park Service, an agency that had been deeply involved in perpetuating and supporting both ideals, found itself in an untenable situation.

Park officials' response is telling and significant. Rather than throw support wholly behind one management tack or the other, they segregated the firescape along the same lines discussed in Chapters 2 and 3. Across the majority of the park they sought the return of "natural" conditions. Today, in vast expanses of backcountry, fire and insects have been allowed back in, though in a somewhat limited way. In the park's frontcountry—along its roads, parking lots, campgrounds, and visitor centers—we behold a management paradigm based on culturally specific concepts of sublime beauty. Here, fire and insects are still not welcome, as evidenced by ardent fire suppression and the use of toxic chemicals to check the spread of insects.

Trees, Morality, and Beauty

Visitors come to Rocky carrying important and interesting cultural baggage including unique notions of beauty, nature, and perfection. During the nineteenth century one important component of how Americans experienced and assimilated constructions of the natural world lay in interpretation of visual art. The act of constructing visual representations (through painting, for example) and the process through which people assimilate such works reveals a great deal about how we understand nature and what we expect it to be in its idealized form. In his classic 1927 text *The Picturesque: Studies in a Point of View*, Christopher Hussey argued that the "impulse of the traveler for pleasure, apart from gain, is, in every variety of degree, to satisfy his craving for the ideal, or to drug his craving by the belief that it is being satisfied." But to first satisfy "his craving for the ideal," that ideal must be created and popularized. In this sense, the visual arts played an important role in cultivating a common understanding of what constituted beautiful. Then, as Hussey argues, travelers set about touring the world looking to find examples of the natural world that embodied what they had come to understand as beautiful and natural.[1]

In this light, the paintings of Thomas Cole, Frederick Church, Albert Bierstadt, and others during the nineteenth century provided more than exquisite examples of landscape art. They infused an idealized natural world with the spirit of God, thereby transforming a hectic and dark wilderness of the imagination into places of perceived beauty and reverence.[2] To those fortunate enough to view the works of American masters, landscape painters of the nineteenth century were doing much more than entertaining viewers with striking scenery; they were teaching viewers how to appreciate nature and exactly what sorts of natural scenes were worth adulation.

One of the earliest and most capable painters to capture the dynamics among nationalism, growth, and nature was Thomas Cole. Cole, who most consider to be the founder of the Hudson River School, dedicated a five-canvas series entitled *The Course of Empire* to these themes. Throughout the series Cole depicted the rise and fall of a society while moralizing its relationship with the natural world.

The second canvas, *The Arcadian or Pastoral State*, reveals the landscape (and nation) that Cole and many of the Hudson River School pined for.

Here, the unwieldy trees deformed by the forces of nature present in the first canvas are replaced with larger, more stately and domesticated ones. Within *The Arcadian* we bear witness to the emerging tensions between unregulated and unpredictable growth and a natural world of order and balance. To many of the painters of the Hudson River School, including Cole, *The Arcadian* reflected the proper balance to be struck: there was growth, settlement, and a modest sort of prosperity—all in accord with nature.[3]

The casual viewer of *The Arcadian or Pastoral State* might conclude that Cole saw only the benefits of progress and none of its messy consequences. Closer investigation, however, reveals that pastoral beauty comes at a cost. Near the foreground of the painting, tucked away to the far right of the frame, squats a nearly clean-cut tree stump with its heartwood thrusting defiantly upward. The inclusion of a stump in this painting—and many others of this school—raises interesting questions. In *The Arcadian or Pastoral State* the stump became a tool to indicate that this landscape had come from something and that it was an artifact of humans and the natural world interacting. Yes, the pastoral landscape is here idealized, but Cole wants and needs his viewers to know that it did not make itself.[4] Material progress came at a cost, and the stump became a sort of trope to capture the price paid for that progress.

In *The Consummation of Empire*, the third canvas, Cole has pushed out nearly all elements of the natural world—the bay is now a bustling port, the stately trees are gone, and towering classical structures dominate the landscape. In every way, *The Consummation* reveals a natural world brought to heel.[5] Trees, which played significant roles in the first two paintings—first as reflections of a wild nature, then as symbols of a domesticated one—are pushed to the very margins and replaced by cold angular stone and the occasional potted floral elements.

Although we witness a clear sense of material progress through the first three paintings in the series, the fourth, *Destruction*, speaks to the dangers of decadence depicted in *The Consummation*. The throbbing commerce is now gone, overcome by conflict and chaos. Ominous smoke has replaced the once placid sky; the escarpment rises once again prominently in the background. A massive and headless stone warrior hefts a fractured shield as men and women savage each other at his feet. Thrusting itself up between the legs of the massive muscular figure is a tree stump. Unlike the stump seen in *The*

Arcadian, this one is central, obvious, and linked directly to the destruction unfolding before us. Trees and stumps became powerful tools that conveyed specific messages about the relationship between human progress and the natural world. Clearly, some semblance of balance was needed.

In the fifth and last painting in the series, *Desolation*, the escarpment still stands, now overlooking the ruins of a civilization gone mad. In the hurly-burly world of the 1830s, Thomas Cole's series reveals an anxiety over material progress and his personal fears of what unchecked growth would deliver. His work also reveals the role of trees and stumps in educating Americans about the natural world, growth, balance, greed, and great loss. Trees, it seems, were far more than trees in the capable hands of this master. They were tools that allowed the artist to investigate and inculcate values and attitudes about the natural world and humans' relationship with it. This tendency to link trees and stumps to deeper moral issues would later become persistent and important elements in the creation, management, and promotion of Rocky Mountain National Park.[6]

Beyond Cole and his contemporaries, there were other ways that Americans came into contact with nature perfected. Urban parks, which offered green grass, winding paths, and shady groves where weary urbanites could refresh minds and bodies, also instructed visitors on exactly what elements of nature were worthy of elevation and protection in nineteenth-century America.[7] The urban park, set as it was in juxtaposition to the dirty city and the thrum of industrial production, was a celebration of the living. Vibrant flowers, carefully placed shrubs, and towering trees were all tools at the disposal of park designers. If employed in accordance with prevailing theories about landscape design, parks would foster contemplation, relaxation, and a sense of peace, all while elevating average Americans above the grit of everyday city life.

Urban parks, however, became much more than a means to retreat into a more naturalized place amid concrete and iron. They also served as aids that "instructed urbanites in the appreciation of other scenic places they might encounter elsewhere. Central Park and other municipal landscape parks therefore advocated picturesque tourism and scenic landscape preservation generally."[8] But not all of "nature" was celebrated within urban parks. Rather, the driving concern behind their creation and function was making places that elevated living elements of the natural world, not cycles of life, death, and rebirth per se. Silently, slowly, powerfully, urban parks forged tight bonds between culture-specific concepts of beauty and nature. Americans would carry such conceptions with them from cities like Chicago, New York, and Kansas City to the park at Estes, where millions expected to see natural beauty that they had been trained to appreciate through lazy Sunday afternoons at the neighborhood park.

"Shadow of the Pines"

The local firebrand Enos Mills became one of the most ardent voices of forest and tree protection in the early twentieth-century West. Trumpeting the message of the U.S. Forest Service in the early years of that agency, Mills traveled extensively across the United States to warn audiences of the dangers of wanton forest destruction. In addition to protecting trees because of their economic value and centrality to national greatness, Mills passionately urged his audiences to embrace trees as friends. Anthropomorphizing trees, as Mills often did, was a powerful rhetorical flourish that enabled him to draw the sometimes disparate threads of conservation together into one fabric.

In a paper titled "Our Friends the Trees," delivered to the General Federation of Women's Clubs in St. Paul, Mills spoke of the inspiration of the gigantic trees of California, which had "endured fire, flood, drought and earthquake, but have never hauled down their evergreen banners." Here, trees were far more than cellulose, bark, and twig; they were inspirations of "steadfastness" and "splendor."[9] Enlightened citizens must, argued Mills, protect trees from fire and axe alike because forested headwaters prevented flooding, retained moisture in the soil, and prevented the wind from "blowing filthy, germ-laden dust into our eyes and throat." Mills concluded his address by stating, "For ages, trees have been our friends, and through the future's golden days I hope we will be theirs. The pathway to the heroic age through the forest lies!"[10]

If Mills's passionate personal pleas did not go far enough in urging would-be conservationists to pick up the mantle of forest conservation, the Denver Chamber of Commerce Board of Trade hoped that its 1905 publication "Forests and Trees: An Arbor Day Souvenir" would raise still more awareness. To help ensure that the message was ably crafted and crowd-tested, the Board hired Enos Mills to coauthor the booklet.

"Forests and Trees" echoed the benefits of a thick-forested nation and paid telling attention to wildfires, which it lumped together with "wasteful methods of lumbering."[11] By linking fire to wasteful human practices like nineteenth-century logging, writers like Mills were essentially moving fire out of the natural realm and into the human one. If conservationists or park managers came to view *all* fires as "unnatural" processes—destructive aberrations that resulted in diminishment of scenery, topsoil, and economic opportunity—they alleviated the possible tension between fire suppression and the broader mission of national parks to protect the natural world. Fighting all fires became a means of protecting the "natural" from an "unnatural" process.

Of course, antifire sentiments and a bias toward healthy-looking forests (as defined by contemporaries) reached far beyond Mills and the Denver Chamber of Commerce. A constellation of significant landscape architects, many of whom played important roles in determining the natural character of state and national parks, contributed to Park Service fire-suppression policy. In this regard, the work of landscape architect Charles W. Eliot II was determinative. At the core of his philosophy was the belief that in the hands of a gifted planner the natural world could be made to yield a result much like a living painting. Accordingly, trees often constituted major design elements for his real-life landscape paintings. It was the duty of the landscape architect "to discover, and then to evolve and make available, the most characteristic, interesting, and effective scenery." Making the scenery "interesting" and "effective" often relied upon the "control or modification of vegetation" and the "devising [of] the most advantageous courses for the roads and paths from which the scenery will be viewed."

As was the case with Mills and others, Eliot often considered fire as something to protect forests from, not a natural process that played a significant role in promoting forest health and beauty. If managed by the gifted and trained hand of a landscape architect and through sufficient planning, argued Eliot, the "forest scenery may . . . in a few years be restored to that fortunate state the beauty of which, barring fires and other accidents" would increase over time.[12] Framing fire as an accident was, in fact, no accident.

It is important to bear in mind that the landscape architects of this era, exemplified by Eliot, focused on improving, enhancing, and maintaining visual beauty as they defined it. By the standards of the late nineteenth century, stately living trees were powerful tools in framing inspirational vistas, just as dead, dying, and downed trees detracted from such views. Men such as Eliot had little trouble promoting the thinning of trees, the clearing of underbrush, and roadside cleanup of trees and shrubs if the above would aid in creating more picturesque scenery.[13] Ardent prevention and control of wildfires and insect infestations—both of which posed significant scenic threats—were logical consequences of this mode of thinking. In time, the National Park Service would wholly embrace this philosophy.

Well before 1915 government officials, promoters, and visitors were imagining the Estes Park region as a sort of natural painting, an exercise landscape architects like Eliot encouraged. In Robert Marshall's report following his exploratory visit to Estes Park in 1913, for example, he encouraged his readers to imagine this swath of the Rockies as a painting. "At first view," he recounted, "as one beholds the scene in awe and amazement, the effect is as of an enormous painting, a vast panorama stretching away for illimitable distances." Within this nature-as-painting, each "view becomes a refined miniature, framed by another more fascinating, the whole presenting an impressive picture, never to be forgotten."[14] Marshall was not alone in using the imagery of a landscape painting to enliven imaginations about this region. The Union Pacific Railroad likewise enticed would-be visitors by promising an experience as perfect as a carefully crafted painting. In describing a photograph of Gem Lake, for example, the UP promised that the "traveler who sees the Continental Divide from this beautiful body of water discovers a setting unequaled on the continent. It is as a cameo before a panoramic painting."[15]

Much more is at work here than mere hyperbole. Informative reports and nicely rendered travel brochures reflected and deepened a "discourse about the park even before visitors came to see the real thing."[16] What is revealed through that discourse is a desire and a need for promoters and visitors to envision Rocky as a carefully rendered painting where the most perfect elements of the natural world could be seen, touched, explored, and internalized. Put another way, the "story of the development of the national parks is the story of people who saw such perfect pictures of wilderness and then wanted to go and see the real thing." As more and more images of the region reached the hands and hearts of more would-be tourists, "the more people wanted to buy train tickets and experience the parks for themselves."[17]

Upon the creation of Rocky Mountain National Park in 1915, a long and complicated set of economic and cultural factors shaped how Americans thought about this region. Rocky Mountain National Park was to be a visual experience foremost, not unlike a painting or urban park. Within this "living painting," thriving trees played a vital role in how contemporaries understood Rocky, just as they provided important motivations for tourists to visit. Although motivations for tree and forest preservation varied from group to group and person to person, a broad and deep coalition of Americans saw real beauty in living trees and made the protection of that beauty a central goal of national parks.

Trees and Parks

Rocky Mountain National Park encompasses no less than nine distinct vegetation types. Some 60 percent of the park is forested, 13 percent lies above timberline, and the rest is a mixture of exposed rock, grassy meadow, and other types of habitat. Here, elevation plays a significant role in determining which trees grow where. At the park's lower reaches, ponderosa pine predominates. Between 8,500 and 9,500 feet lodgepole pine are common, and between 9,500 and 11,500 feet spruce and fir often predominate. Aspect, soil types, available moisture, and competition among other plant species also shape the distribution of trees here. Amid an intricate and constantly shifting mosaic, wildfires and insect infestations provide two powerful engines of ecological change.

Fire is the single most important factor in determining forest succession, as it "controls the age, structure, species composition and physiognomy of the vegetation." Fire also directly impacts "nutrient cycles, energy flows, productivity, diversity, and stability throughout the ecosystem." Because elevation, aspect, available moisture, and forest fuels all shape how often fires burn and at what intensity, it is no surprise that each of the major forest types in the park have a distinct, but interrelated, fire cycle. Fire recurs most frequently among lodgepole pine, which burn on average every 100–150 years. Ponderosa pine typically burn every 22–308 years. Fire is less common at the higher elevations: spruce and fir burn every 300–700 years.[18]

Bark beetles also shape fire cycles and forest composition. When conditions are right, populations can grow dramatically, and their impact on fire cycles and forest composition become more significant. There seem to be at least two significant correlations between epidemic beetle outbreaks and fire. Extensive beetle outbreaks provide an increase in available fire fuel as a function of the dead trees they leave behind. Research on the Yellowstone fires of 1988 has also demonstrated that the more significant long-term impact of beetle kills is correlated to the changes they initiate in stands of trees following an outbreak. Areas where extensive beetle kills take place are more likely to burn in the future, not necessarily as a function of fuel buildup but as a consequence of how forest vegetation responds and rejuvenates in the decades following a beetle outbreak.[19] Trees, insects, moisture, soils, and climate are intimately bound together. Changes to any one part of the equation can, and will, deliver transformations to the entire system.

Through the halcyon days of the 1920s, the dark days of the Depression and World War II, and through the tense years of the 1960s, the staff at RMNP fought year in and year out to gather the men, materials, and expertise that would enable them to keep their dynamic forests picturesque. They reached out to residents and concessionaires, as well as to sister agencies like the Forest Service, to build lasting and reliable partnerships to meet the task at hand. Expanses of charred parkland or insect-infested gray forests were not acceptable to the NPS or to its visitors.

Often taking its lead from the USFS, which emerged from the hellacious forest fires of 1910 as a fire-fighting agency, RMNP began a tradition of stashing caches of firefighting tools at strategic points around the park and in ranger cabins in 1916.[20] Beyond this, RMNP also sold permits for taking dead and downed timber from areas that had burned in the past and along Fall River Road. This work reduced the fire danger while also removing from view unsightly dead and dying trees.[21] Realizing that their meager ranger forces and limited tools were not sufficient to snuff out all would-be conflagrations across the park, the superintendents of Rocky also drew upon local volunteers to aid in fighting fires. In exchange for firewood culled from the park, citizens of Estes Park offered their labor in times of need to suppress forest fires. This policy, which ebbed and flowed in reverse proportion to park resources, often paid dividends. But park superintendents would have to wait until 1922 for the NPS to set aside funds specifically for fighting forest fires. Even then, the initial allocation of $25,000, to be split among all parks, was far short of sufficient.[22] Until the NPS made more money available, parks like Rocky would have to rely upon cooperative efforts, hope, and luck to keep the fires at bay.

In 1918, Superintendent Way and his handful of rangers scrambled to suppress fires across the 358-square-mile park; meanwhile, Secretary of the Interior Franklin Lane was drafting policy for the NPS that put still more importance on enhancing the scenic qualities within parks. Specifically, Lane decreed that rangers had the authority to "thin forests or clear vistas to improve scenic features" and to cut and remove trees to "eliminate insect infestations or diseases common to forests and shrubs."[23] The removal of dead and dying trees dovetailed nicely with the removal of old buildings, remnants of mining operations, and homesteads. All were seen as detracting from the natural beauty of parks, and thus their removal was warranted and desirable.[24]

As was the case with the USFS in the wake of the fires of 1910, the massive fires of 1926 in Glacier National Park pushed the NPS toward more intensive and systematic fire prevention and management.[25] In that one season alone, some twenty-six fires, which burned from May until August and charred some 50,000 acres inside Glacier, were significant enough to draw the superintendent of the NPS himself to manage the fire.[26] Reeling from the destruction those fires delivered, the NPS drafted its first Forest Protection Requirements in 1928.[27]

To park personnel, the busy summer months must have been tense. Although they desperately wanted and needed throngs of visitors to idle through every day, more visitors seeing more nooks and crannies of the park on its expanding road and trail system—on horseback, in automobiles, and afoot—increased the probability of fire while also heightening the need to control what exactly visitors were seeing from each of the new vantage points. Thus, infestations of the mountain pine beetle like the one that occurred in 1927 in Larimer and Boulder Counties posed a major concern for the NPS. Although this outbreak occurred outside the park boundaries, the NPS rightly recognized that it could easily spread to Rocky if not properly contained. Similarly concerned with the negative consequences of a major outbreak, but for different reasons, the Forest Service cut some 8,600 trees that year near Rocky at the expense of more than $12,000. By 1928 RMNP had allocated money and men to stem the tide of insect infestation. In April and May of that year, for example, NPS crews began the arduous task of cutting and piling some 650 infested trees while the USFS continued its treatments outside the park. By 1930, NPS managers were confident that their efforts had "reached a harmless minimum in the park" as the number of "treated trees" dropped to just twenty.[28]

But insects like the mountain pine beetle were not so easily controlled. Like all of the plants and animals in the park, bark beetles in Colorado have a distinct life cycle and play important ecological roles. The mountain pine beetle, for example, has a four-stage life cycle: egg, larva, pupa, adult. In the heat of summer, adult beetles light upon living trees where they mate. Following their romantic interludes, the pairs work at excavating so-called egg galleries, which are essentially tunnels into the tree itself and can be upward of fifty inches long. After eggs have been deposited in the galleries, larvae hatch and continue feeding on the tree, nibbling their own bedrooms adjacent to the "parent" galleries. During the short cold days of winter the larvae remain nestled comfortably beneath the bark of their host tree. Beginning in June, the larvae transform yet again into pupae. As the summer temperatures rise, adults eventually emerge from the trees as they once again leave the host and the cycle repeats itself.[29]

The annual round of mating, house making, growth, and renewal works just fine for the beetle, just as it does the many species that depend on it for food, like woodpeckers, as well as those that rely upon the dead and dying trees they leave behind for habitat. It works less well for the lodgepole, ponderosa, Scotch, and limber pine that play host to them. As the trees are attacked, they produce copious amounts of pitch to push the bugs out. But the mountain pine beetles bring with them a "blue-staining fungus" that inhibits tree sap and water transfer, both of which very often lead to the death of the tree.[30] In any given year, a certain percentage of the area's trees succumb to such infestations. When conditions are right—when the climate warms or large stands of trees are stressed, or when fires have been slow to return to a stand of aging trees—massive outbreaks of bark beetles can occur. Without knowing it, park managers' attempts to suppress fire may have initiated important changes in how the forests of the park functioned, making larger outbreaks of bark beetles more likely in years to come. Ironically, saving beautiful forests from the ravages of fire may well have played a role fostering conditions ripe for unsightly beetle outbreaks.

The fire-suppression efforts of the NPS in general, and of RMNP specifically, raise important questions about the degree to which RMNP reflected upon the early suppression mandate. Although a good portion of the public, the NPS's antifire partners in the USFS, as well as countless elected officials advocated the complete eradication of fire from our nation's forests, there were early signals from the scientific community that could have—perhaps should have—pointed toward a very different management direction.

As early as 1910, for example, scientists had conducted work in the Estes Park region attempting to understand its fire history. In his 1910 article "The Life History of Lodgepole Burn Forests," ecologist F. E. Clements found that fire, even before American settlement, was a significant factor in shaping this section of the Rockies.[31] Clements, who was a professor at the University of Minnesota at the time, had long concerned himself with ecological concepts and processes.[32] Contrary to claims made by Enos Mills and others, Clements demonstrated that fire had always shaped the forests around Estes Park. Clements went so far as to argue that the fires in the region were "extraordinary" in their frequency and unmatched across the entire state. Its climate and topography, combined with comparatively favorable seasonal temperatures, all but ensured a high frequency of fires—both natural and human-caused—in and around Estes Park. For two summers, Clements plodded through the region counting trees, tree rings, pine cones, and burned areas all while creating detailed maps of tree regrowth and distribution of plants following fires.

At the conclusion of the fieldwork, Clements confidently claimed that fires had burned within the region at fairly regular intervals, including the fires of 1707, 1722, 1753, 1781, 1842, 1864, 1872, 1878, 1891, 1896, 1901, 1903, and 1905.[33] In each instance the impact of the fires varied according to intensity, topography, soil type, forest type, rodent population, and a host of other interrelated factors. Although there were instances where tree regeneration was either slow or nonexistent following a conflagration, such was often not the case. Clements recognized fire as a major agent of change and disruption, but not generally one that was wholly destructive. In many cases, previous fires had shaped the forests that contemporaries admired so much.[34] Without periodic fire, for example, the lodgepole forest that characterized so much of the park would gradually fade away. For the lodgepole, fire is a central mechanism that melts away a sort of resin that forms on the outside of dropped cones. Absent fire, the cones remain essentially sealed and dormant on the forest floor. According to Clements, fire gave an ecological edge that enabled the stands of lodgepole to spread into the forests that so many esteemed.[35]

It is difficult to discern when exactly Clements's detailed and convincing research found its way into RMNP. What is certain, however, is that J. D. Coffman, NPS chief forester Ansel Hall, Superintendent Edmund Rogers, as well as the director of the NPS were all aware of Clements's work by 1930. In that year, Coffman compiled the "Report on Fire Protection Requirements of Rocky Mountain National Park," which each of the parks were then compiling, and which each of the men signed. To be clear, Coffman was a man of great importance to the NPS. Prior to being hired in 1928 as the NPS's first real fire-control expert in the wake of the Glacier fires, he was the supervisor of the California National Forest, where he ardently advocated fire suppression.[36] Once on board with the NPS, he worked to create a system of fire suppression within the NPS modeled on the Forest Service. In this regard, the "Report on Fire Protection" in Rocky was indicative of broader intensification of fire control across the NPS.

Coffman's 1930 report on fire in Rocky quoted directly from Clements's earlier research. It cited Clements's conclusion that "the study of burns in the park indicates an extraordinary succession of fires, encountered nowhere else in Colorado. This is due to features of climate and topography both directly and indirectly favorable to fires." Remarkably, Coffman's report at once acknowledged and embraced Clements's conclusions regarding the high natural occurrence of fire in the region. It also echoed Clements's recognition that many, though not all, of the region's fires were the product of lightning.[37] In light of these facts, Coffman's broader recommendations are difficult to fathom.

Like Clements, Coffman recognized that lodgepole pines were important to Rocky's landscape and depended upon fires to propagate; nonetheless, he concluded that fire should be excluded from the park. To support this recommendation, one that was already an established institutional and cultural element within the NPS, he pointed to the 1872 fire in Rocky and the slow forest rejuvenation that followed. Of all of the fires in Clements's report, Coffman drew from the one that reflected the slowest rejuvenation and excluded all of the other data that indicated the important—even central—role of fire in maintaining healthy and diverse forests. Coffman was thus able to conclude that slow rejuvenation following this one fire offered "one very im-

John McGraw at the Shadow Mountain lookout, 1933. Courtesy of Rocky Mountain National Park, ROMO 4017, MSF NEG 2641.

portant reason why every reasonable effort should be taken that no further disastrous fires shall occur."[38]

We can only guess why he so misread Clements's report. Perhaps asking a fire-control expert, a man hired specifically by the NPS to put out fires, to interpret a work of ecology and not focus upon the perceived negative consequences of fire is asking too much. It is also clear that fire had become an indispensable tool in growing the park's personnel and equipment. By arguing year in and year out that fire posed a major threat to the park, one that would have serious negative consequences upon visitation rates, superintendents of Rocky and other parks received more money, hired more men, built more trails, and enhanced the physical plant and visual appeal of the park. Without the specter of disastrous fire looming, growing park resources would have been much more difficult. In any event, 1930 represents an early and rare moment for RMNP employees to think more deeply and critically about their mission, agency practices, the park, and fire. The moment quickly passed, leaving the park still more devoted to fire suppression and prevention than before.

Embracing the spirit of Coffman's report, RMNP continued to devote significant resources to fighting the forces that threatened its forests, to honing its expertise, and to strengthening its fire partnership with the Forest Service. By 1932, forest protection had risen to nearly 10 percent of the park's annual budget. Moreover, five permanent rangers and sixteen seasonal rangers were dedicated to protecting the "park's forests from fire and insects," as well as controlling and guiding park visitors. To further enhance their firefighting capacity, RMNP also hosted Coffman for nearly a week during which he further assessed the park's fire risks and offered suggestions.[39] Each passing season, and each fire that seemed to die an early death at the hands of the watchful and diligent NPS employees, only reinforced their operational assumptions that early detection and suppression were critical to keeping fire out of the park.

Amid their seasonal efforts to keep fire and insects at bay, park personnel undertook an intriguing project. Before RMNP was founded, a logging crew had clear-cut some 10 acres of trees on a plot of land in Hidden Valley, which was visible from the emerging Trail Ridge Road. Once the trees were felled the loggers moved on, leaving behind only the worthless stumps. Beginning in September 1932 crews set about removing the stumps and backfilling the holes. The stumps did not present a fire hazard or interfere with the construction of Trail Ridge Road. Reflecting the power of the stump much earlier hit upon by Thomas Cole, crews at RMNP set about erasing stumps for exactly the same reasons that Cole included them in his paintings. Stumps spoke to the fact that this landscape was the product of humans and nature interacting across time and space. But park managers were not striving to deliver a vision of the Arcadian to visitors. Rather, they labored to present a sublime landscape untouched by human hands, not one where banal economic interests once reigned. Delivering upon that promise, as it turned out, often required significant human intervention.[40]

As in so many places around the nation, 1933 was a watershed year for RMNP. During the peak of the New Deal, the NPS witnessed nearly a tripling of its annual budget from less than $11 million per year to almost $27 million in 1939. Moreover, the NPS benefited from a total of 688,255 workdays dedicated to firefighting alone during FDR's presidency. In 1933 young men from

Remnants of turn-of-the-century logging in Hidden Valley, 1929. Courtesy of Rocky Mountain National Park, ROMO MSF NEG 6223.

around the country converged on Rocky under the auspices of the Civilian Conservation Corps, which was aptly nicknamed "Roosevelt's Tree Army." Initially, the CCC built two camps in Rocky, at Phantom Valley and Horseshoe Park. For a few golden years, Rocky Mountain National Park thrived through this infusion of eager manpower. It is telling, if not surprising, that RMNP superintendents and rangers directed a great deal of the CCC efforts to enhancing the outward appearance of the park. As such, fire and insect control both became significant elements of the seasonal routine at Rocky.[41]

In 1933, for example, the "worst forest insect enemy in the Park," the mountain pine beetle, was making "considerable inroads" within stands of ponderosa and lodgepole pine. This was apparently the worst infestation the park had seen in years, and Superintendent A. E. Demaray was more than pleased that the CCC was on hand to combat its spread. In that year alone, the young men of the CCC treated more than 4,500 acres of the park, cutting and peeling the bark off of some 1,194 trees and exposing the vulnerable larvae to the elements. In all, the CCC contributed more than 855 man days to this work alone.

Even with the massive infusion of strong young backs, treating the entire park was simply not possible. Park managers had to prioritize areas as they decided which should be treated and which should not. Driven almost exclu-

Emergency Conservation workers cutting and peeling beetle-infested trees, 1933.
Courtesy of Rocky Mountain National Park, ROMO 4008, MSF NEG 2987.

sively by concerns for the visual appeal of the park, the majority of work that
the CCC and park rangers completed in felling and barking infested trees
coincided precisely with those portions of the park where visitation was the
most concentrated. In other words, the underlying motivation for removing
insect-infested trees was firmly rooted in conceptions about beauty and the
American public's expectations for seeing "pristine" trees and forests. Dead
and dying trees, irrespective of the fact that rangers and superintendents understood that most of the insect infestations were naturally occurring, were
an affront to their unique concepts of natural beauty. When men and money
were available, both went first to treating the roadsides and campgrounds
that park visitors most often saw.[42]

Although the Depression was a fantastic calamity for the United States, it
did present parks like Rocky with a great deal of opportunity. Through the
New Deal, RMNP saw an appreciable increase in men and material. By and
large, park officials used those resources, such as the CCC, to enhance and
control the visual aspects of the park. As such, fighting fires and insect infes-

tation were among their most significant contributions to RMNP. As the nation stepped closer to World War II, however, men, materials, and attention turned away from places like Rocky. The danger of fire remained, as did the perennial threat of insect infestation. Gone, however, were the strong young men that had so effectively combated these twin evils for nearly a decade.

Just as the park braced itself for the possibility of a wild summer season, still another threat loomed. Although rangers were confident that the mountain pine beetle population had been held in check in 1941, a troublesome new guest—the spruce budworm—came knocking. By 1942, the spruce budworm was making serious inroads across the park. Worse yet, this outbreak was most concentrated where the unsightly infestations were easily seen by visitors.[43] In years past, the NPS could have met the challenge by directing CCC men to cut and peel increasing numbers of trees. By 1942, however, park budgets were rapidly shrinking in the face of wartime demand, and the bustling CCC camps were all but a memory.

With the park inadequately staffed and short on money, Superintendent Canfield decided to try another approach. Focusing initially on the Endovalley campground and its immediate vicinity, rangers treated some 80 acres of trees with no less than 23,600 gallons of lead arsenate solution, which equates into nearly 300 gallons per acre. Such measures were needed, reasoned Canfield, to prevent the "likelihood of ghost forests through comparatively large sections" of the park. Because they did not have an advanced application delivery system or a sufficient supply of the chemical to treat the entire park, they instead focused on "areas of heavy public use" such as popular campgrounds.[44]

By 1943 the outbreak was reaching "alarming proportions below 9,500 feet in elevation along the east side" of Rocky. The budworm had defoliated countless trees in the park's Northern District, most of which would soon die. Although the park received considerable cooperation, oversight, and advice from the Bureau of Entomology and Plant Quarantine, limited funds, manpower, and equipment hamstrung widespread control efforts. Facing a difficult situation, and fearful of "ghost forests" spreading across the region, rangers again focused their control efforts on roadways in the eastern side of the park where visitation was highest.[45]

During this pitched battle between Park Service personnel and the spruce budworm, a powerful new weapon arrived: DDT. Although it was available only in limited quantities, rangers nonetheless applied it in the Endovalley

campground to determine its potential impact. Following the promising results of their initial application, rangers treated 12 acres in and adjacent to the
Endovalley campground in May 1945. Meanwhile, the USFS was conducting
its own experiments adjacent to the park. Rather than limited spraying from
the ground, as had been the practice of the NPS, the Forest Service acquired
the means to treat a much larger percentage of affected trees through aerial
application. The NPS watched this "experiment" with great anticipation in
the hopes that it could, in the near future, embrace the same approach.[46]

Thanks to a late cold snap in the early summer of 1946, RMNP was spared
widespread aerial application of DDT.[47] The timing of the cold weather delivered a massive blow to the budworm population just when the insects
were most vulnerable. Still, it is hard to escape the irony of the situation.
Motivated by concerns over physical beauty, the park staff applied copious
amounts of dangerous chemicals to the very places where they were attempting to maintain an appearance of pristine beauty. In the end, those places
became the most toxic areas of the park.

Although the spruce budworm outbreak was effectively over, the massive die-off of trees that it left behind presented still more challenges for
park managers. Not only were the large sections of dead and dying trees unsightly, they also presented opportunities for subsequent infestations and an
increased potential for fire. During the previous ten years, for example, the
Douglas fir bark beetle took up residence behind the swath of destruction
left by the spruce budworm. By 1950, the Douglas fir bark beetle had gained a
foothold and was reaching alarming proportions within and adjacent to the
park. There were some 2,000 infested trees, and as the park lacked the means
to combat the outbreak, the superintendent concluded that "the infestation
will probably be much greater next year." Part of the reason that Superintendent Canfield had planned for no Douglas fir bark beetle control was because
the park had already devoted a crew of thirty-five men, in cooperation with
the Bureau of Entomology, to combating blister rust across the park.[48] This
ongoing work involved attempts to eradicate the blister rust by attacking its
hosts, which were deemed to be ribes plants. Accordingly, the NPS eradicated
more than 228,000 ribes plants in 1951 and some 89,000 the following year.[49]

After more than three decades of struggle, one thing was becoming pain-
fully clear: managing a natural garden as large as Rocky required continuous
and intensive weeding, spraying, and fire suppression. If efforts on any one

of those fronts came up short, the garden itself would reveal the imperfections of nature and the painting would yield a view that few would esteem. Reflecting this tension, in the summer of 1956 Eldon Knecht of Lincoln, Nebraska, spent a week touring the park. While there he was appalled to find that a fire had burned some 900 acres of the park. This lightning-caused fire attracted the attention of some 150 firefighters, including 100 Native American firemen flown in from Montana. Despite intensive efforts to suppress the fire, Knecht chastised RMNP, stating that "we are endeavoring to preserve our parks and national forests for generations still unborn" and that without proper manpower and oversight the national parks would be lost to fire and other disasters.[50]

Knecht's complaint demonstrates the untenable position of RMNP and other western national parks during the postwar era. Fantastic increases in visitation, which the NPS needed and wanted, brought growing fire risk. More visitors hiking, driving, and riding horses through more distant corners of the park increased the chances that a stray cigarette or untended campfire could become a conflagration.[51] The NPS simply did not have the resources to snuff out every fire that threatened the parks. Something had to give.

Fire's Warm Embrace

Events in the newly created Everglades National Park provided the breaking point. In 1950 three large fires broke out in that park. Unable to fight all three simultaneously, the NPS did what it could to contain them, with only limited success. The lack of infrastructure, planning, and equipment in the park, combined with recent plans of the U.S. Army Corps of Engineers that would further reduce the amount of water available in the area to fight future fires, forced the NPS to rethink its strategy there. Moving forward, managers hoped to be able to use controlled burning to mitigate the danger of larger uncontrollable fires. This idea, which had been occasionally advocated and unofficially implemented in other parks, found its way to the NPS director's desk in 1957. Surveying all of the information, Conrad Wirth "approved the first controlled burning plan within the national park system in more than thirty years."[52] The wedge had thus been driven. In due time, the NPS would begin to reconsider its approach to forestry in other parks as well.

Also driving the shift was mounting evidence from researchers studying the relationship between forest health and fire regimes. The work of forester Harold Weaver exemplifies this trend. At the 1964 Tall Timbers Fire Ecology conference in Tallahassee, Florida, for example, Weaver presented "Fire and Management Problems in Ponderosa Pine." To Weaver, who had served for some 35 years as a forester, the absence of fire in ponderosa pine forests was causing considerable harm. Echoing research that stretched back at least to Clements, Weaver argued that "light surface fires, that had occurred at frequent intervals over countless centuries, were responsible" for creating open ponderosa pine stands. Prior to the arrival of fire-suppression regimes, frequent surface fires "consumed dry grass and accumulations of dead needles, twigs, cones and exfoliated bark scales under the larger trees, thus preventing heavier fuel accumulations that might someday support much hotter fires."[53] Decades of concerted fire suppression and the buildup of forest fuels that resulted, cautioned Weaver, made it very difficult and expensive to control such fires when they did erupt.[54]

Research like Weaver's indicated a deepening appreciation for the role of fire in maintaining healthy and vibrant forests, but still more powerful forces were at work in pushing the NPS toward new management practices. Facing withering criticism of its elk reduction program in Yellowstone, during which the Park Service killed more than 4,500 elk in that park alone, Secretary of the Interior Stewart Udall put together a team to review various elements of NPS wildlife management. A biology professor at the University of California–Berkley and the son of Aldo Leopold, A. Starker Leopold headed this committee of "highly respected wildlife specialists." The official 1963 report, popularly known as the Leopold Report, argued for a fundamental shift in how the NPS managed many of its resources.[55] At the core of that shift, the report asserted, should be the recognition of the "enormous complexity of ecological communities and the diversity of management procedures required to preserve them" across the whole of the park system.[56]

Implementing this transformation would not be easy. It would require that the NPS distance itself from other agencies that it had long relied upon for support, insight, and manpower. Arguing that the "objectives of park management are so different from those of state fish and game departments, the Forest Service, etc.," the committee urged the NPS to take charge of its own research programs so that they better reflected the agency's unique mission. This break, in turn, would put the Park Service in a position to think about forest management, fire, and insect infestations in ways not possible as long as their efforts were so heavily shaped by partnerships with other agencies. The committee also strongly advocated that "every phase of management itself be under the full jurisdiction of biologically-trained personnel of the Park Service."[57]

Embracing ecological health, as opposed to nineteenth-century romantic beauty or the conservation tactics of the Forest Service, enabled the committee to challenge a wide range of practices that bore directly upon forest management in the NPS system. Viewing parks though ecology-colored glasses, for example, the committee saw the "mass application of insecticides in the control of forest insects" as dangerous. The use of insecticides, they argued, could herald "unanticipated effects on the biotic community that might defeat the overall management objective." The committee also advocated the use of fire as a powerful—and affordable—means to manage vegetation within parks.[58]

Not since the founding of the NPS in 1916 had such a restatement of its mission and philosophy been proffered at such a high level. For generations, the overriding management paradigm for the NPS embraced outward beauty of park resources—as defined by nineteenth-century aesthetics—and high annual visitation. True, there were times when the ecological health of the park bubbled to the surface, but previous instances were often not as systemic, sweeping, or enduring. Reflecting the rise of ecology as a respectable science, as well as its growing cachet among the broader public, the Leopold Report was a clarion call to embrace a very different way of looking at national parks. Shortly after its release, the Leopold Report became official NPS policy.[59]

In the past, Enos Mills and his contemporaries saw fire as an aberration, an unnatural accident that threatened a beautiful but fragile living painting. By the late 1960s, however, "fire had come to be seen as a natural force" and it was slowly granted readmission into the parks.[60] In the first nine months of 1974 alone, for example, the NPS let lightning fires burn across some 15,000 acres. More surprisingly, they set fire to an additional 11,000 acres through prescribed burns.[61] Embracing a more nuanced approach to fire management that recognized the great diversity of park lands and fire needs, the NPS "scrapped the centralized control of fire that stemmed from Coffman and the New Deal era" and instead allowed individual superintendents to implement their own fire policy.[62] Nine parks, including Rocky, crafted new policies that allowed far more latitude for natural fires to go unchecked, as well as the careful use of prescribed burning.[63]

In October 1974 *Time* magazine ran an article entitled "Let 'Em Burn" in response to a fire that had been burning in Grand Teton National Park since July of that year. By October the fire had burned some 3,500 acres, giving testament to the NPS's commitment to the new fire management policy. *Time* pointed out that the "practice seems to contradict Smokey the Bear's highly publicized advice to extinguish all fires," but the author added that Smokey was "no ecologist" and did not know that "natural" fires were "good" for forests. Echoing the research of Weaver and others, the article argued that contrary to popular belief, "far from depriving animals of food, the fires make way for a prodigious growth of succulent sprouts. Moreover, they eliminate accumulated deadwood and underbrush—the fuel for more dangerous holocausts." Although the article does an admirable job of popularizing ecological understanding about the importance of fire and of reflecting the NPS's new position on the issue, it also reveals the tension, apprehension, and disdain that the new policy provoked.

The Teton fire, which represented an early "public test" of the new policy, claimed *Time*, raised the ire of many. For example, Mrs. Miles Seeley, who was a summer resident of Jackson, Wyoming, called the new approach a "'scorched earth policy'" and launched a petition to reverse it. According to Seeley, the unchecked fires had "'burned up one of the most beautiful areas in Teton County'" and were responsible for deteriorating air quality as well. The complaints, however, went far beyond locals. "Tourists," claimed *Time*, had "been complaining all summer." To one New Yorker, part of the problem was the difference between his vacation expectations and his actual experience. "'I thought I'd see beautiful mountains up there,'" complained the man, but "'all I saw was a bunch of smoke.'"[64]

Within this broader context, RMNP drafted its Master Plan for 1976. Master Plans allowed managers to state clearly the park's resources, to outline problem areas, and to point toward management strategies that they hoped would benefit the park and its visitors moving forward. In fascinating ways, they offer a snapshot on how NPS managers view the park at any given time. In a remarkable disclosure, RMNP's 1976 Master Plan lamented a range of self-induced changes that the NPS had actively sought in earlier eras. The document pointed to the reintroduction of elk, the propagation of sport fish, as well as "zealous efforts to extinguish all natural and man-caused fires," which "unnaturally favored selected species at the expense of those developing after a fire," as misguided.[65] The inclusion of such language speaks to the degree to which ecology had become—at least for many—the guiding principle of park management. Through the eyes of a twentieth-century ecologist, previous attempts to beautify parks through insect eradication and fire suppression were less than beautiful.

One of the core objectives of RMNP moving forward was to "restore the native ecosystems" of the park. Whereas decades of promotional material, as well as many visitors and park personnel and managers, saw fire as an aberration—a scourge that only destroyed the outward beauty of the park—the Master Plan argued that "Rocky Mountain forests are ravaged occasionally by windstorms or natural insect epidemics. Lightning fires have always denuded vast areas and changed vegetative patterns for decades." In effect, what was happening in Rocky and other parks was a formal reversal of an environmental attitude that had held sway during nearly the entire history of U.S. national parks. Naturally ignited fires and insect infestations were not accidents. They were not unnatural. Decades of scientific research demonstrated that both were eminently natural and absolutely integral to an ecologically healthy place. Having drawn fire and insect infestations back into the realm of natural events, it was logical for the planning document to conclude that "natural wildfires should be allowed to burn themselves out where they do not threaten an undesirably large area, lands outside the park, prime scenic resources near roads, trails, or developed areas."[66] J. D. Coffman would have flipped his lid.

Building on initial plans in 1973 and 1974, Rocky drafted its 1977 Fire Management Plan to balance the ecological importance of fire against the complicated range of variables involved in allowing fire back into a park surrounded by national forest lands and small towns. To do so, the plan contained two sections: the first dedicated to fire suppression, and the second to the new parameters for letting some fires burn. Recognizing that the 3 million people who visited the region every year were coming to "enjoy the scenic beauty of the areas and engage in various recreation activities," the superintendent stated that it was "imperative that the Service maintain a high level of preparedness to combat undesirable wildfire."[67]

Drawing largely from the 1970 "Administrative Policies for Natural Areas of the National Park System," which contained the entire Leopold Report,[68] the second section of Rocky's 1977 Fire Management Plan created new space for prescribed burning and lightning-caused fires. The new policy was based on the division of the park into three different fire classifications: low, moderate, and high-risk. Of the three, the areas of the park located above 10,000 feet were part of the low-risk zones where naturally occurring fires would ostensibly be allowed to burn. The NPS would not suppress naturally occurring fires within the moderate risk zone if the National Fire Danger Rating System number was low, or if the fire was burning in the fall as colder, wetter weather moved in. Those areas within the high-risk zones, including visitor centers, campgrounds, the ski area, and backcountry ranger cabins, required full suppression.[69] Ironically, the 1977 Fire Management Plan, a document that sought to restore fire as a major ecological component of the park, was responsible for further cleaving Rocky into distinct places, some reflecting the importance of ecological processes, and others deeply imbedded notions of natural beauty. Nonetheless, the departure from generations of fire policy in RMNP was stark, as was the overall sense that the plan's architects thought they had fire behavior pretty well figured out.

Park on Fire

On August 9, 1978, a storm passing through RMNP ignited a fire in one of the park's low-risk fire zones near Ouzel Lake. Adhering to their freshly minted plan, park officials allowed the fire to burn as they monitored its progress, ensuring that it stayed within the confines of the low-risk criteria. After burning slowly for two weeks, the fire flared on August 23 and "intermittently crowned." For the next week the fire burned erratically. Then, on September 1, "high winds caused more persistent crowning and spotting."[70] Fearful that the fire would soon spread beyond control, a crew of twenty-eight firefighters was dispatched to contain the blaze. After two days of intense labor the fire was back under control, and the on-site fire crew was reduced to twelve.[71] Then, on September 15, winds again fanned the flames. Park personnel concluded that the fire was again likely to escape their control and so they initiated fire-suppression tactics. Additional firefighters and equipment arrived on September 16 as the fire raged. At the fire's peak, some 600 people were fighting this single blaze.

A great deal was at stake for the NPS as the Ouzel Fire burned. The shifting attitudes toward fire that had been building for decades, finally embodied in RMNP's 1977 Fire Management Plan, were drawn immediately into question. Making matters far worse for RMNP and for natural fire advocates everywhere was the fact that the small town of Allenspark, located just outside the park boundaries, was very nearly destroyed by this fire. Apparently, a small ridge adjacent to the town deflected the "chinook wind up and over the town, sparing it." Finally, on September 30 the unruly fire was back under control, though it continued to burn until December. Local outrage at the NPS for the perceived failures of the new policy, which many only tepidly accepted to begin with, was widespread. Boulder County went so far as to fine RMNP for violating its air-quality standards.[72]

To be sure, parks like Rocky were in a nearly intractable position. For generations they contributed to and benefited from the fruits of fire and insect suppression. Both were powerful tools in drawing men and money to the parks, and such efforts delivered what many Americans expected from living paintings. When the NPS failed to deliver upon this implicit promise, a good number of its constituents voiced deep displeasure. Starting in the 1960s and accelerating rapidly thereafter, however, more and more people inside and outside the NPS clamored for the return of fire and its foundational contributions to ecosystem formation and health. Attempting to please both sides of this debate, RMNP drafted a series of fire plans in the 1970s that at once promised the limited reintroduction of fire while also promising that it had the knowledge, equipment, and manpower to bring fire fully to heel if the situation warranted it. These were difficult, if not impossible, promises to keep.

Although many members of the scientific community were ardent supporters of allowing fire back into RMNP, many park visitors continued to believe that beholding "a dead tree [was] like looking at a dead body" and that most people "don't come to see the natural beauty of a fire-killed tree." As was the case with J. D. Coffman and his 1930 "Report on Fire Protection Requirements of Rocky Mountain National Park," the seemingly slow plant rejuvenation after the Ouzel Fire gave anti-fire advocates a rallying point and a stark reminder of the dangers of letting fires burn.[73]

Rocky Mountain National Park is preparing yet another Fire Management Plan. Only time will tell the degree to which this newest plan will re-

Impact of Ouzel Fire, 1978. Courtesy of Rocky Mountain National Park, ROMO MSF NEG 5068.

flect the latest ecological understanding and just where that may lead. In the earliest years of the park, the science of the USFS guided and supported the NPS in its fire-suppression efforts. At this stage, the science behind fire suppression dovetailed with traditional notions of wild beauty. During the second phase, the cultures of ecology and tourism existed in rising tension. For decades, there has been a widely held belief that fire suppression in places like Rocky was not just wrong but that it was bad. According to this opinion, fire suppression led to the buildup of forest fuels, greater likelihood of insect outbreaks, and a "shift in the severity of fire from non-lethal surface fires to stand-replacing [wholly destructive] fires."

Recent studies, however, are once again drawing previous scientific paradigms into question. Regarding the subalpine forests in RMNP, some scientists are now positing that "fire suppression does not appear to have created unnaturally low amounts of burning nor unnatural landscapes in the subalpine forests" of the park.[74] Rather, fewer, less severe periods of drought conditions during the twentieth century are now thought to be the primary drivers behind "low fire frequencies" in the park's subalpine forests.[75] Still other research indicates that unlike the ponderosa pine–Douglas fir forests of the Southwest, those of RMNP are not characterized by frequent low-intensity burns. Hence, fire-suppression efforts of the past century have not "clearly and uniformly increased fuels or shifted the fire type from low- to high-severity fires."[76] Meanwhile, revealing the ascendancy of climate science over the past 15 years, researchers like William Baker are making strident and convincing arguments that climate cycles, not necessarily forest fuel buildup, are central to determining fire cycles and intensity in many of the forest types common in Rocky. If they are correct, generations of costly fire suppression in Rocky may have mattered far less than many have assumed.

Conclusion

As RMNP moved cautiously toward the partial embrace of fire again in the 1990s, the specter of insect-riddled ghost forests once again arose. The mountain pine beetle, which had been a periodic and unwelcome visitor to the park, returned in the late 1990s with shocking force. Driving through the park, especially along the western side, a sea of dead and dying trees unfolds before the eye. The park's current position regarding insect management stretches back to 1970, when it ended most insect control efforts, which had included the cutting and peeling of thousands of trees during outbreaks. Like fire, even the troublesome bark beetles had become recognized as important members of a healthy ecosystem. Although the new policy presented a significant change from the past, it nonetheless contained language that left plenty of room for mitigation efforts to protect the scenery of the front-country. Once again, park staff were attempting to reconcile an ecological philosophy with political and cultural realities, both of which are reflected across the park's geography.

To date, this infestation has touched more than 41 million acres of forested land in the United States and more than 6.5 million acres in Colorado alone. According to the U.S. Forest Service, the agency that has borne the brunt of this problem, over the next ten years an astounding 100,000 trees *per day* will fall as a consequence of mountain pine beetle mortality. Each tree that crashes to the forest floor may impact the state's roads, recreation sites, trails, ski areas, transmission and power lines, and water supplies. The USFS spent an incredible $97 million between 2008 and 2011 on this single outbreak.

The magnitude of this problem has sent researchers scrambling to find explanations. Although their findings have varied, it seems likely that generations of forest management centered on fire suppression, combined with a prolonged drought during the 1990s and early 2000s, in addition to the warmer winter temperatures associated with climate change, are all prime suspects.[77] Reacting to the outbreak, RMNP initiated a Bark Beetle Management Plan Environmental Assessment in 2005 to outline the problem and to put forth management strategies.

It is interesting to note that during the beetle outbreak of the 1940s RMNP had the desire, but not the manpower, to treat the entire park. As such, it focused on those aspects of the park with the most visual importance. Campgrounds, roadsides, and other high-traffic areas received the bulk of attention and healthy doses of deadly chemicals. During the most recent outbreak, the NPS does not have the desire to treat the entire park, but it has chosen to continue its long tradition of protecting "the visual character, screening, and other important qualities that trees provide RMNP, particularly in developed and culturally significant areas." To an agency that still trades a great deal in outward signs of natural health and beauty that stretch back more than a century, "healthy trees near visitor centers, campgrounds, picnic areas, employee housing areas and national historic districts within the park are especially valuable and should be protected."[78]

Decades after the arrival of ecology into the NPS and its percolation into portions of the American public, nineteenth-century conceptions of beauty remain integral to how we envision, and manage, our parks. RMNP is planning to remove an estimated 1 million dead and dying trees from the park by 2014 to improve visitor safety and satisfaction.[79] The works of Thomas Cole, Frederick Law Olmstead, Enos Mills, and others continue to shape the park and how we experience it.

Eerily similar to the outbreak of 1943, protecting high-value trees has once again put the NPS in the position of using chemicals to treat insect infestations in those areas in or adjacent to campgrounds, picnic areas, visitor centers, parking lots, and the like.[80] According to its 2005 Bark Beetle Management Plan, when conditions warrant it the NPS will apply Sevin brand XLR Plus Carbaryl to treat threatened areas.[81] In 2009 the park treated an estimated 5,000 high-value trees and planned to treat at least another 4,000 through the 2010 season. Areas receiving the application of Carbaryl included the "Beaver Meadows Visitor Center and Headquarters, Moraine Park Visitor Center, Kawuneeche Visitor Center, Aspenglen, Moraine Park, and Glacier Basin Campgrounds, Bighorn Ranger Station, McGraw Ranch, Holzwarth Historic Site, Timber Creek Campground Water Tank, Leiffer Cabin, Kaley Cottages, Lumpy Ridge Trailhead, and the east and west side park service housing areas."[82]

Mild exposure to this product, according to its makers, may cause "salivation, watery eyes, pinpoint eye pupils, blurred vision, muscle tremors, difficult breathing, excessive sweating, abdominal cramps, nausea, vomiting, diarrhea, weakness, [and] headache." In more severe cases, exposure can prompt convulsion, unconsciousness, and respiratory failure "rapidly" following contact. Sevin brand XLR Plus Carbaryl is also "extremely toxic to aquatic and estuarine invertebrates" and should not be applied "directly to water, or to areas where surface water is present or to intertidal areas below the mean high water mark." It should not be used "when weather conditions favor drift from area treated," and it is "highly toxic" to bees.[83] Remember this the next time you are eating a sandwich in one of the park's well-shaded campgrounds that we all find so irresistible.

There are few pleasures greater than finding a secluded tree in Rocky Mountain National Park and settling beneath its outstretched arms. What you see before you is not a static forest set loose from the bounds of history. Rather, the trees and forests across Rocky are the product of humans and nature interacting across time and space. When we pass through the park's gates we do not enter empty-handed. We carry with us unique, complicated, and shifting ideas of beauty, science, reason, and right and wrong. These ideas, in turn, bind us to these wonderful trees and to the fires and insects that consume them.

5

Growing Elk

The sound rises on crisp September mornings throughout the Rocky Mountains. It ricochets across canyons, screams through gold-splashed aspens, and raises gooseflesh on those who hear it. It is an almost otherworldly sound that defies written description. It begins with a low, growling, and powerful whistle that rises to higher and higher octaves and then finishes abruptly. This bugle, as it is called, is often followed by a series of guttural harrumphs. To the human ear, the bugle of the elk might be reminiscent of a bagpipe gone bad; to an elk, it is an invitation to make love and war.

Elk are as much a part of Rocky Mountain National Park as Trail Ridge Road, Bear Lake, or flipping an elk hair caddis under the out-stretched branches of a bankside willow. For decades families have piled into cars, donned hiking boots, and lifted binoculars with hopes of seeing one of the park's most beloved and recognized animals. Take a drive this summer through Moraine Park or over Trail Ridge Road. Not only are you likely to see elk in diverse habitats, but you are just as likely to see ogling tourists pressing forward, cameras at the ready.

In this sense the proliferation of elk across Estes Park and RMNP has been a boon for both. Even before the creation of RMNP in 1915, a host of people and organizations worked to associate the park with specific icons. As demonstrated in previous chapters, this iconography included good roads, diverse trails, and pristine forests. Just as important was the opportunity to see beautiful (and bountiful) game animals. For tourists making the train ride from Chicago or the quick jaunt from Denver, rumors of roadside deer, majestic bighorn sheep, and rutting, bugling, and sparring elk were indeed great attractions. Realizing the close connection between robust visitation and ubiquitous game animals, the NPS dedicated significant efforts to maximizing encounters between visitors and the park's ungulates. These efforts included an extensive extermination of predatory animals, such as bobcats, lynx, coyotes, and mountain lions, as well as other measures.

Through an active predator reduction program and a moratorium on hunting within the park, the NPS was able to grow its elk population from a few dozen in 1913 to as many as 3,500 by the late 1990s.[1] As early as the 1930s, however, the NPS found itself in an increasingly difficult position. Although park officials and others had successfully linked the RMNP experience to the expectation of seeing elk, those very same elk—once released from predation—were damaging other beloved attractions. Trampled meadows, eroded soil, scarred and dying stands of quaking aspen all spoke to elk's power to transform the park.

The ecological side of this management problem was relatively straightforward: employ the necessary means to reduce and control the park's elk population. The political and cultural side of the equation has proven much more intractable. For generations, the NPS and others advertised Rocky as a place to see—from the comfort of an automobile—one of these majestic creatures. For this reason and others, culling Rocky's elk herd has been wildly controversial, and the NPS has only sporadically been willing to buck public opinion on the matter. All the while, Rocky's elk continue to eat themselves out of house and home.

Cervus elaphus

The North American elk (*Cervus elaphus*) has roamed the Rocky Mountains for some 40,000 years.[2] For much of that time, these animals have been of great interest to humans as a source of food, raw materials, and, of late, inspiration and entertainment. The North American elk is a ruminant, meaning that it has a single stomach comprised of four parts including the rumen, reticulum, omasum and abomasum.[3] Through complicated biological and chemical processes, elk are able to transform grass, forbs, and other vegetal matter into blood, bone, meat, and fur. Considering the average size of a mature elk, often in excess of 1,100 pounds for males and 600 pounds for females, it should come as no surprise that they require an impressive quantity of forage to maintain themselves.[4]

The feeding habits of elk are flexible, depending on season and available forage. Elk can and do select from a range of edible plant species but often focus on those with the highest caloric benefit as compared to the caloric expenditure of eating them.[5] Prevailing season and the individual elk's caloric requirements further complicate which foods it will eat and when it will move to a different location. For example, a cow supporting a calf through the bountiful summer months will consume in the neighborhood of 18 pounds of "good quality forage" per day. Taking into consideration the size and structure of their mouths, that same cow elk would have to dedicate some 13–14 hours per day just in cropping, chewing, and digesting. The majority of the elk's diet consists of grasses, followed by shrubs like willow (*Salix* spp.), as well as aspen (*Populus tremuloides*) and forbs.[6]

In addition to meeting daily caloric needs, male and female elk spend much of the year in the business of reproduction. The cycle begins in August with the rut, which often stretches through October. The purpose of the rut, from a purely biological point of view, is to select the most fit males for breeding with the largest number of females. In their effort to build up the largest breeding pool possible, bull elk partake in a range of behaviors to demonstrate their virility, including bugling and dominance fights. As it is understood, the bugle is essentially an open invitation to other bulls to challenge dominance. In cases where an immature bull challenges a mature one, a head-on rush accompanied by a show of teeth and hissing is often enough to drive the lesser of the two adversaries from the field. In cases where the challenger is also a mature bull, the proceedings look much different.[7]

Rather than run the risk of serious bodily harm or the fruitless burning of precious calories just before the onset of winter, a harem-tending bull will often first resort to a series of postures to drive off a well-matched opponent. Such postures might include thrashing the ground with antlers, spraying urine, and loud bugling. If these actions fail to dissuade the challenger, then fighting is likely to ensue. Fights vary widely but often entail a shoving match with locked antlers. This process, which is often played out several times a day, is serious business. On average, a rutting bull sustains several dozen wounds per season, some of which lead to infection and even death.[8] The

Bull elk tangled in barbed wire while fighting. Courtesy of Rocky Mountain National Park, ROMO 10680.

prize for the bugling, urinating, charging, and fighting is copulation with the females in his harem.

During the cold days of winter an impregnated cow begins gestating its fetus, a process that takes about 255 days.[9] Cows typically give birth around the beginning of June. The rigors of predation and impending seasonal change put a premium on all ungulates' ability to grow quickly, and elk are no different. At birth the typical calf weighs perhaps 110 pounds, but the fat- and calorie-rich milk from the mothers promotes quick growth, and by their first spring they typically weigh 310–350 pounds.[10]

Such is the life cycle of *Cervus elaphus*. Viewed from afar it is a wonderfully choreographed movement of animals across time and space: large herds gathering in the fall and winter, fighting and making babies; the diffusion of herds in the spring accompanied by the birth of calves into the bosom of lush summer grasses; and the drawing together in fall to start the cycle anew. Although they have specific caloric reasons to stay in one place and thereby maximize the ratio between caloric intake versus expenditure, the changing seasons and predation keep elk herds from settling into one place for too long. In a perfect world, this is how it works.

Branding a National Park

To those in the business of promoting and selling, *branding* refers to efforts intended to associate a product with a certain sentiment that might compel a person to purchase it. Managers of RMNP have sought to associate the park with certain images, hopes, and attitudes, including smooth and commodious roads and trails as well as powerful and pristine scenery. In seeking to broaden the appeal of RMNP, NPS officials and others also worked diligently to associate the park experience with viewing "game animals." In this sense, the history of RMNP is little different than Yellowstone, Yosemite, and the Grand Canyon. As originally conceived, national parks were to be vast "living museums" where visitors could witness fish, fowl, and furred animals in their natural habitat. It was a strategy that worked well for the promotion and growth of the National Park System. After all, driving across a smooth road casting one's gaze upon splendid peaks is one thing; being close enough to see, smell, and almost touch an elk, mule deer, or bighorn sheep from that same automobile is an altogether different experience.

Not surprisingly, some of the earliest promoters of big game in the area were the very same groups that touted fishing and driving near Estes Park. In the Union Pacific's "Colorado for the Tourist," for example, the railroad lauded the state's fecund wildlife through both prose and picture. Given that this pamphlet was designed to advertise all of Colorado, and because it was published in 1911, before the creation of RMNP in 1915, hunting rather than viewing animals was the focus. According to this advertisement, the mountains of Colorado abounded in "deer, bear, elk and grouse. Bear and grouse may be hunted ad libitum, but the elk and deer are protected by statute. Flocks of mountain sheep can be seen, but they are protected for the present. For the hardier hunter there are mountain lions, bob-cats and wolves, and there is no better sport than an extended search for these dangerous beasts."[11] Advertising the plentiful opportunities to hunt the wilds of Colorado was an effective strategy. As several historians have argued, American men were increasingly interested in tapping into masculine activities in a world where their manliness seemed to be slipping away. The ever-perceptive UP used such concerns to boost the railroad's bottom line.

In its 1924 publication "Colorado's Mountain Playgrounds," the Union Pacific continued to promote the region's abundant wildlife, but the tone had changed. Rather than celebrating the state as a hunter's paradise, the pamphlet touted it as a "Sanctuary for Bird and Beast." Within this sanctuary, promised the UP, "forests and streams have many inhabitants now safe from trapper and hunter. The beaver has countless dome-shaped tenements in the streams, where he may be seen by patient watching. The foremost mountain climber on the globe, the bighorn sheep, roams the precipices of the highest peaks. Deer are often encountered, but bears are few and rarely seen; marmots, woodchucks, rabbits and conies are common."[12] The creation of RMNP in 1915, with its emphasis upon watching rather than shooting wildlife, clearly worked its way into the promotion of the region. Whether the park was viewed from the working end of a rifle or that of a Kodak, corporations like UP were well aware that abundant wildlife along their rails held the promise of more patrons, and thus they dedicated significant time, money, and effort to promote their presence.

Elkhorn Lodge, which entertained guests as early as 1880, also made an obvious connection between itself and wildlife simply through the selection of its moniker.[13] Beyond naming the lodge the Elkhorn and festooning the hotel with copious antler sheds and animal heads, its advertisements and brochures also used faunal iconography to draw tourists to Estes Park. In one brochure (likely printed in the late 1910s), the Elkhorn promised that Horseshoe Park was a place where "mountain sheep are becoming so tame that they will allow you to approach within fifty feet and take photographs." In addition to such promises, the Elkhorn also claimed that "in an effort to reinstate a condition that existed in former times, the State has lately turned a band of Elk into the Park, which still roam in the neighboring hills and can be frequently seen."[14]

The concerted effort to promote the area's abundant wildlife makes historical sense. To the growing class of Americans with the time, money, and motivation to escape more urban settings, the chance to view wildlife was a great attraction. The Earl of Dunraven knew this; so did the members of the Estes Park Improvement Association who originally conceived of RMNP as a game preserve. The Union Pacific Railroad and the National Park Service were also well aware that an abundance of animal life in and around Estes Park—whether for sport or for viewing—promised to please the growing number of people annually attracted to the region. Through brochures, pamphlets, and other printed materials, boosters linked Rocky Mountain National Park with the opportunity to view wildlife. The desire to see wildlife, especially the park's ungulates, put the NPS in a position to manage those animals in such a way that increased the likelihood that a visitor would encounter them.

Replanting Elk

It is impossible to know with certainty when the last elk was shot in the Estes Park region, or whether or not elk were indeed completely extirpated, as is commonly thought. What is known, however, is that the rapid growth of Denver and surrounding mining camps in the 1860s and 1870s put tremendous strain on the plant and animal life up and down the Front Range. According to one of the earliest residents of Estes Park, Abner Sprague, the elk "lasted about three years. They came down from their high range just before Christmas, 1875, by the thousands and were met by hunters with repeating rifles and four horse teams; hauled to Denver for three or four cents per pound. In 1876 fewer came down; in '77 very few were seen on [the east] side of the divide. In 1878 I killed my last elk, and to get him had to go over Flat Top [sic][Mountain]."[15] By the middle of the 1880s, it appears that there were few, if any, elk in the Estes Park region.

To restock the area, the first of two shipments of elk arrived from Yellowstone National Park in 1913. The following year an additional twenty-five were shipped in, bringing the total number to about thirty.[16] As early as 1917, park officials reported that "conditions for wild animals in the Park have been excellent. The weather has been exceptionally mild, and the abundant feed of the earlier months promises to last well into the fall."[17] Monthly tallies of animals seen supported the optimistic tenor of the report. In November of that year, for example, park staff counted a total of "48 grouse, 19 elk, and 60 mountain sheep."[18] Under such favorable conditions, the park's elk herd grew quickly, much to the pleasure of the NPS. According to its official count, by 1918 there "were 5 herd of elk in the park" with a total population of about sixty individuals, and they were "increasing rapidly."[19] For park

First shipment of elk from Yellowstone National Park to Estes Park, 1913. Courtesy of Rocky Mountain National Park, ROMO MSF NEG 989.

managers eager to attract visitors as quickly as possible, herds of multiplying game animals meant nothing but good things.

By the close of 1918, just three years following the park's creation, Superintendent L. Claude Way was already keenly aware of the connection between visible game animals and increasing visitation. In his 1918 annual report, he reported that good days brought many visitors to the park to see the wild game, the numbers seen being "exceptionally great." Because visitors could not harvest these animals to hang on a wall back home, they settled for keeping tallies of how many animals they saw. One party proudly reported seeing eighty-two deer, forty-one sheep, and twenty-seven elk in less than an hour from the comfort of their automobile.[20]

The elk shipped to and released in Estes Park, combined with the existing herds of mule deer and bighorn sheep, gave prospective visitors much to ponder in anticipation of a trip to RMNP. From the NPS's perspective, however, there was one significant problem. Although gray wolves and grizzly bears—both top-tier predators of deer, elk, and bighorn sheep—had been extirpated prior to the establishment of the park, many predators still lurked in the park's shadows in search of their next meal.[21] Any animal that threatened the existence of so-called game animals was thus a threat to the mission of the NPS.[22]

Although the NPS was created with a mission very different from that of the U.S. Forest Service, the U.S. Biological Survey, and the U.S. Fish and Wildlife Service, its initial interpretation of the organic legislation often reflects the philosophies and priorities of those other agencies. This is especially true for game management. As historian Thomas Dunlap demonstrates, sportsmen and so-called nature lovers loathed predatory animals. The sportsman's animus came from a fear that predators removed valuable game from the range; nature lovers loathed predators because they saw them as base and cruel. In any case, when the NPS was founded, wolves, coyotes, and any other predators found little sympathy in the United States.

Making matters worse, at least as far as predators were concerned, was the fact that the NPS was a small and relatively unstable organization upon its founding. As demonstrated in previous chapters, this put the NPS in the position of relying on outside organizations (both private and public) for assistance in carrying out various programs. In the case of wildlife management, RMNP turned often to the help and expertise of the Biological Survey. As originally conceived, the Biological Survey was charged with the regulation of hunting and fishing, as well as putting in place policies that enhanced both. The Biological Survey was an early and ardent proponent of predator control as part of the broader effort to enhance the killing of game animals by sportsmen. The NPS's reliance upon organizations like the Biological Survey to carry out its mission is reflected at least in part in the NPS's adoption of similar predator-control practices. The major difference between the two agencies, however, lay in motivations behind the policy of extermination. The Biological Survey was able for many decades to promote predator reduction as a means to enhance hunting. For the NPS, however, which strictly prohibited hunting within its administered lands, predator control was pursued largely to promote the population growth of game animals to please the tourist.

To encourage the growth of the tiny band of elk and to protect further the viable populations of deer and bighorn sheep, RMNP began an extensive program to exterminate a wide range of predatory animals that threatened other members of the park's faunal community. In its first year of predator reduction in 1917, for example, the NPS killed foxes, coyotes, and martens.[23] Of more concern still was the presence of mountain lions in and around the park. These big cats were often blamed for killing elk, deer, and bighorn sheep, all of which park visitors esteemed. The NPS and others fervently hunted and killed them to protect other game animals.[24] In 1919, for example, the superintendent of RMNP reported that although the "deer, elk and sheep are coming down from the higher altitudes, and are in very good condition," there were "more mountain lion . . . reported this year than ever before," compelling him to acquire "lion dogs" and to initiate "an intensive campaign against predatory animals."[25] The winter of 1919–1920 brought the death of six mountain lions in and adjacent to the park, five of which were females.[26] December 1920 brought the destruction of two more cats, one hunted with dogs, the other caught in a trap.[27]

Anxious to build upon the previous season's success, RMNP issued permits to five men to trap predators within the park in 1922.[28] Park staff also hosted Predatory Animal Inspector Stanley P. Young and the hunter John Crook, both of the U.S. Biological Survey. As Superintendent Roger Toll of RMNP accompanied the two men through the park, the Estes Park Fish and Game Association held a meeting regarding the killing of predators in and around Rocky. After setting seventeen poison stations, the NPS killed two coyotes and a bobcat. More important, they tracked and killed a mountain lion that they claimed was responsible for killing a five-point buck. As reported, the lion was over six feet in length and was the mother to three kittens.[29] Year after year, the monthly game counts increased, giving managers clear evidence that their predator eradication program was having its desired effect. By the fall of 1922, during the rut, elk sightings were "numerous," with some herds as large as sixty.[30]

As more people came into contact with the park's elk, an important change began taking place: the elk began losing their natural fear of humans. One band of elk in particular that traditionally fed in the vicinity of Deer Mountain and Horseshoe Park in December, for example, had long been visible to visitors. By 1926, park personnel reported that although it "has always been possible to see these elk from a distance," the "present season marks the first year when they could be termed all tame." In late November 1926, a "group of about 100 of these elk were visited by large numbers of Estes Park people, who had no difficulty at all in taking whatever photographs they desired from the very short distances of 100 to 200 feet. The elk showed not the slightest degree of fear of the visitors."[31]

More animals within the park—especially ones lounging roadside—held great promise for pleasing the growing throngs of visitors. By 1927, with the park's elk herd estimated at 200 head, park personnel continued to report the correlation between visitation and wildlife viewing.[32] In March of that year, Superintendent Toll reported that "never before have such large numbers of deer and elk been seen at points close to the public highways throughout the park. This attraction brings more and more visitors from the valley towns for trips along park roads during the winter season." The novelty of watching 1,100-pound animals stomping, bugling, and thrashing their way through the rut was powerful enough to draw visitors to the park on moonlit nights, with carloads of visitors seen "every night" in Horseshoe, Moraine, and Beaver Parks watching the elk graze and delighting at their nocturnal bugling. [33]

Signs of Trouble

Between the founding of the National Park Service (1916) and the beginning of the Great Depression (1929), ecology was virtually nonexistent within the National Park Service. The reasons for this are many, but they stem primarily from the very limited budget of the agency, its need and desire to pour resources into promotional efforts to grow itself, and the fact that the field of ecology was relatively new and practiced by only a handful of scientists. In fact, in 1930 the NPS employed only one research scientist, nine wildlife rangers, and six naturalists to oversee its seventy-four national parks and monuments.[34] Moreover, the NPS's wildlife rangers and naturalists spent the bulk of their time in visitor education and resource protection and relatively little time conducting anything approximating scientific study.

Ecology eventually came to the NPS, but not through institutional initiative. Rather, it arrived through the privately funded research of the "independently wealthy biologist" George M. Wright.[35] Working in iconic parks like Yosemite, Wright had come to the conclusion that the NPS did not know enough about the natural resources it managed, and he also realized that the NPS was reluctant to fund such research from its own budget. Accordingly, he proposed to fund and direct the first in-depth and comprehensive scientific investigation into the parks in 1928. Between 1929 and 1940, scientists like Wright and others "promoted an ecological awareness in the Service and questioned the utilitarian and recreational focus that dominated the bureau."[36] As the NPS came to employ more scientists, the widely accepted aesthetic standards for judging park landscapes that dominated so much of the administrations of Mather and Albright were challenged by new standards derived from the application of ecological principles.

In the summer of 1930, Wright and fellow biologists Joseph Dixon and Ben Thompson began their investigations. After concluding their fieldwork in the spring of 1931, the research team wrote and soon published *Fauna of the National Parks of the United States: A Preliminary Survey of Faunal Relations in National Parks,* more widely known as Fauna No. 1.[37] At its heart lay a recognition that "the parks' faunas have been extremely sensitive to the influences of civilization" and that immediate steps were needed to better understand and temper the influences of "civilization" upon park resources. The authors contended that the parks were valuable in part because they represented landscapes that had been rescued "from the immediate dangers of private exploitation" where "climax examples of Nature's scenic achievements" remained.[38]

Fauna No. 1 was remarkable in many ways. Regarding RMNP, it recognized that the original park boundaries, which reflected political realities and prevailing attitudes of sublime beauty, had not paid sufficient heed to the biological needs of plants and animals.[39] Expanding the borders of RMNP to include natural barriers such as major mountain ranges, argued the authors, "would greatly alleviate the present unsatisfactory condition" of the park. This recommendation, in turn, was largely guided by what the research team viewed as a growing elk "crisis" within the park. In the winter of 1930 the elk population was reaching a tipping point, as elk turned increasingly to aspen as winter forage to stave off starvation. If the park's boundaries were expanded to include more winter range, the researchers believed, the problem would be "largely corrected." If, however, strategic expansions of the park failed to achieve a "natural balance," then some "form of artificial control may be necessary."[40]

After its publication, the NPS adopted Fauna No. 1's recommendation that all NPS wildlife management decisions be based upon scientific study. Also revealing the embrace of science within the NPS was its increased willingness to fund scientific inquiry. For example, in 1931 the NPS agreed to fund half of Wright's endeavor, and it assumed full financial responsibility for his work in 1933. In large part because of Fauna No. 1, the NPS also created its own Wildlife Division in 1933. Headquartered at the University of California–Berkeley, the Wildlife Division employed biologists in the pursuit of scientific understanding of NPS resources.[41]

In response to its growing elk problem, and speaking directly to the rising authority of an ecological way of viewing the park, RMNP purchased nearly 4,500 acres of private land within the Thompson River drainage as well as nearly 8,000 acres in Mill Creek, Beaver Meadows, and Horseshoe Park. Privately owned stock had grazed much of this land since before the creation of the park, thereby reducing the range's ability to support elk populations, especially through winter. Once under NPS control, private grazing rights came to an end and available elk forage increased.[42] Much more is at work here, however, than a simple redrawing of park boundaries. At its very core, the expansion of the park along biological—as opposed to purely scenic— lines was an early and powerful indication of the ways that both tourism and ecology tugged at the imaginary lines that constituted the park itself.

Although the NPS sought to add acreage to the park through the purchase of private land, it did not yet have either the will or the backing to implement artificial controls to contain elk within the carrying capacity of the range. Managers' reticence to do so is understandable given the growing popularity of elk in the park. But popularity came with as many challenges as it did opportunities. In addition to winter range degradation, the NPS also began reporting that visitors were becoming aggressive and careless in their zeal to get closer to the elk. For example, Superintendent Edmund Rogers reported that the elk were so popular and so tame that it had become "necessary during the early part of the month to barricade many old roads and obliterate the beginning of new ones where visitors in their cars had been running over the parks and meadows in an effort to see, or get closer to, the elk."[43]

By 1935, with nearly all available private grazing land now in the hands of the NPS, the park took further steps to address the growing elk crisis. Admitting the limited options, Superintendent Rogers concluded that the time was soon coming when lethal force would have to be applied to keep the elk "within the natural carrying capacity of the range." The superintendent assigned a park ranger and a wildlife technician to the project of determining how many elk the park could support. By 1935, the total elk population within RMNP was estimated at 425, 75 more than roamed the park when Dixon, Wright, and Thompson surveyed the area just five years earlier.[44]

Between 1935 and the winter of 1943, the NPS made no move to implement lethal herd reductions, and the number of estimated elk in the park grew with each passing year. In 1937, for example, there were some 555 elk in the park in the winter, and nearly 650 in the summer.[45] The next year's figures showed yet another rapid population growth, with nearly 800 in residence during the summer and 675 in the winter.[46] Although an increasing number of experts agreed that culling the herd was a necessary and proper course of action, the NPS chose not to implement this strategy.[47] The desire on the part of hundreds of thousands of visitors to experience the park's elk was just too strong. But each passing year brought more reports of range damage and the crystallization of a new and different way of looking at the park's elk. Meanwhile, the NPS continued to search for more palatable options.

Binding the Bounty of Nature

Amid the growing concern about the park's elk population, biologist Fred Mallery Packard initiated a study into aspen decline in the park.[48] Packard concluded that the most significant threat to the park's aspens were fungal diseases, "chief among which [was] dieback, caused by *Cytospora chrysosperma*," which is introduced into healthy trees by wounds in the bark.[49] Although bark wounds could result from a range of factors, elk were the leading culprits. In scraping their antlers on the trees, eating the shoots and leaves, and most significantly eating the bark and cambium off the trees, elk exposed aspens to the deadly fungus and thereby became significant agents of aspen mortality.[50] Although aspens across the park were suffering due to elk overpopulation, the problem was most apparent in Beaver Meadows. In one stand of trees, reported Packard, the "trunk of every aspen [was] heavily scarred as high as the elk [could] reach, and no branches survive[d] below that height." Just as disconcerting was the discovery that "the trees bordering the meadow [were] dead or dying by the hundreds." Under such conditions, Packard predicted that it was "almost certain that in comparatively few years all of these aspen will have died, and there is little chance that they will be restored."[51]

Responding to mounting scientific evidence of their growing elk problem, RMNP staff wrote an Elk Management Plan in 1943.[52] Of most importance was the decision to finally use lethal force to reduce the number of elk win-

Elk rub on aspen tree, circa 1932. Courtesy of Rocky Mountain National Park, ROMO MSF NEG 3377.

tering in the park. After receiving approval from the director of the NPS in 1944, the staff at RMNP began an intensive culling campaign. In the span of just two months, the Park Service shot a total of 301 elk and 113 deer in RMNP.[53] Although the culling efforts held the promise of solving the population problem, the assistant director of the NPS, Hillary A. Tolson, wrote to the park in 1946 that "the Director's office had a 'strong dislike' for reduction programs either inside or adjacent to NPS units." Accordingly, further reductions were halted until 1949.[54]

Despite the extensive herd reduction during the 1944 season, scientists continued reporting extensive range degradation. For example, Packard conducted further research on the park's deer and elk herds and published his findings in the *Journal of Mammalogy* in 1947.[55] According to Packard, elk within the park were reproducing at a rate of 29 percent to 50 percent per annum, which was responsible for the continued range degradation.[56] With the number of elk expanding so rapidly, it is no wonder that Packard's report echoed the findings of previous investigations. "In spite of a number of natural and artificial checks," argued Packard, "the elk herd is increasing rapidly, and already exceeds the optimum carrying capacity of the winter range."[57] Despite the efforts of the NPS throughout the 1930s and the culling campaign of 1944, Packard found "serious deterioration" of forage plants on the winter range.[58]

In light of the worrisome trend, the NPS initiated another intensive culling campaign in 1949–1950 that resulted in the removal of an additional 340 elk and 100 deer from the park. Following the heavy reductions of that season, the NPS committed itself to an annual herd reduction with the hope of stabilizing herd growth. Between 1950 and 1959, 507 elk and 309 deer were culled from the RMNP winter range.[59]

Although control measures continued throughout the 1950s, the number of elk killed each year became less and less as some indications pointed toward minor improvements in range conditions.[60] This was not, however, the only reason that annual herd reductions diminished between 1950 and 1959. In his annual report for 1950, RMNP Superintendent David Canfield confided that "considerable public relations work was necessary to acquaint the people at large, and especially the various sportsmen's organizations, with the need and purpose of the reduction." Close cooperation with the Forest Service and the Colorado Game and Fish Department, reported the superintendent, "aided in carrying the reduction to a successful conclusion with little opposition."[61] Although the superintendent reported "little opposition" to the program, the record tells a different story. In 1951, for example, fewer animals were killed—eighty-five elk and 105 deer—than in previous years, and the culling efforts were "carried out over a prolonged period in order to cause less stir among the public."[62] The following year, the NPS opted to trap rather than shoot deer to limit "public outrage." Regardless of the possibility of causing an uproar, the NPS did kill eighty-nine elk that winter season.[63]

Careful to keep hidden the messy process of removing tens of thousands of pounds of elk from the park, the NPS took several precautions to reduce the likelihood of public outcry during the culling process. To keep the killing and the visiting as far apart as possible, the NPS closed off areas when culling was taking place. Once the deed had been completed, the carcasses were tucked beneath tarp-covered truck beds and spirited away. The meat was then "given to the Izaak Walton League and various local sportsman associations for distribution to charitable groups, to schools for lunches, to churches, etc."[64]

According to the park ranger Stanley Brownman, every precaution was used to ensure that "no evidence of the program was exposed to park visitors."[65] With opposition to culling efforts already high, the NPS could not afford to let little Suzy or Jimmy see the park's most beloved animal crumple following the crack of a well-placed shot, especially considering that about one in five elk shot were calves. The trauma and bad publicity such an incident could produce had the potential to seriously tarnish the NPS's image.

But there is more at work here than sparing visitors the potential trauma of the culling process. For decades, the NPS and many of its partners had touted the natural fecundity of the park through the presence of copious elk. To most contemporaries, abundant elk reflected the vitality of Rocky and served as a constant reminder of the wisdom of protecting such natural places in the first place. Lethal herd reduction raised many uncomfortable questions about the past and future of the park and its elk. If the elk were representations of the natural world set free from human pressure, how could they be responsible for destroying other parts of the park? Elk could not, in other words, be symbols of natural order and disorder at the same time. Witnessing the lethal reductions would force visitors to confront the thorny question of just how separate humans were from these wild animals.

Despite the efforts of the NPS to avoid public outrage, the elk reduction programs greatly dismayed many visitors. Mrs. R. J. Thornburg, for example, was especially upset with the reductions, and her opposition captures vividly the feelings of many park visitors. Her letter also expresses some of the deepest fears of the NPS. According to Thornburg, since "Mr. Public foots the bill" for national parks, "maybe he should be considered" when decisions are made regarding the killing of fauna within them. In a not-so-veiled threat to the park, she continued: "If in hiking around a national park the size of Rocky Mt. you can't see anything bigger than a squirrel or a cony [the taxpayer] might get the idea it wasn't worthwhile to spend so much money for upkeep of the area." Not relenting, she contended that "many felt this, for we heard lots of griping about the paucity of wildlife last summer." Moreover, a "national park devoid of the larger species of wildlife isn't very inspirational and you can't help feeling something is wrong." Reaching her boiling point, she then blasted, if "all those thousands of acres in Rocky Mt. park won't support enough deer so you can see more than six or eight in six weeks of travel on trails and roads, turn it back to the Indians, they did a lot better job of managing than that."[66]

And there it was. To many park staff and a growing cadre of ecologists, the park had a serious elk problem. Dead and dying trees, soil erosion, and shortages of winter forage told them as much. To Thornburg and others who brought the culture of tourism with them to Rocky, however, those very same herds of elk lazily eating their way through the park were the very epitome of nature and a central reason for visiting the area. As was the case with the park's roads, trails, and forests, Rocky's wildlife was becoming a front on the ideological turf war between two distinct philosophies. The NPS, who had soldiers in both camps, stood in the middle and groped for answers.

To further hasten range recovery, the NPS began drafting its "Long Range Management Plan for the Eastern Rocky Mountain Elk and Deer" in 1960.[67] According to the plan, which was released in the fall of 1961, the NPS's chief objective was to reduce the populations of elk and deer on the park's winter range to levels conducive to regrowth of forests, shrubs, and grasslands. The plan also recognized the detrimental impact that elk were having on beaver and bighorn sheep within the park and stated that restoring their populations was also a primary goal. To accomplish the above, the NPS intended to reduce the elk population on the winter range to a total of 400 animals "as soon as possible" and to initiate a more concerted monitoring program to determine future reduction needs.[68]

The Elk and Deer Management Plan speaks to a broader shift taking place within the rank and file of the NPS. For example, prior to the completion of the plan, park biologist James Cole wrote to the superintendent of RMNP, stating that although the "National Park Service should give Park visitors opportunities to observe wildlife," the "emphasis should be upon wildlife in a normal habitat." Rather than promoting an appreciation of abundant wildlife, the NPS should promote "fewer good examples of sleek elk and deer, even though the visitor must expend some energy to find them." Only once this was accomplished could the NPS maintain "healthy and vigorous plants upon which the condition and existence of all wildlife ultimately depends." To Cole, managing for ecological balance—not the proliferation of a few key animal species—was the NPS's fundamental charge as "custodians of Park wildlife."[69] The 1961 plan represented a significant—if not easy—step in that direction.

Anticipating public opposition, the Elk and Deer Management Plan also called for an active public relations campaign to inform the public of the need for reductions. The NPS issued a press release in 1961 designed to educate the average visitor in the hopes that understanding would lead to support. According to the release, the problem of elk overpopulation was a function of an "unhealthy imbalance . . . between the wildlife and its habitat due principally to the lack of natural predators, and the fact that old herd migration routes to winter range areas outside the Park have been blocked more completely each year by human habitation." To help visitors understand the connections between the park's plant and animal communities, the NPS stated that it was "not only the animals that suffer, but plant species on which the deer and elk feed are badly over-browsed and overgrazed. . . . In addition, the loss of this important protective ground cover leads to damaging soil erosion."[70]

If thoughts of soil erosion and overgrazed grass were not enough to win public support, the NPS intimated that there was "no natural remedy for this vicious cycle of imbalance except the cruel one of a true famine, which will be avoided at all costs."[71] To protect the park's soil, plants, and the elk themselves, the NPS announced it would "remove" an estimated 200 elk from targeted portions of the park. Doubtless hoping to assuage visitor angst that culling would diminish the experience, the NPS promised that at RMNP "every effort will be made to prevent interference with visitor opportunities to observe wildlife in a natural and appealing setting, and yet encourage migration outside the Park where animals would be available to hunters."[72]

Despite the public relations campaign, backlash to the 1961 plan was fast and fierce, coming from several organizations, individuals, and government agencies. One of the plan's most vocal opponents was the Colorado Game and Fish Commission. To them, the elk living in Colorado belonged not to the NPS but to the state. For its part, the NPS believed that any elk living within the park fell under federal jurisdiction. Although the two agencies had cooperated between 1939 and 1961 in managing hunting on state land adjacent to the park, Game & Fish was increasingly troubled by RMNP's removal of so much game from the park itself. To the commission, culling within

RMNP amounted to "wasteful slaughter." Although Game & Fish was not opposed to the idea of culling, it believed that reduction should be accomplished through "limited, controlled public hunting in the [national] parks" or "by trapping and transplanting excess animals" to lands where they could then be hunted. The interagency friction is not surprising given that Game & Fish was primarily in control of regulating hunting and fishing in Colorado and received significant revenue from the sale of licenses.[73]

The Game and Fish Commission was not alone in voicing opposition to NPS culling efforts and in proposing public hunting within the park as a solution. Representing a large contingent of outraged hunters, former Forest Service employee and wilderness advocate Arthur Carhart had long been an opponent of NPS culling programs. Earlier writing to NPS Director Conrad Wirth, Carhart argued that past efforts to control the elk population had failed. Predators, he claimed, had not "kept the balance" in terms of elk population, and neither had the NPS's hired guns. Rather than "controlling game herds" through unseemly "starvation and epidemic," argued Carhart, public hunters must be allowed to hunt within the park.[74]

Although Carhart was outspoken in favor of hunting within the park as a way out of the morass, he was not blind to the public relations dynamic. In closing his letter, he warned the director that he would "catch hell" from those who refused to open their eyes and minds to public hunting in the park, and so he proposed that it be conducted "after season, when parks are generally closed to tourists, and to the benefit of every factor and facet in the whole complex business of maintaining the 'park idea.'"[75]

Carhart was right about one thing: the NPS did "catch hell" following release of its elk management plan. The *Denver Post* reported, "seldom has the National Park Service taken a worse public beating than it's now suffering over the planned program of killing elk. Belted with charges of ineptness, stupidity, even of inhumanity, the NPS has been pictured as a ghoulish, kill-crazed monster with blood dripping from its bureaucratic jowls."[76] Culling had always been a sensitive matter, but the reductions proposed in the 1961 Elk Management Plan were met with more resistance than in the past. In part, the stiffer opposition was due to the fact that elk reductions in Rocky Mountain coincided with a much more intensive culling campaign in Yellowstone. As in RMNP, elk populations in Yellowstone had careened out of control in the absence of human and natural predators. But the problem in

Yellowstone was far more grave and the solutions far less palatable. While Rocky Mountain prescribed the eventual taking of 200 elk, Yellowstone was gearing up to reduce its herd by some 5,000.[77]

As pressure to halt culling in RMNP mounted, NPS urged the RMNP managers to stay the course. The regional director wrote to Superintendent Hanks commending his efforts to trap elk but he urgently cautioned that park staff make "all efforts necessary to affect your intended reduction of 200 elk this winter." Alluding to the ecological and public relations disasters in Yellowstone, the regional director continued: "We know you are aware of the consequences in reaching an excessive overpopulation of your resident elk herd and wish to avoid at all costs a duplication of the intensive operation which has become necessary in Yellowstone."[78]

In the winter of 1961–1962 RMNP was at a crossroads. On one hand it had irrefutable scientific evidence that RMNP's winter range was in dire condition and that more than a decade of lethal elk control was working to ameliorate the situation. On the other hand, it faced stiff opposition to future culling. Under tremendous pressure, RMNP management attempted to find a solution that would please all parties while managing for the NPS's evolving understanding of ecological health.

To the relief of many, in early February 1962 the *Rocky Mountain News* reported that the "control program for thinning the elk herds of Rocky Mountain National Park by execution" had been halted after only fifty-eight elk were killed. In comments to the press, Superintendent Allan Hanks revealed the direction that the NPS had instead chosen. According to the newspaper, Hanks stated that "hopes were high that a transplanting program could be carried on next year" and he "gave assurances [that] there always will be a surplus of elk in the park."[79] In other words, the NPS would use nonlethal (and far more publicly acceptable) means to remove elk from the park. Hanks's assurances spoke directly to visitor concerns that NPS's elk-reduction program—through whatever means—would not diminish the viewing opportunity to behold the majestic wapiti within the park.

Accordingly, RMNP managers called for an intensive trapping and marking program to gather data on the migration of the elk between Rocky and the Roosevelt National Forest. To achieve the above, the NPS signed a Memorandum of Understanding with the National Forest Service and the Colorado Game and Fish Commission to undertake the cooperative research and

Trapping elk in Rocky Mountain National Park, 1967. Courtesy of Rocky Mountain National Park, ROMO MSF NEG 4912.

they hired wildlife biologist Neal Guse to participate in the studies. Better understanding the migratory patterns of the elk, they hoped, would allow Colorado Game & Fish to set appropriate seasons and harvest levels adjacent to the park.[80]

The NPS and Game and Fish had long known that a substantial number of RMNP elk migrated out of the park near the end of December. Although they had allowed hunting in the game refuge on the park's eastern and northern borders since 1939, the hunts took place in October, well before most RMNP elk migrated out of the park. This was the prime reason, surmised Guse, that hunting outside the park had failed year after year to control elk populations.[81] What was needed instead were interagency studies designed to "gather information on elk migration and distribution habits to effect additional harvests outside the Park, thus eliminating the annual reduction programs on the winter range."[82] In other words, if the NPS could obtain accurate and reliable data on the annual migration of elk, it might well be able to use licensed hunters outside the park to solve a problem. For an agency facing a major public relations debacle, Guse's suggestions were warmly received.

Together, the NPS, Forest Service, and Game & Fish designed and executed a research program through 1962 and 1963. To aid in determining elk migration patterns, they orchestrated a trapping program both inside and outside the park boundaries. After animals were captured, they were fitted with ear tags and neckbands, both of which would aid researchers in collecting data. In all the agencies trapped and tagged a total of ninety-four elk within the park as well as two beyond its boundaries.[83] With tagged animals roaming across the region, researchers eagerly collected data.

Overall, the research program provided valuable information on seasonal movements and confirmed Guse's suspicion that many elk wintered beyond the park's boundaries. Somewhere between one-half and two-thirds of the summer elk population left the park after the first significant winter storm.[84] The majority that wintered east of the Divide, where elk overpopulation was the worst, however, did not typically leave the park until January. With this realization, the NPS and Game & Fish orchestrated an additional public hunting season on land adjacent to the park in January and February, instead of October as they had in previous years. The NPS then collected data on how many elk were killed as a result of the newly established season. In its estimation, hunters had killed as many as 500 elk that left the park.[85] Deeming the season "highly successful," Guse reported that "for the first time in approximately 20 years desirable winter elk herd numbers were achieved."[86]

And there it was—a true panacea. If the data was reliable and the experiment reproducible, hunting outside the park was an understandably attractive option. Not only did the NPS have preliminary evidence that the season could keep park elk populations under control; it also meant that NPS would be able to disassociate itself from the unseemly killing of a park icon. This solution also promised to placate hunters who bemoaned the "wasteful killing" of game animals by government officials, while still providing license revenue for Colorado. Obviously overcome by all of the above, the NPS moved to embrace hunting adjacent to the park as the primary means of elk population control.

Between 1969 and 1992 the NPS has based its elk management on the above model. Despite park managers' hopes, however, the elk population within and around RMNP increased dramatically.[87] The causes of the increase were many, but the primary reason lies with the ineffectiveness of hunting outside the park to reach the numbers optimistically reported by Guse and his research team. Research conducted between 1968 and 1992 found that a decline in the tolerance for sport hunting, combined with increasingly limited access to private land for hunting, were the primary reasons for the policy's failure. Making matters worse, the Colorado Division of Wildlife watched elk populations on USFS land adjacent to the park plummet, eventually prompting it to "drastically" curtail the number of hunting permits allowed in areas adjacent to the park starting in 1992.[88]

For these reasons elk harvests adjacent to the park never came close to the harvest of 500–600 elk per year required to stabilize elk population growth. Between 1968 and 1987, the average elk harvest amounted to 442 ± 78 per year. Since that time, the average annual harvest has dipped to 302 ± 36. Despite the NPS's efforts (or perhaps as a direct result of them), the overall population of elk within the park has witnessed a threefold increase since 1968.[89] The high-water mark came between 1997 and 2001, with an estimated 2,800–3,500 elk in the park—several *thousand* beyond the estimated carrying capacity of their winter range.[90]

The Price of Failure

To understand fully the implications of elk management in RMNP—to grasp the connections between managing for the satisfaction of tourists and the natural world—we would do well to see the park from the perspective of a willow or a beaver. Not surprisingly, elk are part of a complex and dynamic matrix of plant and animal life. Their rutting, eating, defecating, calving, and migrating are all tied to the health of other plant and animal systems where they roam. In the nineteenth century humans had already drastically altered the relationship between elk and the ecosystems to which they contribute. The reintroduction of elk into the Estes Park region, combined with the establishment of RMNP, created a unique set of circumstances that tied human desires to the natural world in new ways.

According to the prevailing research, at the root of the elk problem in RMNP are two interrelated facts: there are too many elk for the winter range to support; and elk in the park are less migratory than they have been in the past, which further compounds the problem of overpopulation.[91] Both situations are tied directly to human decisions regarding the management of ungulates—specifically elk—in and around the park.

Studies conducted in the 1990s found that there were approximately 1,000 elk that spent their winter days inside the park pawing through the snow to meet substantial caloric needs. An additional 2,000 elk wintered on land immediately adjacent to the park, wandering the streets, lawns, golf courses, and gardens of Estes Park while searching for edible plants. The overabundance of elk during the winter season, in turn, has a compounding dynamic of its own. Even under the best of circumstances, winters present forage problems for elk, as their preferred food choice, grass, is in shorter supply. When population dynamics are out of balance, however, the problem of winter forage is heightened, and plants that lie at the outer edges of elk preference are more intensively browsed. Over time, the implications for many of the park's aspens and willows—not to mention other plants and animals that rely upon them—have been dire.[92]

But more is at work here than simply having too many elk in the park. The second significant problem—one that complicates the first—is that elk in the park are less migratory than they would be under more natural conditions. Under ideal circumstances the elk within RMNP would migrate between their summer range in the "Kawuneeche Valley and subalpine and alpine areas," and their winter range, which lies primarily on the eastern side of the park and in Estes Park.[93] The seasonal movement of elk, in turn, would ensure that no single part of their range is overgrazed.

With the vast majority of the park's predators long since removed, the human population adjacent to the park increasing with each passing season, and the institution of late hunting seasons adjacent to the park, the elk have become less willing to migrate out of the park. According to the NPS, between 10 percent and 15 percent of all the elk within the park remain on the primary winter range during the summer. As more elk spend more time on the winter range within the park, its ability to rebound from elk grazing is curtailed, the range of elk food choices decreases, and the elk turn increasingly to secondary and tertiary food choices during all seasons.[94]

One of the plants most directly and negatively impacted by the elk population imbalance is the aspen (*Populus tremuloides*). Beginning in the early 1930s, managers of RMNP began reporting significant "barking" of aspen and interpreted it as evidence that the population of elk within the park was not healthy. The intensive overgrazing of aspen by elk was evident by the 1960s, as park staff commented that the exclosures in Horseshoe Park built in the 1930s stand "out like an oasis surrounded by herbs and grasses. After twenty-five years of protection, thirty-one aspen stems were growing" in the exclosure, and there were none outside of it.[95]

Researchers William L. Baker, Jennifer A. Munroe, and Amy E. Hessl relied upon the park's exclosures to gather information on elk herbivory, and their work produced stark conclusions. Not only were aspen populations outside the exclosures declining, as demonstrated by "high mortality among established trees, including entire stands that are dead"; evidence also reflected a "low density of live suckers" not sufficient to regenerate the trees. Perhaps most important, the researchers concluded that due to overgrazing by elk "almost no cohort regeneration" had taken place "since the adoption of natural regulation."[96] In other words, mature aspen within the park were aging, but successive generations of aspen were not in place to replace older, dying trees. According to the most recent assessment by the NPS, the "continuation of the high elk densities in Rocky Mountain National Park [will] result in the complete loss of aspen trees or, at best, existence in a shrub-like state on core winter ranges."[97]

Aspens, and the many plants and animals that rely upon them, are not the only flora put at risk by too many elk in the park. Willows (*Salix* spp.) have also suffered as a result of the booming elk population. Although willows are not a primary food choice for elk within the park, absent other preferred grasses elk will turn to them for food. As a result, elk have significantly inhibited riparian willow reproduction, as seedling survival has become "almost non-existent." Further, the pressure from elk is so great that few willows "attain a height greater than the herbaceous layer, which is the layer of non-woody plants such as grasses, forbs, and herbs."[98]

Observations of the exclosures built and monitored since the 1930s told this story of transformation. By the early 1960s, less than three decades following their "release" from ungulate grazing, willow covered some 70 percent of the three exclosures in Beaver Meadows and Horseshoe Park. Where the plants were not protected by such exclosures, park biologists concluded that the willow were rapidly diminishing. As a prelude to the damage that was yet to come, park staff concluded that although the loss of streamside willow would not "alter the landscape picture so much," it would have a significant and detrimental impact on both elk and beavers.[99] The above process, well under way by the 1930s, greatly accelerated as elk populations soared following the cessation of lethal herd reductions in the 1960s.

It is important to bear in mind that the processes at work are not linear but dynamic. The increase in browsing pressure from elk upon willows, and the subsequent decline in streamside willows within the park, has in turn significantly impacted beavers within the elk range. Beavers, which rely upon willows for both building material and food, have declined over the previous fifty years. In part this was the direct result of trapping, as in 1922 when forty-six beavers were trapped in and near the park. However, competition with elk over a finite and overlapping resource base is a more significant factor in beaver decline in RMNP. Although there were "an estimated 300 beavers living in Moraine Park alone in 1939, that number had plummeted by more than 90 percent by the dawn of the 21st century."[100]

Too many elk eating too many willows have had more complicated impacts than simply reducing the number of beaver in RMNP, which park staff has been cognizant of since at least 1960. Many iconic meadows like Horseshoe Park, which once held robust populations of willows, were now largely covered with grass. The loss of willows also meant fewer beaver dams, which reduced the watertable in such areas, which further curtailed willow fecundity. In some places, like Moraine Park, the above processes have reduced overall surface water by some 70 percent.[101]

Overabundant elk posed still more problems. As elk crop, chew, and digest some species—like aspen and willow—at higher rates than they would under healthier ecological conditions, opportunity is created for other plant species to spread. For example, areas where elk herbivory is heavy can witness significant increases in the presence of invasive plant species like Timothy (*Phleum pratense*). This plant, which was likely introduced into the park as a food stock for cattle, showed an increase of 54 percent between 1978 and 1988.[102] Intensive elk grazing can also result in upturns in bare ground, soil compaction, increased sediment yields in water adjacent to over-grazed areas, and "warmer, or drier soil microclimate," which can have a direct bearing on plant growth.[103] In all of these ways, and countless others, the impacts of tourism and scientifically based choices have been scribed across Rocky Mountain National Park.

Conclusion

Millions of people travel to Rocky every year expecting to see elk. They push cars through wandering herds of cows, calves, and bulls and stride to within feet of them in the hopes of capturing an evocative image that commemorates the moment they stood so close to a wild animal. Local and regional businesses, the NPS, and other agencies created such expectations and then set about making certain that they were met. The result, after nearly a century of tinkering, is a park chock-full of elk.

In time, however, copious elk in Rocky complicated assumptions about nature and tourism. The elk, which many understand as wild or natural, have become remarkably tolerant of humans and automobiles; they enjoy lives largely free from predation; and they have drastically altered the park's ecosystems. Often unwittingly, the NPS created, nurtured, and protected a powerful force that has long been eating, stomping, and pawing at other cherished aspects of the park. Fading stands of willows and aspens, desiccated meadows, and soil erosion all tell us as much.

Beginning in the 1930s, an alternate way of conceptualizing elk began challenging previously held assumptions and desires. Whereas most of the traveling public esteemed large herds of elk, ecologists and park managers came to see so many elk as disturbing reminders of ecosystems out of whack. Accordingly, they supported measures to reduce the number of elk within the park itself. Similar to tourists like R. J. Thornburg who chastised the NPS for failing to present enough animals to admire, biologists like Neal Guse and others also championed a specific view of the park. Trapping, shooting, and eventually hunting elk—all measures deemed necessary when viewing Rocky through the lens of ecology—were attempts to reconcile what the park was with what *they* thought it should be. For decades, their successes and failures have also contributed much to making Rocky Mountain National Park.

After years of study, debate, and contemplation, the NPS released its "Final Environmental Impact Statement Elk and Vegetation Management Plan, Rocky Mountain National Park, Colorado" in 2007. The plan, more than 400 pages, takes a hard look at the elk problem in Rocky and the NPS's role in its manifestation. Once again, the agency has embraced lethal means to control the number of elk in the park. According to the Plan, qualified government employees and volunteers may now use—under the cover of darkness—silenced rifles to kill elk within the park.[104] The NPS has also initiated experiments whereby cow elk are given the birth-control agent Gonacon.[105] Although the NPS should be credited for their willingness to once again grapple with this complex and volatile issue, it is revealing that many of their leading solutions rely upon the dark of night or invisible chemical agents to keep the elk population under control. Despite decades of dealing with the complex consequences of doing so, we continue to draw stark lines between nature and culture.

6

Fishing for Tourists

Wicker creels bursting at the seams; stringers of fish pulled taut between the proud hands of an angler; trout ordered by size and laid thoughtfully upon the summer's green grass: these are all images that were part and parcel of the fishing heritage of early Colorado. Such scenes were memorialized in photos and tucked away in shoeboxes and albums, later to provide entertainment and reflection on a winter day too cold to fish.[1]

Beyond a treasured memento of a successful day with rod in hand, these images tell a more significant story. The picture on the next page, featuring at least sixteen individual trout, tells us something about the relationship between a fisherman and his quarry. The photo, we must remember, was staged. We can assume first that this day was an exceptionally successful one. We also can at least infer that simply catching the fish was not enough. The fisherman was compelled to keep some or perhaps all of the fish he (or she) caught and memorialize them in this photo.

More important, this photo also speaks to an ecological revolution playing out in the state's waters well before the turn of the twentieth century. Due to the fact that the picture is not in color, it is difficult to ascertain with much certainty the type of trout spilling from the creel. Although it is possible that they are rainbow trout, a fish introduced first from the waters of California, they may also be greenback cutthroat or Colorado River cutthroat. What is fairly certain, however, is that the fish perched atop the wicker basket—the one that the fisherman placed above all others—is an eastern

Fish in a basket, circa 1900. Courtesy of the Denver Public Library, P-2270.

brook trout. The spot pattern on the fish's side and the white tipped fin on his underside tell us as much. And as the name implies, the brook trout is no native of Colorado.

Well before 1900, local and regional boosters, railroad companies, and eventually the National Park Service all advertised and promised great trout fishing along the Front Range and in the Rocky Mountains. In relatively short order the advertising campaign showed signs of success as increasing numbers of fishermen plied Colorado waters. As more people traveled to Colorado to fish, concern over diminishing angler success grew, prompting many to look for solutions. Not willing or able to strictly regulate daily catches, but still hoping to grow tourism, the state of Colorado, Estes Park residents, and the Park Service turned almost exclusively toward technical solutions to fisheries decline.

An embrace of science was understandable. Fish culture, which had been growing in popularity and prestige in the second half of the nineteenth century, offered an appealing solution. If interested parties could hatch and rear a high volume of fish annually, then rivers, streams, and lakes would teem with fish and continue to draw fishermen. To those involved in the early history of fisheries management in and around RMNP, the problem was a simple one of supply and demand. Understanding the situation thus, a range of organizations and agencies planted billions of nonnative fish attractive to anglers, including the rainbow trout, brown trout, and brook trout.

The embrace of science in growing fish for stocking or planting—terms that reveal much about how managers viewed fish—created as many problems as solutions. More than planting fish that were easy to rear and ones that anglers prized, managers unknowingly stocked fish that held a variety of competitive advantages over the native greenback cutthroat trout. Within a few decades, the greenback was losing ground in the streams and lakes across the state as brook trout and other types became more common.

As long as fisheries management revolved around only pleasing tourists with full creels of trout, all was well. During the 1930s, however, a competing way of viewing and understanding the park's fish arrived. Whereas many fishing tourists valued only large catches, many scientists inside and outside the NPS came to see stringers filled with nonnative brook, brown, and rainbow trout as painful reminders of unwanted, human-wrought changes in the park's waters.

From the 1930s to today, park rangers and scientists have waged a sometimes intensive campaign to restore native trout within the waters of Rocky. But fish, as it turns out, have historical agency, too, and the popular brook trout has not yielded the waters of the park so easily. Decades of incredible efforts, which included the poisoning of some lakes and streams, helicopter assaults wherein thousands of trout dropped from the sky like shimmering green berets, and the closing of some park waters to all fishing speak to the tension between a tourist landscape and one more firmly rooted in a different definition of nature. After decades and decades of concerted efforts, it seemed as if ecology and persistence were finally paying off and the greenback was on the way to victory.

Recent discoveries, however, have thrown a dark pall over restoration efforts. A graduate student from the University of Colorado first discovered, much to the dismay of nearly everyone, that the battle over the park's waters was also being fought on a genetic level. The majority of greenbacks that park personnel and others had so carefully raised for decades—which scientists viewed as natural and rightful citizens of the park—were not greenback trout or, in some cases, were genetic combinations of greenbacks and other species. Same fish, mind you; but yet another way of understanding them and their place in the park. Now, restoration efforts must grapple with the difficult question of exactly what makes a greenback a greenback.

Oncorhynchus clarkii stomias

Colorado once maintained at least four different native cutthroat subspecies, including the Colorado River, the extinct yellowfin, the Rio Grande, and the greenback. Each subspecies, having evolved in different environments, varies in color, size, average number of gill rakers, pyloric caeca (fingerlike appendages of the intestine), and scale counts. Of the four cutthroats listed above, the greenback lurked in the eddies and ripples of the South Platte and Arkansas River headwaters, in addition to the waters of what is now RMNP.[2]

Although casual observation may not reveal it, trout are a territorial species. According to fisheries biologists the social unit of trout is a "hierarchy with infrequent subordinate revolt," meaning that the most dominant fish gains access to that portion of a stream that is food-rich while less dominant ones vie for control of less productive sections. On occasion, subordinate fish take part in behavior that is intended to squeeze out a high-ranking fish from its dominant position. This behavior generally falls into two categories and seems to be followed by all trout regardless of subspecies. In some cases, upstarts will employ a "frontal threat display," which entails approaching an adversary from the front with "dorsal fin flat, all other fins fully extended, mouth opened, and the bottom of the mouth pushed downward."[3]

In other cases, upstarts might rely on a "lateral threat display," in which it exposes its side, "stretches out its body and assumes a rigid pose . . . with all fins, including the dorsal, fully extended." Of the two tactics, scientists believe that the frontal display is the more aggressive, as it "more often than not ends in an attack with the threatening fish moving in to nip or chase its opponent."[4] The reward for successful posturing and chasing is access to the foods greenbacks prefer, including adult Hymenoptera (ants, bees, and wasps), Diptera (flies), and other terrestrial and aquatic invertebrates like stone and caddis flies.[5]

In most cases, greenbacks spawn in the spring when water temperatures reach 41°–46.4°F. Because greenback spawning is tied directly to water temperature, and because so much of the fish's historic range within the Colorado Rockies includes high- and middle-elevation waters, greenback spawning times vary according to location. In warmer lower waters, for example, greenbacks may spawn as early as April; in colder waters they might not spawn until mid-July.[6] As the fish begin anticipating the spawn, male fish jockey for breeding position near places where females tend to spawn. As the breeding male fish fight for access, females turn onto their sides over gravel and sand and flutter in place to clear a spawning bed (called a redd) using their tails. Once the redd is in order, "through some mechanism of male supremacy and female decision, one dominant male will move in alongside the female over the redd."[7] At this time, the fish partake in a "dramatic dance in unison" as the female releases her eggs and the male his milt (sperm). Following this remarkable display, the female covers the eggs and often remains in place, guarding her redd from other fish, for several days.[8]

After successful fertilization and hatching, the life cycle of the greenback begins anew, with the smallest fish working day and night to become larger, more dominant ones. Depending on water conditions, within a couple of years greenbacks reach sexual maturity, and the process begins again. Unlike other subspecies of cutthroat, greenbacks do not attain a large size, with one- and two-pound fish common.[9] Similar to the reproductive habits of elk, the fighting, mating, and growing that makes greenbacks what they are has played an interesting role in shaping human history in RMNP.

Angling for Anglers

As early as the 1860s, writers recognized and amplified the great fishing to be found in the territory. Their words offer an entertaining blend of fact and boosterism so common in the frontier writing of the nineteenth century. Take, for example, an 1868 article in the *Rocky Mountain News*. According to the writer, "Trouting was never better than at present, it being an easy task to take with a hook, from thirty to fifty pounds a day from almost any stream in this neighborhood. The fish are also especially large and fat, varying from three quarters of a pound to three pounds each."[10] Just two years prior to the state's founding, another writer claimed to have wandered throughout the Rocky Mountains, where he had "never seen such an abundance of fine trout in any of the mountain streams, as in the Grand river and its branches." In some locations like Troublesome Creek, the author boasted, "one could catch with a hook two hundred to three hundred pounds of fine trout in a single day."[11]

Word spread quickly, and those with the means and desire to fish in the territory began making the trip. Fall River, located in Rocky Mountain National Park, was an especially popular destination. According to one eyewitness in 1874, the stream had "its full share of tourists," with an estimated 200 crossing it on their way to Middle Park that year alone. Beyond great fishing and striking scenery, Estes Park also had the power to impart to "young ladies a golden bloom upon their cheeks" from "a bit of captured sunshine that they can't catch in the east."[12]

Perhaps attracted by stories of great fishing or rumors of golden-cheeked ladies blooming in the summer sun, C. F. Orvis (founder of one of the longest-lived producers of fly-fishing accoutrements) made the trip to Estes Park in 1875. Although Orvis recalled encountering many tourists along Fall River and in Horseshoe Park, the waters were not yet "fished out." In fact, recounted Orvis, the "trout struck and I landed them so fast that the sport began to be monotonous." He had filled his creel by noon. Later, Orvis encountered his companion, who had filled a 16-pound lard can with his catches and carried an additional "dozen upon a stick."[13]

By one estimate, during the summer season as many as a thousand trout were removed daily from Fall River, the Big Thompson River, and other waters around Estes Park. Given that reported catches of forty or fifty fish were common, and given that "camps are to be found on all the trout streams," the thousand-fish-per-day number does not seem unreasonable.[14] Such large catches, however, led many to fear that the waters in the region would soon be depleted and thus compel the traveling angler to seek more pristine waters to practice his art. To prevent the depletion of the state's fish stock and the loss of tourist revenue, the state and several individuals looked to the artificial propagation of fish as the answer.

The development of artificial propagation in Colorado was part of a broader national embrace of fish culture during the same period. According to historian Joseph Taylor, the development came "in response to declining fisheries in the eastern United States," where industrialization and agriculture "had driven many Atlantic salmon and shad runs into sharp decline or extinction during the late eighteenth and early nineteenth centuries." Responding to a declining resource base, those with the means and motivation to get involved turned to the creation of more fish as the answer.[15]

In response to this situation, Congress established the United States Commission of Fish and Fisheries (known as the U.S. Fish Commission, or USFC) in 1871, and "the federal government assumed a more visible policy-making position" in the realm of fisheries management.[16] Although the USFC was originally created to conduct scientific research on fisheries issues, it struggled mightily through its first years. Spencer Baird, its first director, desperate to secure a future for his fledgling organization, embraced technology generally and fish culture specifically in his bid to protect fisheries and promote the new agency.[17]

To establish the USFC as a valuable tool in restoring declining fish stocks, Baird hired Livingston Stone as assistant commissioner to oversee operations on the Pacific Coast. Stone was an active proponent of fish culture and a "leading authority on salmon propagation." The USFC hired others who also embraced fish culture—as opposed to more stringent regulation—as the key to restoration and management. James Milner, who was hired to investigate the failing Great Lakes fisheries in 1871–1872, was also a proponent of fish culture. In relatively short order, the rank and file of the USFC had come to fully support rearing and stocking as the most practical, efficient, and expedient means to fix failing fisheries around the country.[18]

Colorado quickly embraced the solutions proffered by the USFC and initiated a program of artificial fish propagation of its own in 1871. Over the course of more than a century, the state and other entities would stock Colorado waters with billions of fish, a large percentage of which were nonnative species. Although a modern-day environmentalist may cringe at the thought of a government agency dedicated almost wholly to the introduction of nonnative species, contemporaries saw things much differently. Lacking anything like ecological awareness, those who stocked fish saw themselves as taking an active part in improving the state's waters through the application of science and expertise. More trout—of whatever variety—meant more excitement with rod and reel, and that translated into more tourists.

Pumping trout into Colorado's waters required science, money, and expertise—all of which the newly formed state was acquiring by the 1880s. In his Biennial Report, Colorado Fish Commissioner Wilson Sisty assured readers in 1880 that although "there was a time when the successful propagation of fish . . . was questionable," that time had passed. Using state-of-the-art techniques, Colorado could now "take advantage of and profit by the practical and successful results laid before her by so many fish-farming States." The state thus required a "hatching house" and a supply of eggs, which were to be procured from "the East and West in large quantities" in order to "plant the young fish throughout the waters of the State."[19]

In a few short years, Sisty's vision became a reality with the construction of the state's first hatchery in 1881. By 1886 Colorado implemented a stocking policy that persisted for decades. According to Fish Commissioner John Pierce, the state gave preference to distributing young trout to "streams which were in the vicinity of the leading places of resort." Of special importance in such efforts was Estes Park, which was "situated on the head waters of both the St. Vrain and Big Thompson [Rivers]" and was the "best point from which to stock both these magnificent streams." Revealing the economic calculus behind the stocking policy, Pierce stated that "even if every fish planted at such points as these is caught each year, it will pay the State to keep on putting them in."[20]

News of great fishing continued to spread through the 1880s, and more fishermen headed to Colorado to investigate. A *Sports Afield* article titled "Trout Fishing in Estes Park" contended that no "point within easy reach from Denver offers greater inducements to the fisherman than Estes Park." Here, claimed the author, trout "seemed to be everywhere and of all sizes." More than puffing up the region's angling opportunities, *Sports Afield* unknowingly spoke to an ecological revolution taking place around Estes Park. As late as the 1870s a fisherman in the Estes Park area would expect to catch greenback cutthroat, called "natives" by contemporaries, or the "red-horse sucker," a bottom-feeding "trash fish" also native to the region.

By the 1890s, however, *Sports Afield* reported that fishermen visiting the region could expect to catch "the mountain trout" *and* "his Eastern cousin," which sported "red spots and pugnacity that go with them." This pugnacious fish with red spots was the brook trout—a nonnative species that government agencies eager to keep catches high and tourism strong introduced into western waters. In the same *Sports Afield* article, the writer referred to interspecies competition for food in waters where both brook and native trout lived, stating that the brook trout was "present to contest with the native for possession of the fictitious food that trailed behind the treacherous and almost invisible snell."[21] Although the writer is referring to competition for an artificial lure, it is no great leap to conclude that the two species were competing for all food types. And indeed they were.

Although no one was aware at the time, brook trout hold several biological advantages over greenbacks. Whereas greenbacks spawn in the spring and early summer, brook trout spawn in the fall. This means that "young-of-the-year" (YOY) brookies have already hatched and begun growing well before most greenbacks even emerge from the ova. For trout, especially those in streams and rivers, size is directly tied to the ability to inhabit those portions of the water column where food is most plentiful and the caloric expenditure of maintaining that position is minimal. Due to the different spawning period, more YOY brook trout are able to occupy more advantageous stream positions. Underwater observation and analysis conducted in RMNP's Hidden Valley Creek, for example, found that where greenback inhabited an overlapping section of stream with brook trout (or *sympatry*), greenbacks held stream positions with "higher focal point velocities," meaning that the current at their snouts exerted more force. They also found that greenback juveniles in sympatry with brook trout occupied positions farther from cover. In the absence of brook trout (or *allopatry*), however, greenback juveniles were able to move to stream locations with "lower focal point velocities" closer to cover. The higher focal-point positions assumed by YOY greenbacks mean that they were forced to exert more energy—that is, burn more calories—in order to feed themselves. This disadvantage, in turn, results in "decreased growth and lower overwinter survival for YOY cutthroat trout."[22] This process, played out year after year, pushed greenback cutthroats to the very margins of existence.

Unaware and unconcerned with the displacement of native fish by non-natives, Colorado Fish Commissioner J. S. Swan confidently claimed in 1898 that as "a result of the restocking of the clear streams of the state, most of such streams are now well supplied with trout, and Colorado in consequence has lost nothing of its reputation as being the country of beautiful streams from which the expert with the rod, line and fly is always rewarded with a good string of the speckled beauties."[23]

Anglers at Bear Lake, circa 1890. Courtesy of Rocky Mountain National Park, ROMO 5518, MSF NEG 2208.

Several railroad lines that operated in Colorado also participated in the stocking program. Like state officials, railroads recognized that it was in their interest to promote and protect the growing reputation of Colorado as a great trouting destination. According to Commissioner Swan, railroads transported young fish throughout the state free of charge.[24] In 1905 alone, *Outdoor Life* estimated that some 3 million more trout had "been planted in streams along the Denver & Rio Grande railroad this year than [were] planted in 1903." Their stocking efforts, which grew annually, gave a Denver & Rio Grande spokesman confidence that there was no cause to worry that the supply of "fish in the state was decreasing."[25]

Also concerned with the negative consequences of overfishing to the region's economy, a group of Estes Park citizens drew together under the banner of the Estes Park Protective and Improvement Association (EPPIA) in 1895. It is no accident that among the organization's founders were Estes Park residents whose livelihoods relied on tourist revenues, including local resort owner and newly elected EPPIA president Abner Sprague. In the broadest terms, the organization was dedicated to preventing the "destruction of the fish in the rivers of the Park, the illegal killing of game, and the destruction of the timber by camp fires." Responding to what they perceived as a "mania among parties . . . to catch the greatest number of trout" in a single day, EP-PIA implored fishermen to return smaller fish to the streams.[26]

As was the case with the USFC and the state of Colorado, Estes Park residents understood the fisheries problem largely as one of limited supply. The key to drawing fishermen toward the budding community lay, at least in part, in ensuring a reliable and robust supply of fish. To accomplish this, EPPIA contributed to protecting and enhancing the bounty of the waters around Estes Park through the construction of a private fish hatchery. According to the *Estes Park Trail*, EPPIA realized that rivers packed with fish "would be one of the greatest advertising features of the Park" and thus began drumming up public support for the idea.[27] Raising money for the endeavor posed a challenge to the small community, but many local businessmen threw their support behind a project that promised measurable returns. Through a series of dances, bazaars, and vaudeville shows, EPPIA raised more than $900 for the completion of the project, and construction began in 1907.[28]

Once complete, the facility was a "model of efficiency" and had the capacity to hatch 500,000 eggs at a time three times per year.[29] Proud of the accomplishments of the local organization, the *Trail* claimed that the Estes Park Fish Hatchery (EPH) was responsible for stocking more than 6 million fish in the vicinity of Estes Park during its first five years in operation. Although the number paled in comparison to the estimated *8 billion* the federal government planted nationwide, the addition of millions of fish to the waters promised good fishing even for novices.[30] The *Trail* was also impressed with the fact that the local hatchery had "transported fish from other waters, and even from foreign countries," and introduced them to Colorado streams. As was the case with Colorado, the EPH planted a large percentage of nonnative trout such as brook, rainbow, and brown. The reasons for doing so were many.[31]

Obtaining native eggs or fry was a difficult endeavor. Hatcheries in Yellowstone and Glacier would later provide the state of Colorado with Yellowstone cutthroat eggs, but in the meantime the state substituted available trout—rainbow, brook, brown—for greenbacks. Also, greenbacks were more difficult to hatch than other strains. For instance, the federal fish hatchery in Leadville, Colorado, attempted to hatch and raise greenback cutthroat but found that they were difficult to rear in captivity. Making matters worse, locals despised the hatchery's spawning traps in Twin Lakes and used dynamite to clear them.[32] Over time, the availability of other strains of trout, combined

Interagency stocking effort in Rocky Mountain National Park, circa 1930. Courtesy of Rocky Mountain National Park, ROMO 4008, MSF NEG 3036.

with the difficulty in rearing greenbacks, resulted in a stocking policy that favored nonnative fish over native ones.

But more was at work here than planting available fish. A large percentage of those who sojourned in Estes Park came from the Northeast, as had been the case with Orvis and his companion. The brook trout that the state introduced as early as the 1880s (and which the EPH actively stocked) were native to Northeast states. The brookie was the subject of a body of fly-fishing literature that held it in high esteem for beauty, fighting ability, and willingness to rise to the fly. The rapid decline of brook trout habitat along the Eastern Seaboard in the nineteenth century prompted stocking efforts to replenish them in the eastern United States.[33] Planting fish that anglers were familiar with solved two problems. Brook trout provided Colorado with a rapidly breeding, easily reared fish that was familiar to, and highly prized by, the anglers the state hoped to attract.

Of course, contemporaries knew very little about the population dynamics of fish they planted—nor did many seem to care. They sought to fill local waters with desirable fish and enjoy the reputation of a premier trouting destination. In other words many locals held a different fishing ethos than supporters do today—one that valued high-volume catches of game fish regardless of speciation. The state of Colorado and the EPH acted in concert to promote this ethic. Among a populace not yet cognizant of modern ecology, trout were trout.

Although the Estes Park Protection and Improvement Association had played a leading role in building the EPH and stocking the area, it decided in April 1912 to turn over control of the facility to the state. This arrangement allowed members of EPPIA to devote more effort and attention to the national park movement and strengthen their hatchery's connection to a broader network of state-hatched fish and eggs.[34] This did not mean that citizens of Estes Park were losing interest in stocking local waters. The community continued to play an active role in fish propagation, primarily through efforts to secure "sizing ponds" around Estes Park and through the donation of time and materials to stock the fish raised at the local hatchery.

Fishing for National Parks

For two full decades following the park's establishment, the philosophy and aims of fisheries management remained unchanged. Through this period, groups and individuals stocked so-called virgin lakes and redoubled efforts to keep the park's waters flush with quarry. Although the park's creation did not change the direction of fisheries management in the area, it did add weight, institutional authority, and pressure to expand current practices. As was the case with the state and the EPPIA, the NPS sought to draw anglers to boost visitation. In this sense, the early policy was a complete success.

Rocky Mountain National Park was not alone in its attempts to bolster fish populations to attract fishermen. Yellowstone, which the U.S. Fish Commission had stocked as early as 1889, operated an egg-collection station on Yellowstone Lake. This facility provided eggs and fry for local and regional hatcheries, including at Bozeman, Montana, and Estes Park.[35] According to historian James Pritchard, Yellowstone's desire to protect and bolster fish populations eventually led to measures to control populations of pelicans in the park, which were thought to have been responsible for consuming large quantities of trout and trout eggs.[36] Although RMNP never attempted to limit nonhuman fish predation within its boundaries, it enthusiastically pursued fish culture and stocking to promote its sport fishing.

More than stocking streams and lakes already containing fish, however, RMNP Superintendent Roger Toll and others recommended that NPS stock fishless lakes. Doing so, contended Toll, would add to the availability of good fishing and disperse fishermen, thereby easing the pressure on streams and lakes near Estes Park.[37] Toll's point did not fall on deaf ears. National Park Service Director Arno B. Cammerer also realized that aside from inspirational vistas, "fishing undoubtedly presents the greatest recreational feature of the national parks to attract visitors, and it is therefore a matter in which the national Government is very greatly interested."[38] To aid Toll in his bid for more fish, Director Cammerer contacted the federal Bureau of Fisheries (BF) and requested his assistance in providing the expertise required to bring still more fish to the park. Over the following years, the relationship between the two federal agencies worked well in securing additional eggs for the Estes hatchery.

Eager to expand the fishing frontier within the park, rangers planted some 30,000 fish in Sky Pond in August 1930 expecting that it would become "the most popular fishing lake in the vicinity in three years."[39] Two years later the NPS boasted that "each year two or three more of the unstocked lakes are added to the list" of newly stocked ones.[40] Yet stocking fishless lakes, perhaps an effective tool in drawing more fishermen to the park and dispersing them throughout, wrought irreparable ecological change.[41]

The processes of glaciation responsible for carving many of the vistas tourists admired were also responsible for creating many mountain lakes, "most of which were separated from downstream fish populations by impassible barriers on rivers and streams." Isolated from the movement of fish, these mountain lakes were "colonized by a diversity of aquatic species, many of which required fishless habitats for their persistence."[42] Rocky Mountain National Park contained several of these lakes, including the breathtaking Sky Pond.

Introducing fish into historically fishless waters can cause a cascade of ecological changes. According to aquatic biologists, "studies have repeatedly demonstrated that fish introductions dramatically alter native vertebrate and invertebrate communities, often resulting in the extirpation of . . . amphibians, zooplankton, and benthic macroinvertebrates."[43] Such stocking

Ranger Walter Finn stocking a pond, 1936. Courtesy of Rocky Mountain National Park, ROMO 4017, MSF NEG 2643.

practices can be especially detrimental to local and regional populations of amphibians. In their study of sites in the Frank Church–River of No Return Wilderness, David Pilliod and Charles Peterson found that the presence of trout in historically fishless water drastically reduced the "abundance of amphibians at all life stages."[44] Apparently, introduced fish limit amphibian breeding success because female "amphibians avoid laying their eggs" in such sites. Furthermore, if egg-laying does occur, "fish [i.e., introduced trout] prey upon the embryonic and larval stages," thereby reducing annual amphibian fecundity. The researchers also found that the detrimental effects of fish upon amphibians are amplified in mountain lakes, which often offer "less habitat structure" and shorter reproductive seasons for amphibians.[45]

Furthermore, stocking high-elevation fishless lakes can "provide a geographic and demographic boost to their invasion of stream networks, thereby further endangering the native stream fauna."[46] Although planting nonnative fish at lower elevations can initiate ecological change, the consequences of this practice are often geographically limited by upstream barriers, such as waterfalls, and the fish's apparent unwillingness to move upstream when the streambed slope exceeds 17 percent. When planted in lakes and streams near headwaters, however, brook trout in particular are able to move downstream with relative ease and thereby inhabit a greater geographical range.[47]

It is telling that the NPS literally planted millions of highly efficient predators inside the park in the form of trout, which wreaked havoc with native fauna, at the very same time they sought to exterminate other predators like coyotes and mountain lions. The difference is in what was being preyed upon. Trout fed upon frogs, salamanders, plankton, and insects, which few (if any) visitors came to view. Over the past hundred years, at least eighty-one of RMNP's historically fishless lakes and ponds were stocked with fish.

It is evident that the ecological change that began with the first planting of nonnative species in the 1870s and 1880s was fairly complete by the mid-1930s.[48] In May 1936, for example, hundreds of catchable fish in a Moraine Park beaver pond became trapped when the Big Thompson changed course. In response, rangers seined the pond and replanted the fish into the Big Thompson. Some 701 trout were moved, of which 97 percent were brook trout, 1 percent rainbow, and 2 percent cutthroats.[49]

Going Native

The 1933 release of Fauna No. 1, as discussed in Chapter 5, heralded a new and powerful way of viewing national parks.[50] Dixon, Wright, and Thompson were deeply concerned with protecting deer, elk, and mountain lions, just as they were with the introduction of invasive animal species and the marginalization of native ones. Still, they made interesting exceptions regarding fishing and fish culture in national parks. According to the authors, "Wild flowers are to be enjoyed in place and the timber in the trees is not to be utilized. No animal is hunted, and only the fish is angled from its native waters. Fish culture is practiced to prevent depletion and to extend the pleasures of the sport to waters not naturally stocked." Defending traditional fisheries management, the authors contended that in the case of this "important exception" the "direct benefit to man overrules the disadvantages which are incidentally incurred" through fish harvest and stocking.[51]

The NPS's willingness to allow anglers to harvest fish, a rare exception to the agency's resource policy, begs the question of why it did so. Historian Lisa Mighetto explored the development of animal rights through her *Wild Animals and American Environmental Ethics* and found that a rising consensus that animals were sentient beings capable of feeling pain was a driving force in the historical evolution of animal activism.[52] Speculating on why Americans have not put fish in the same category as other animals, Mighetto mused that "fishing has been viewed traditionally as a contemplative activity" and thus "it was difficult to portray its participants as bloodthirsty savages." She also posited that "fishing also failed to inspire strong protest because it involved animals that were not attractive in the traditional sense." In this regard, the lack of empathy for the plight of fish was a function of the "humane movement's emphasis on the kinship between people and animals," which "encouraged the perception that only humanlike creatures deserved moral attention."[53] Whatever the reason, the NPS broadly—and Dixon, Wright, and Thompson specifically—was ambivalent about fishing in national parks.

This is not to say, however, that the authors of Fauna No. 1 were wholehearted supporters of stocking and fishing in parks, either. Although they did not challenge fishing or stocking, they did argue that at least "one watershed shall be set aside for the preservation of the aquatic biota in its undisturbed primitive state" within each park. But even here, where there should "never be any planting of fish or fish foods," fishing would be permitted, though under tighter regulation. Further reflecting an ambivalence, the authors confided that the "time is rapidly approaching when these would be the only places on the continent where the native trout could be seen and studied in their primitive haunts unmodified by human interference."[54]

By May 1936 the acting director of the National Park Service, A. E. Demaray, apparently agreed: the National Park Service would no longer stock nonnative fish at the expense of native ones. Reversing decades of practice, Demaray announced that "native fish in our national parks and monuments henceforth will be safeguarded by policies of conservation similar to those long adhered to by the National Park Service in its administration of the fauna and flora of these areas. . . . That is to say, natural conditions will not be interfered with by man." After twenty years of allowing individual parks the latitude to introduce and stock nonnative sport fish, the new NPS policy held that "scientific study" demonstrated that introducing nonnative species "disturb[s] the system and order carefully worked out during long periods of time by nature." But, lamented Demaray, "heretofore this policy has not been generally applied in the case of fish."[55] Organizations like the Council of the American Association for the Advancement of Science had been encouraging a native-only stocking policy in national parks since at least 1921. At that time, however, the NPS was more interested in colonizing the park's waters with other varieties of trout.[56]

Interpreting the previous decades of fisheries management across all NPS-administered lands, Demaray stated that in the past if "it seemed advisable, for the sake of better angling . . . to import species not native to the lakes and streams, this was frequently done. Experience has shown, however, that nature makes no allowance for good intentions on the part of man," and such a policy had worked to disrupt natural systems. The NPS would now largely "forbid the introduction of exotic species of fish into waters which at present contain only native varieties." Just as striking was the announcement that "even non-game native varieties, reduction of which might be considered conducive to better angling, will be left to increase and multiply unmolested."[57]

Although a deviation from previous policy, the new directive contained language that allowed the partial continuance of traditional stocking programs. Specifically, it excluded "areas where exotic species have proved to be best suited to the environment, and of higher value for fishing purposes than the native fish." In other words, in those waters where the damage had been done and ecological systems already reworked, stocking of nonnatives could continue. The stocking of such waters, however, was contingent on case-by-case approval by the park superintendent and the director of the NPS.[58] The era of laissez-faire fish management within national parks was coming to an end.

Demaray's press release raised important questions about exactly which "native" fish should be stocked in the park. Most believed that greenback cutthroat—the only true native trout to the eastern portion of RMNP—was extinct by 1931. Therefore, when park rangers recommended the stocking of "native trout" in RMNP they were not speaking of greenbacks but rather Yellowstone cutthroats, which had been stocked east of the Continental Divide prior to the 1930s. One could make the argument that stocking Yellowstone cutthroat was little different from stocking rainbow or brook trout, as none were truly native. Lacking many options, RMNP turned to the stocking of nonnative cutthroats—which looked nearly identical to greenbacks—to meet its institutional mandate.

To aid in restoring the park's waters to something approximating natural conditions, RMNP instituted a series of lake and stream closures for the 1938 fishing season. Among those were the very popular Bear Lake, Emerald Lake, the ponds in Hidden Valley, and portions of Fall River.[59] To further restore these waters, the NPS planted an estimated half-million Yellowstone cutthroats, which had been shipped the previous spring from Yellowstone National Park and hatched at Estes Park, Fort Collins, Denver, and Grand Lake. In all, the fish were planted in "35 lakes and 20 streams in scattered sections of the park" by rangers and CCC enrollees.[60]

By the early 1940s RMNP had planted well over 2 million Yellowstone cutthroats to fulfill the NPS directive for native stocking.[61] To measure progress, the supervisor of fish resources from the Fish and Wildlife Service, David Madsen, conducted a survey of the park's waters in 1940. Despite years of concerted efforts to reclaim the park on behalf of cutthroats, Madsen found that the park as a whole continued to suffer from overpopulation of brook trout, especially in beaver ponds located at the headwaters of major streams.[62]

Beyond offering a valuable accounting of the park's waters at midcentury and a condemnation of stocking of nonnatives as "a serious mistake," Madsen's report is important for other reasons. Between the NPS policy shift of 1936 and 1941, managers at RMNP continued to frame the fisheries problem within the park as directly related to a supply issue. Park managers long perceived a correlation between stocking programs that favored nonnative fish and the proliferation of those fish across the park. Lacking any real scientific understanding of the processes at work, it was easy to conclude that the reason brook trout were so common in park waters was a direct function of stocking efforts, not a result of ecological and biological processes.

By understanding the situation in this way, restoration of native fish required little more than a stocking policy that favored native fish over nonnative ones. In this instance, the rise of ecological thinking within the NPS had given its managers the sense that previous policy was flawed but did not de facto give them the scientific and technical knowledge needed to adequately adjust it.

As managers soon realized, however, the restoration of native fish would require far more than a stocking program that favored cutthroats. Between 1938 and 1941 RMNP planted cutthroats almost exclusively (only two small plantings of rainbow trout took place), yet brook trout continued to reign supreme. Madsen was the first to understand that something beyond planting more cutthroats was warranted. Specifically, he argued that the current situation would not be corrected until the NPS found "some means of greatly reducing the brook population." Admitting that he did not know what factors specifically were responsible for the cutthroat's inability to compete with brook trout, he urged that "some person with the proper training and background be assigned to a thorough study" of the problem in the hopes that brook trout population could be curtailed.[63]

Although money and manpower were in short supply during World War II, the stocking of cutthroats continued. In 1943, for example, the NPS planted more than 700,000 eggs and 255,000 fry in the park.[64] Despite continuance of the policy, however, progress was slow at best. Again attempting to ascertain the efficacy of the new stocking program, Stillman Wright filed a report on the "fishery problem" in RMNP in 1944. According to Wright, the "plan of planting only the Yellowstone Lake trout has not produced satisfactory results," as some of the park waters had received nothing but cutthroats since 1937, "yet brook trout [were] excessively abundant and cutthroats [were] rare."[65]

Making matters worse, the successful conclusion of World War II brought a period of unparalleled growth in the number of annual visitors to RMNP and greatly threatened the park's ability to meet the expectations of its fishing clientele. During the postwar era, the NPS faced steady criticism that fishing across the park was poor and it begged for additional resources to study the park's stocking program.[66]

Going Green

With budgets still at wartime levels and visitation exceeding the park's ability to protect itself from nature lovers, the solutions to the management difficulties were scant. Making matters all the more complicated was an exciting discovery made in 1955 when professor Howard Tanner of Colorado State University found what he hoped were isolated populations of greenback cutthroat in the waters of Albion Creek near Nederland, Colorado.[67] After his discovery, Dr. Tanner collected and shipped specimens to Robert Miller, curator of fishes at the University of Michigan, for identification.[68] Upon close inspection, Dr. Miller concluded that "these fish represented a kind of cutthroat different from any others we know today, and that they may or may not be *Salmo* [*Oncorhynchus*] *clarkii stomias*," otherwise known as the greenback cutthroat.[69]

In the wake of the discovery, RMNP biologist James E. Cole, Superintendent James Lloyd, and the NPS's principal naturalist, Gordon Fredine, requested a preliminary study of the habitat of greenback in 1957.[70] The objectives of the study included securing additional fish so that positive identification could be made, collecting enough to serve as brood stock, and surveying the lakes and streams across the park with a "view toward establishment of sanctuaries in Rocky Mountain National Park." The researchers also conducted extensive surveys for additional locations that had not been tainted by the introduction of nonnative species.

The researchers concluded that the Faylene–Fay–Caddis Lake drainage provided the best location for stocking greenbacks, as it provided ample spawning habitat and isolation from downstream nonnative fish populations.[71] They also found that the portion of the Big Thompson River running through Forest Canyon would be a prime location for the restoration of greenback, as it contained a "series of falls and cascades," which provided an "effective barrier to any upstream movement" of fish, thereby preventing nonnatives below Forest Canyon from interfering with the restoration efforts. More significant, the researchers also found "no record of any fish stocking" in Forest Canyon, and they doubted whether "pack horses could be brought down into the drainage for stocking purposes." Hence, they came to believe that the "cutthroat trout present in the streams appear to be native to the area."[72] They subsequently took twelve specimens from Forest Canyon that appeared to "have the characteristics of green-back trout," believing that they would provide "an excellent source of fish for propagation purposes." Hoping to use the suspected greenbacks found in Forest Canyon as brood stock, the research team made arrangements for poisoning the Fay Lake drainage in 1958 to remove all fish in preparation for stocking greenbacks in 1959.[73]

Once the lakes were devoid of all fish life, the NPS and its partners at the Bureau of Sport Fisheries and Wildlife turned their attention to finding pure strains of greenbacks with which to stock the lakes. Drawing from the conclusions of the 1957 report, they selected the Big Thompson River at Forest Canyon as the most likely site for pure strains of greenbacks. Accordingly, researchers took "by hook and line, by electric shocking, and by treatment with cresol" several samples of suspected greenbacks from Forest Canyon. Once captured, the fish were carried out of Forest Canyon on horseback and transferred to the Estes Park Hatchery.[74]

By August 1959 the NPS and the federal Bureau of Sport Fisheries and Wildlife were poised to make a run at stocking the alleged greenbacks. Using a helicopter and bucket, crews made one drop into Fay Lake in August and another in early September. In all, well over 100 suspected greenbacks were planted, with no evidence of mortality with either drop. The NPS also moved "an additional 83 fish by truck to the US Fishery Station in Leadville, Colorado to serve as a brood stock" for future stocking efforts.[75] By 1959 the brood stock had successfully reproduced, and more than 1,000 eggs were harvested.[76]

Amid these developments, RMNP staff turned to the expertise of the Bureau of Sport Fisheries for further guidance. During the 1961–1962 season, aquatic biologist Robert Azevedo undertook a comprehensive study of the lakes of Rocky Mountain National Park. In all, Azevedo gathered data on twenty-five lakes and made recommendations. Echoing the findings of previous investigations, Azevedo stated that "pristine conditions have been vastly altered by active programs of stocking of non-native species and strains of trout in nearly all park waters." The nearly century-long effort to stock the waters of Colorado and RMNP with available and popular trout species, believed Azevedo, meant that any attempt to "determine the original composition and distribution of the native park fishes" would be extremely difficult.[77]

Aside from pointing out the difficulties that lay ahead in repairing and managing aquatic resources in the park, Azevedo's report revealed other bad news. According to Azevedo, Robert Miller of the University of Michigan Museum (to whom specimens of suspected greenback trout were sent in 1957 and 1958) concluded that the fish gathered from Forest Canyon were not *Oncorhynchus clarkii stomias.*[78] In addition to Miller's conclusions, the NPS had also discovered that "160,000 cutthroat trout, listed as 'spotted natives,' [likely Yellowstone cutthroats] were planted in the upper end of Forest Canyon in 1922 and that 130,000 were released in 1923." As was common during the early 1920s, the fish stocked in Forest Canyon were planted by "the Estes Park Fish and Game Association in cooperation with the National Park Service and the Rocky Mountain Transportation Company." In other words, the closing of Fay Lake, the removal of exotic fish from them, the capture of fish from Forest Canyon, and the eventual aerial dumping of those fish were all for naught. Hence, concluded Azevedo, "efforts to protect and perpetuate them as such are without valid purpose," and the lakes should be reopened to fishing.[79]

By the early 1960s, with ecological understanding on the rise, native fish in short supply, and the number of fishermen increasing, a new solution was required. At this most critical time, the NPS turned to a concept referred to initially as "fishing for fun." In a paper presented in 1963 before the National Convention of Trout Unlimited in Allenberry, Pennsylvania, NPS naturalist Orthello L. Wallis told crowds, "Fishing-For-Fun is a concept that there is more to fishing than filling one's creel. It is a philosophy that numerous authors have expressed and that a multitude of anglers have enjoyed for many years. Now this concept is being translated into trout management plans."[80] At the heart of "fishing for fun" (more commonly called catch-and-release) was the belief that a true sportsman did not desire the wanton destruction of fish for mere amusement but rather respected his quarry enough to practice angling techniques that ensured the safe return of the fish from whence they came. Such practices included the use of barbless hooks, using artificial flies and lures that fish were less likely to swallow, and keeping fish submerged while removing hooks. Each of the above, if followed diligently, greatly enhanced the likelihood that a fish would survive the trauma of being caught so that it could be caught another day.

Although the introduction of a catch-and-release policy may have been a radical step for the NPS, it was not an entirely new concept. According to Wallis, "Writers have long extolled the pleasures of angling amid scenic and placid surroundings and not the thrill of the kill alone."[81] In fact, the concept likely originated in the 1870s when writers began calling for the use of barbless hooks. As the idea of fishing for fun spread, regulations designed to encourage the behavior became more common, with the Michigan legislature enacting one of the first fly-fishing–only laws to protect the Au Sable River. In 1949, likely responding to the postwar demand for recreational fishing, the Pennsylvania Fish Commission adopted the motto, "Kill Less—Catch More!"[82]

The concept of catch-and-release fishing was attractive to the NPS for many reasons. Facing a slew of difficulties in keeping parks like Rocky stocked with adequate numbers of catchable native trout, catch-and-release had the capacity to effectively recycle trout. Recycling the trout through catch-and-release alleviated fishing pressure and allowed the NPS to keep stocking budgets relatively low while not violating the its mission to support native species. The NPS was aware, however, that enacting such a fundamental shift in fishing regulations also came with a greater chance of upsetting the fishing public so long accustomed to keeping whatever it caught.

RMNP completely abandoned stocking as a tool to support sport fishing in 1968. The era of fishing for tourists had effectively come to an end as scientific concerns came to dominate the ends and means of how the spaces along rivers, streams, and lakes were used within the park. Although RMNP abandoned stocking, it continued searching for "pure" strains of greenback trout in the following years. By 1973 it seemed likely that it had found two pockets of greenbacks still swimming the waters of the eastern side of Colorado—one in Como Creek and one in South Fork–Cache la Poudre River. These two streams, both part of the South Platte River drainage, held what scientists believed to be an estimated 2,000 pure greenbacks inhabiting an estimated 4.6 kilometers of stream.[83]

After the passage of the Endangered Species Act in 1973, the greenback trout was officially listed as endangered and afforded all the legal protections of the law. As part of their restoration efforts, fisheries researchers chemically treated Hidden Valley Creek in RMNP to remove the brook trout and then stocked it with greenbacks in 1973. Further hoping to establish stable and naturally reproducing populations of greenbacks, the NPS and U.S. Fish and Wildlife Service also removed all brook trout from Bear Lake and restocked it with greenbacks in 1975.

The 1977 season brought more developments for the restoration of greenbacks. Researchers completed the first comprehensive greenback trout recovery plan and located another likely pure population of greenback trout in 2.8 kilometers of Cascade Creek. To give it a wider range of tools to aid in restoration of greenbacks, including the introduction of angling for non-greenbacks, the trout recovery team recommended the downlisting of greenback from endangered to threatened. The reason for doing so was simple. If greenbacks were listed as endangered, no angling could take place in water that contained them as part of the legal protection that prevents the taking of endangered species. If they were listed as threatened, however, the legal protections against taking would be somewhat relaxed, and limited fishing could take place in waters containing greenbacks. As the NPS had hoped, the greenback was downlisted in 1978. By 1981 an estimated 630 greenback subadults and more than 16,000 fry had been produced through the broodstock program and stocked in restoration projects in the South Platte River drainage.[84]

With several projects under way, the restoration team and its partners in Bozeman had finally bred enough greenbacks to allow for stocking at a rate of 1,000 fry per hectare, a level high enough to open many of the restricted areas to limited fishing. Beginning in 1982, RMNP implemented the very first season of catch-and-release fishing in many of the park's waters that contained the precious greenback. Driven both by the desire to allow angling opportunities in the park and the desire to protect greenbacks from invasive species like brook trout, the NPS designed its catch-and-release program to achieve both. Specifically, in waters like Hidden Valley Creek, RMNP allowed angling with artificial flies and lures but required that fishermen release all greenback caught, while encouraging them to keep all brook trout. This catch-and-release/catch-and-kill policy is still in effect for most of the waters in the park today.

The Estes Park Hatchery, which had been badly damaged by the floods that ripped through Estes Park in July 1982, was finally slated for closure in January 1983. The Colorado State Division of Wildlife planned to replace the old Estes Park Hatchery with a larger-capacity facility located closer to Denver. Although many in Estes Park were concerned that the closure of the EPH would negatively impact tourism in the town, it was clear that the facility was no longer needed.[85]

The closure of the hatchery bears witness to the vastly changed nature of fisheries management in RMNP. When the facility was originally built, fish culture was truly a local endeavor. Although the state soon assumed control of the hatchery, fisheries management remained a largely local affair as the citizens of Estes Park contributed time, money, and energy to stocking the waters in and around RMNP. The newly established NPS welcomed this high level of community involvement. In fact, for the first twenty years of RMNP regional and national NPS officials had relatively little input into the species, numbers, and locations of fish stocked in the park. It was not until 1936 that the NPS regional and national management began taking a more active role in what individual parks were stocking. From that point on, the operations at the EPH grew less central as scientists both within and outside the NPS began assuming a more central role in fisheries management.

With the hatchery closed and greenback restoration well under way, RMNP continued to expand its catch-and-release policy. Between 1988 and 1994, for example, the NPS opened thirteen lakes and streams containing stable populations of greenback to catch-and-release fishing.[86] The marriage of catch-and-release angling for greenbacks and catch-and-kill for brook trout and other species, however, has produced mixed results. Beginning in the 1960s "fishing for fun" captured the moral high ground in persuading fishermen to release fish so that they may be enjoyed another day. Although this new fisherman's ethic was slow to find its way into RMNP fishing regulations, it had done so by 1982. In ways that the NPS did not anticipate, however, fishermen have not reserved catch-and-release only for greenbacks. In 1982–1983, for example, anglers reported having released in the neighborhood of 60 percent of all brook trout caught. A similar survey for 1984–1985 reflected that fishermen released anywhere from 45 percent to 100 percent of all brook trout caught. Additionally, it was estimated that as many as 7 percent of all greenbacks caught were kept by mistake.[87] If the catch-and-release program did not work exactly as managers had hoped, it nonetheless offered one tool that is essential to RMNP fisheries management still today.

Just as important as finding, breeding, and stocking greenbacks was the sometimes difficult and tedious process of educating the public about the importance of restoration efforts and the value of native fish. Beginning in the early 1990s, the greenback restoration team began to work more closely with conservation groups such as Colorado Trout Unlimited. Doing so allowed for "increased educational opportunities" through Trout Unlimited publications and meetings. The restoration team also reached out to local schools and members of Trout Unlimited to make the greenback the state fish. In 1994 the greenback trout ousted the rainbow trout as the state's official fish and it seemed as if the counterrevolution was nearly complete.[88]

Not often do trout find their way into the pages of the *New York Times*, but in September 2012 the greenback did just that. A postdoctoral fellow at the University of Colorado, Jessica Metcalf, used DNA analysis to question much of what we thought we knew about greenback trout. Her dissertation,

"Conservation Genetics of the Greenback Cutthroat Trout (*Oncorhynchus clarkii stomias*)," first rocked the NPS and its greenback restoration partners in 2007, arguing that the hybridization among other subspecies of cutthroats and greenbacks, combined with hybridization between greenbacks and other trout, meant that decades of efforts to save the greenbacks were for naught.[89]

Her most recent research, published in *Molecular Ecology* in September 2012 and covered by the *Times*, further highlighted the troubled future of greenback trout restoration. Comparing historic samples of DNA kept in specimen jars for more than a century to samples taken from a wide range of trout in Colorado waters, Metcalf concluded that there are, in fact, no pure strains of greenback cutthroats in the waters of Rocky Mountain National Park—or the vast majority of eastern Colorado, for that matter. She and her team of researchers found but one tiny pocket of greenbacks in Bear Creek, a small stream located just south of Colorado Springs. A hotelier had apparently stocked the four-mile section of the historically fishless alpine stream in the nineteenth century in hopes of bringing guests to his establishment.[90] Tourism, which has for so long been a powerful force in pushing greenbacks to the brink of extinction, may now provide the sole remaining hope for future greenback restoration.

Although disappointing news for those involved in restoration efforts, Metcalf's findings fit into a much broader historical pattern within the park. For generations, the NPS and its partners stocked and protected fish that they thought were the beloved greenbacks. Thus, the greenbacks that lurked the eddies and riffles of Hidden Valley Creek were a beautiful symbol of the resilience of nature and the power of science to point the way forward. Now, those very same fish viewed through a new and different scientific lens are no more native, no more natural, than the millions of other trout dumped into the park by those who vied for the fishing tourist.

Conclusion

The fish that now swim the waters of Sky Pond and the brook trout that do not lurk in Bear Lake both offer an opportunity to understand the connections between tourism and ecology and the material world. Fishing tourists and those who understood the park in ecological terms both sought to manifest a national park that fit their definition of "nature" and "parks."

Both required sometimes drastic acts of creation and re-creation, and they have helped foster a patchwork parkscape that reflects both ideologies. But humans have not controlled the history of the lakes and streams of Rocky. Fish—and their eating, mating, fighting, and migratory patterns—have been powerful historical agents, too.

Many tourists still cross through the gates of the park to fish. But much differentiates the fisherman in RMNP in 2012 from one in 1900. Fishermen now travel to the park knowing that catches will likely be low and that most of what is caught requires prompt return to the waters from whence it came. Fishermen have also come to terms with the fact that not all of the park's waters are open to the sport. Yet folks still come to fish. Their desire to do so, at least in part, is tied to the flexible genius behind those who advertise for tourism. Front Range Anglers, a guiding service based in Boulder, advertises the opportunity to catch the vaunted "grand slam" of trout fishing. The waters of Rocky Mountain National Park, they claim, offer the guided fisherman a rare opportunity to catch brown, brook, rainbow, and greenback trout in a single day.[91] As Metcalf's research seeps into park management and as the business of tourism adjusts to the new understanding of what exactly is and is not a greenback, it will be interesting to see if people still travel to the park, rod in hand, to hit a much less exciting triple.

7

Slippery Slopes

Two hundred dollars. If you do not include the price of gasoline or any of the high-fashion cold-weather gear needed to survive a surly day on the mountain, and if you have a free place to stay, $200 will buy you lunch, equipment rentals, and a lift ticket at Aspen Mountain. The scenery is otherworldly. The Silver Queen Gondola, for example, deposits skiers at a breathtaking 11,212 feet above sea level. Perched atop the run, skiers do not look up at the Continental Divide; they look across it. The Aspen Mountain experience also comes with the thrill of plunging down the slopes while keeping watch for celebrities who frequent the mountain. For a princely sum, anyone can purchase the excitement of a day on a pair of skis and the illusion of belonging in this world of fantastic wealth and conspicuous consumption. Meanwhile, your shillings—and tons just like them—feed the gilded behemoth that is Aspen.

Aspen was not always Aspen. Telluride was not always Telluride. Winter destinations like these were made through promotion, construction, and the artful ability to convince people that these were the places to be and to be seen. They are deeply cultural landscapes. While many of us associate the wintertime West with posh rustic resort towns, Rocky Mountain National Park has a long, rich, and engaging skiing history all its own. But skiers no longer flock to Hidden Valley to ski. No one who labors up any of the park's steep mountainsides expects to see a movie star whizzing down the slopes beside them. Why not? The answer is complicated and tells us a great deal about the powerful impact of tourism and recreation upon the landscape, the shifting environmental attitudes that ebb and flow from such activities, and the role of the National Park Service in mediating between the two.

In the earliest years of the park, skiing at Hidden Valley held the promise of great things for all parties involved. But skiing at Rocky eventually became an affront to the mission and ideals of the NPS and many of its patrons. The ski area had to be removed. Now the NPS waits patiently for the trees and shrubs to fill in the runs once opened by axe, saw, wind, and fire. Ironically, the accessibility of Hidden Valley, its proximity to Trail Ridge Road, the rising popularity of skiing, and the assumed innocuous environmental impact of the sport—many of the same factors that brought development in the first place—later provided the most powerful ammunition for closing the ski area and erasing it from the landscape decades later.

Skiing for Gold

Like so many modern recreational diversions, skiing in the American West sprang from necessity, not whimsy.[1] The discovery of precious metals in the second half of the nineteenth century drew tens of thousands of argonauts to Colorado. Placer deposits quickly dried up and more capital-intensive mining moved in, intent upon piercing the earth's skin to find veins of gold and silver. As a consequence, settlements popped up in some of the most unlikely and inhospitable corners of the Rockies, giving miners a place to sleep, eat, and live as they chipped and blasted their way into the mountains.

Although summer in the high Rockies is blissful, the season is crowded at both ends by the early arrival and late departure of winter's snow. No reasonable person would locate settlements at high-elevation mining camps like Camp Bird or Tomboy. But the search for wealth often makes people do unreasonable things. There were many challenges in living at elevations well over 10,000 feet year-round, not the least of which was staying connected to the outside world. During summer months, hauling supplies to the string of mining towns and camps across the state was hard enough. With the onset of winter the task became nearly impossible. Knitting the mining towns together and tying them to larger flows of goods was a crucial task. Norwegian immigrants, who had a long cultural tradition of using skis to navigate their world, offered skiing as an early solution to the problem. In short order "skiing became a necessary part of the local economy and daily life" across western states like Colorado. Especially important were those men who used skis to deliver mail to isolated mining towns. In addition to letters from friends and relatives, these skiing mailmen also brought "greenbacks," which gave the miners "access to a larger economic system, let them cash in on their digging, and also helped define their bearers as powerful and successful."[2]

Surviving the endless tedium of winter required more than keeping the fire stoked and getting occasional mail from the distant world below. For many, ski racing provided a welcome diversion that offered release from the endless grind of work, a chance to socialize with others, and an opportunity to demonstrate male bravery and fitness to the community. Although racing was a male-dominated activity, women also found occasion to ski, using it as a means to build and sustain relationships with friends and neighbors, though they did occasionally compete in women's races.

The arrival of the railroads and other more reliable means of transportation into the once isolated mining towns brought an eventual end to the skiing mail carriers. The novelty and exhilaration of skiing, however, had become firmly established in the Centennial State.[3] Like fishing, hiking, and horseback riding, skiing would soon become an activity that promised those with sufficient disposable income access to clean outdoor air, invigoration, and an escape from bustling cities all while engaging the rugged West. To celebrate the sport and to find other enthusiasts, the citizens of Denver formed the Denver Ski Club in 1913 and the Denver–Rocky Mountain Ski Club the following year. The Colorado Mountain Club, which advocated for the creation of RMNP, also embraced skiing as an organized activity in 1915 with its first winter event at Fern Lake.

Towns across the state also embraced winter carnivals to break the winter boredom and to promote economic activity and community development. Full of hot cocoa, coffee, or a stiff nip of whiskey, winter carnival spectators enjoyed the companionship of their neighbors and thrilling events including ski jumping, cross-country races, dances, and skijoring, which entailed pulling a skier with a horse.[4] Tapping the growing enthusiasm for skiing and hoping to attract winter visitors, Rocky Mountain National Park held its first winter carnival in 1917.[5] By 1919 the winter outing was "becoming deservedly popular," with the number of participants exceeding local accommodations.[6] Popularity of winter excursions continued to grow, and by 1923 an estimated 500 people had enjoyed expanding ski and sled runs at Fern Lake. Hoping to nurture the budding trend, the NPS dedicated resources to blasting several large rocks and removing brush that interfered with the emerging ski run as well as building a new run for beginners.[7] Although still in its nascency, the culture of skiing was already making its mark upon the park.

In 1926 Estes Park hosted the State Ski Tournament, attracting some 1,500 paying customers and another 1,500 who came to town but did not attend the event.[8] Local businesses and the NPS were, during the early years of the park, of the same mind regarding winter sports in the area. Promotion of winter use bolstered NPS visitation and introduced visitors to a different side of the park, while ski carnivals, CMC outings, and ski tournaments raised the profile of Estes Park and held the promise of economic growth during the winter doldrums. What park managers did not foresee, however, was the tangle of ideological conflicts that would attend the development of more capital- and technologically intensive skiing. The culture of the sport was dynamic and difficult to anticipate, as were the market demands that drove its cycles of expansion and contraction.

Not-So-Hidden Valley

Stretching between 9,000 and 11,000 feet in elevation, Rocky Mountain National Park's Hidden Valley is a glacier-carved headwater drainage that feeds into Fall River. The valley is clad in climax spruce–fir forest with lodgepole and aspen stands growing at its lower reaches. Toward the upper end of the valley, "characteristic stands of stunted conifers . . . fade into true alpine tundra on the ridge."[9] Like so many of the park's nooks and crannies, Hidden Valley had a human history well before Rocky's founding. In the 1880s, for example, locals built a sawmill at the bottom of the valley. The mill, which was eventually owned by F. O. Stanley and operated to cut lumber to build the Stanley Hotel and Elkhorn Lodge, extensively reshaped the appearance and ecology of the valley. By generating the power to hew the materials needed to build two of the region's most iconic buildings, the mill denuded a significant portion of lower Hidden Valley, later providing the opportunity for winter recreation among the cleared areas.

On the evening before Halloween 1915, some 200 Estes Park residents were enjoying a costume party when a man wearing singed clothing riding a nearly

Hidden Valley sawmill, circa 1900. Courtesy of Rocky Mountain National Park,
ROMO 5512, MSF NEG 2866.

broken horse arrived at the gathering. Once there, he announced to the partygoers that there was a fire fast approaching town. Demonstrating the early
cooperation between locals and the NPS, Estes Park residents—still dressed
in their Halloween costumes—dashed from their party to extinguish the fire.
"There in the light of the fire," reported the *Rocky Mountain News*, "the bizarre costumes of the masqueraders mingled strangely with the uniform of
the foresters." In what must have been a sight truly befitting All Hallow's
Eve, "Romeo and Satan worked side by side with the kaiser and a Chinese
dragon" to extinguish the blaze.[10] By the time the "ragged, blackened band,
dressed in their panoply of Hallowe'en came straggling back to Estes Park"[11]
the fire had burned a significant portion of Hidden Valley.

The late 1920s and early 1930s brought still more changes to the valley by
providing contractor W. A. Colt a staging area for equipment and material for the construction of Trail Ridge Road. Hidden Valley was also the
campsite for the nearly 200 men who labored on the project. In maximizing
the road's vistas, planners plotted its course in such a way that it bisects the

lower portion of Hidden Valley and then "entirely circumscribes" the valley's upper reaches.[12] As planners had hoped, the road became one of the most popular elements of Rocky, with tens of millions of visitors enjoying the views of Hidden Valley and beyond.

By the early years of the Great Depression, local and regional support for more winter recreational opportunities within Rocky was mounting. Loveland's Chamber of Commerce, for example, passed a resolution supporting winter sports in RMNP in 1932.[13] That same year, the NPS authored a brochure listing winter sports as one of the park's leading attractions.[14] Subsequent printings of the brochure in 1937 and 1941 reflect the same attempts to entice visitors to Rocky in the winter months.

Meanwhile, ski clubs across the state had sought to expand the boundaries of their sport. In 1930 the Colorado Mountain Club made arrangements for railroad service from Denver to the West Portal of the Moffat Tunnel for interested skiers. This innovation, which made skiing in the state possible in ways that it had not been before, remained in place until the road over Berthoud Pass was later completed. With the road complete, skiers from Denver began the tradition of using automobiles to deliver skiers to the top of slopes. The practice became so prevalent, in fact, that the Colorado Mountain Club bankrolled a ski bus at Berthoud beginning in 1936. For just 15 cents per shuttle ride, a member of the Colorado Mountain Club could enjoy the comfort of the bus ride to the top of the hill and the thrill of descent to its bottom.[15] The marriage of roads, automobiles, shuttle buses, and skiing would soon prove crucial to the further development of Hidden Valley.

One of Rocky's most iconic rangers, Jack Moomaw, also played a direct hand in shaping Hidden Valley and in making future development possible there. By his own admission, he had spent some of his time in the 1920s and 1930s clearing "old logging roads and skid trails" to make portions of Hidden Valley and other locations within the park more amenable to skiing. Unauthorized clearing of any trees in a national park was, as Moomaw later discovered, a very serious matter. In the early 1930s locals and the NPS were debating the merits of hosting the National Championship Ski Races at Hidden Valley. Not surprisingly, the Estes Park Chamber of Commerce ardently supported the idea, but NPS officials expressed concern that clearing ski trails needed for the event would "mar the scenery of Hidden Valley." Moomaw apparently "chuckled" and stated that the ski trails, which he had opened himself without authorization, "had been there for years" and no one seemed to notice. The admission left his superiors fuming at the behavior of their rogue ranger, and his "career almost ended then and there."[16] Moomaw apparently won the day, however, and he was granted permission to further open the area to skiing by cutting what became known as the "suicide" run in anticipation of the National Down Mountain and Cross Country Ski Races of 1934.

Amid the growing popularity of winter sports in the park, Superintendent Edmund Rogers took occasion to further articulate his evolving position to the director. Although Rogers was a staunch supporter of winter recreation, he did not favor transforming the park into a commercialized center of skiing or ski jumping where some "professional could establish a world's record." To him, "neither the physical scar nor the flavor of the thing" was appealing.[17] But there was a problem. Following a ski-jump fundraiser event in June 1931, Director Horace Albright had spoken with the *Estes Park Trail* about winter recreation in RMNP. It seems that Albright was willing to give assurances that the NPS stood firmly behind winter recreation of the sort Rogers favored, but the *Trail*—either intentionally or by mistake—gave the impression that the NPS favored full development of a winter recreation area within the park. Rogers, who stood between the mounting local pressure for full development and the measured approach of the NPS, understood that "the local people are without a doubt thinking in different terms from what the Director has had in mind, [and] it will take a lot of explaining to repudiate the promises that they feel have been made."[18] In fact, the perceived promises from the director gave locals hope, a rallying point, and a fulcrum needed to transform Hidden Valley into a ski area over the following decades.

Going Up

Rocky Mountain National Park was not the only western park embracing winter sports as a means to increase year-round visitation. In 1917, for example, locals cleared a substantial run in Yosemite National Park west of Camp Curry. The completion of the All-Weather Highway in 1926 and the Ahwahnee Hotel in 1927 further promoted winter access and use of Yosemite. The Yosemite Curry Company, which held the concession to run the hotel,

worked desperately to find the means to increase winter business; skiing provided that opportunity. In 1928 the concessionaire founded the Winter Club
to raise the profile of winter sports in the park, and the NPS began flooding
a portion of the Camp Curry parking lot to create an ice rink. Furthermore,
the NPS hired the Swiss national Ernst Des Baillets as director of winter
sports for the park, and he soon established a ski school for Yosemite.[19]

Although winter recreation showed great promise at Yosemite, the Winter Club sought a location more amenable to downhill skiing, which they
found in Badger Pass. In 1934 the NPS installed a cable-drawn toboggan to
pull skiers up the mountainside. Although technologically crude, the new lift
system was a far better alternative than post-holing one's way up the mountainside in exchange for a few moments of downhill pleasure.[20] The Winter
Club estimated that some 15,000 people visited the area in the 1933–1934 season alone. Hoping to further develop the park's winter use, the Yosemite
Park & Curry Company assiduously lobbied for more expansive facilities to
meet growing demands. The NPS approved plans to develop the Badger Pass
Ski Area, and by 1935 Yosemite boasted a first-rate ski lodge built in the Swiss
chalet style.[21]

The success and rapid growth of the Badger Pass Ski Area gave Estes Park
promoters hope. Prospects of a ski resort at RMNP, however, soon dimmed
as the NPS clarified its approach to winter sports development. Concerned
about the "injuries" that could occur to parks like Rocky, such as the building of roads and cutting of trees, NPS Director A. B. Cammerer instead embraced a measured approach. It was wise, thought Cammerer, to "confine"
intensive winter development to Yosemite, Mount Rainier, and Crater Lake,
where facilities were already in place, and to "open all other western parks
for winter recreational use but . . . not develop specialized winter sports programs therein."[22]

Not surprisingly, the *Estes Park Trail* and the Estes Park Chamber of
Commerce ardently opposed the NPS position on the matter. According
to the *Trail*, "Quibbles about 'scarring' the park have never seemed to us
more than the poor argument of obstructionists. It might just as easily be
argued that roads and trails should never have been built in Rocky Mountain National Park."[23] The *Trail* had a point. Hidden Valley had not—for a
very long time—been anything approaching a "pristine" section of the park.
Sawmills, construction camps, anthropogenic fire, swaths cut for ski and

sledding runs, and an iconic NPS road had all made the valley a decidedly cultural landscape. The NPS argument that a more systematic development would undermine the scenic value of the area speaks volumes about how naturalized roads and other developments had become within the minds of the NPS—and how incredibly short their historical memory was. It also demonstrates that major ski runs and their accompanying lifts were not, at least at this point, sufficiently naturalized to fit seamlessly into the park.

But the managers of Rocky were in a difficult position. They had drawn a line regarding future development of winter recreation in the park, but they still needed and wanted locals to lend a hand fighting fires and tending to other emergencies as they arose. Perhaps hoping to smooth things over a bit, RMNP Superintendent Thomas Allen made the decision to keep Trail Ridge Road open to the headwaters of Hidden Valley Creek for the winter of 1936–1937. Allen's innovative idea allowed visitors to drive their automobiles up the road, park, and ski down the valley. With a bit of carpooling, skiers could enjoy a day on the slopes without the need of lifts and tows. Park rangers and CCC workers also leveled the ice on one of the beaver dams in the lower valley for ice skating.

The scheme worked well, and skiers and skaters came from out of state to play at Hidden Valley. More important, the "little village of Estes Park, which usually goes more or less to sleep in the winter time . . . had more winter business than they ever contemplated." In a moment of proud reflection, Superintendent Allen boasted that they had "done no construction work and have built no structures." Rather, they "merely took advantage of natural facilities and made it possible for the public to reach them."[24] Trail Ridge Road, referred to as a "natural facility," was crucial to development of Hidden Valley as a winter playground.

Allen's seemingly innocuous solution to the problem, which at once pleased development interests, quieted concerns over eyesores, and bolstered Rocky's winter visitation, was pivotal. It is impossible to say what direction development of Hidden Valley might have taken had Allen not decided to keep Trail Ridge Road open. Had he and his superiors weathered another season or two of criticisms about being obstructionist and antidevelopment, the matter very well may have played itself out as other ski areas opened around the state. As Allen and others would soon discover, however, keeping the road open and promoting Hidden Valley created conditions that increased pressure to develop larger facilities. More promotion meant more skiers. More skiers meant that ski runs had to be wider to minimize accidents. As the profile of Hidden Valley rose, more skiers pressed for more and better slopeside services. Better accommodations, in turn, began the cycle anew.

Transforming Hidden Valley into a "mecca [for] winter sports enthusiasts" required constant promotion and advertising, which Estes Park businessmen were happy to provide.[25] By 1938 there was solid evidence that their efforts were working. In mid-February 1938, for example, more than 1,700 people visited the park, and the parking lot at Hidden Valley was "overflowing."[26] To accommodate the growing crowds, the NPS allowed installation of shelters at the upper and lower runs with a warming shelter open for skaters. They also directed Ranger Moomaw and CCC workers to widen the ski and sledding trails.[27] As the popularity of Hidden Valley increased, Roe Emery, owner of the Rocky Mountain Transportation Company and RMNP concessionaire, gave permission for Paul Hauk and Charles Hardin to operate a ski school in the park.[28] Meanwhile, the whole of the NPS witnessed impressive growth of its winter use, with as many as 400,000 people coming to the park system during the 1939–1940 season.[29]

The outbreak of World War II dampened momentum for winter use at Hidden Valley, but important developments were afoot. Revealing an overall lack of oversight and regulation within the park, a group of local high-school boys installed a ramshackle ski tow in Hidden Valley. Such unauthorized development would be unthinkable today, but the war did much to siphon men and attention away from Rocky, thereby creating the opportunity that the boys seized. Like Superintendent Allen's decision to keep Trail Ridge Road open, the installation of a rope tow at Hidden Valley—even an unauthorized one—was an important milestone that foreshadowed changes yet to come.[30]

Building Hidden Valley

The conclusion of World War II and the embrace of recreational activities by millions of Americans presented Hidden Valley boosters with fresh opportunities. George Hurt, who had served in the famed 10th Mountain Division and was a native of Estes Park, returned to the area following his service and began pushing for formal development at Hidden Valley.[31] Specifically, Hurt asked the NPS for permission to install the first authorized ski tow and a small concession stand in 1945. The Park Service, still hesitant to allow Hurt's request, delayed approval as it launched a feasibility study during the winter of 1945–1946.[32]

By 1946 Hidden Valley reflected decades of physical changes at the hands of the NPS and Estes Park residents. Still, the valley was a far cry from what anyone might consider developed. It had a few open but fairly narrow runs, a small ski jump from which brave souls could launch themselves as far as 60 feet, and a toboggan run that stretched some 250 feet up the valley. Surveying the situation after the war, the NPS came to what should have been another crucial realization. Although the park showed the potential of heavy winter use, officials concluded that further development at Hidden Valley was not desirable. In addition to the limited size of the area, which they feared demand would soon outstrip, Hidden Valley was too close to Trail Ridge Road. In the not-so-distant past, the proximity of the valley to Trail Ridge Road was a boon. Now, however, the NPS concluded that "widened trails or permanent ski facilities would impair the scenic value of this location" as seen from the iconic park road.[33]

Trail Ridge Road, arguably one of the park's most popular attractions, was too valuable of an asset to risk in pursuit of winter recreation. Skiing, although increasing in popularity, served a comparatively small clientele, and further development risked undermining one of Rocky's most popular activities: driving. During the previous eight years the NPS had also conducted studies into the Mill Creek Basin to discern if it might better serve as a future location for skiing in Rocky. The Denver Chamber of Commerce had also conducted its own study of the area and reached the same conclusion. The snow was better and the wind less fierce at Mill Creek; also, it was tucked away and not visible from Trail Ridge Road and required only minimal clearing to open up good ski runs.[34] Still hoping to take advantage of promises from the Union Pacific Railroad to run weekend specials from Chicago, Omaha, St. Louis, and Kansas City if RMNP moved forward with ski development, it seemed that momentum was shifting toward Mill Creek Basin.[35]

Given the NPS's conclusions regarding the liabilities of further development at Hidden Valley and the feasibility reports for development of Mill Creek Basin as a ski resort, it is puzzling that the NPS gave the go-ahead to continue development at Hidden Valley. Perhaps seeking to quiet local displeasure, in 1946 rangers cleared three ski trails at Hidden Valley of logs and other hazards and gave George Hurt permission to install his 1,000-foot rope tow at upper Hidden Valley and to operate a lunch wagon slopeside. The NPS also granted permission for the Rocky Mountain Parks Transportation Company to provide shuttle services between Estes Park and Hidden Valley and from Lower Hidden Valley to the point at which Trail Ridge Road bisected the ski runs. From there, skiers could use the new rope tow to access upper Hidden Valley.

Enthusiasm for the developments ran high, and more than 12,000 people enjoyed skiing, skating, and sledding at Hidden Valley during the weekends of the 1946–1947 season. But by the end of the season, Hurt's profits were not as robust as hoped. Not counting the cost of installing the new rope tow, the ski area generated $789 in net revenue. If the $3,700 that the Park Service spent to keep the roads open and to ensure the safety of the visitors is included, Hidden Valley operated at a net loss of more than $2,900 during its first full season of operation—an omen of things to come.[36]

Although skiing was quickly becoming a centerpiece of American winter recreation, not everyone was willing to trade in warm winter hearths for a set of skis. In a 1947 article, for example, *Rocky Mountain News* reporter Robert C. Ruark lambasted skiing as a dangerous waste of time. After a day on the slopes at nearby Winter Park, where readers assume that things did not go well, the reporter recounted that he had been "dumped into the heart of the ski-country where little children are born with barrel-staves strapped to their feet and the adult with the un-frostbitten nose is a sissy." Decidedly unimpressed with the sport, Ruark concluded that skiing was "the most involved way [he knew] of to break your neck while dying simultaneously of pneumonia."

Packed with fantastic hyperbole that fills the mind's eye with colorful images of his day on the slopes, Ruark's article reveals a great deal about the sport and its gender assumptions at mid-century. To Ruark, this new craze wherein "ordinary sane adults" go to "unbelievable lengths" to make themselves "miserable" was driven, in large part, by "magazine covers and movie shorts depicting people soaring birdlike off peaks." There was little inherently fun about skiing, which, by the author's estimation, was mainly the pursuit of mimicking the beautiful people happily whizzing down powdery slopes as seen in magazine articles and advertisements.[37]

"Snow bunnies" at Bear Lake, 1940. Courtesy of Rocky Mountain National Park, ROMO MSF NEG 1707.

By his reckoning, "some giddy broad swooshed off a hill and didn't crack a pelvis and decided that here was a marvelous opportunity to buy clothes for still another occasion." In the earliest days of skiing in places like Hidden Valley the clothes and gear of skiing was largely utilitarian. Now, groused Ruark, skiing was an expression of "high fashion" where it cost "more to outfit a skier than to prepare a debutante for the big ball." Although Ruark's comments about women being attracted to the sport as an opportunity to buy more clothes are patently sexist, he is right in that skiing had been undergoing significant changes. As early as the 1920s, skiing was becoming a reflection of disposable income and free time. Advertisers, who played an important role in depicting appropriate roles for skiers, continued to promote the idea that men skied to demonstrate skill and achievement, while intimating that the activity was largely social for women. As the ads suggested, high slopeside fashion offered women the opportunity to flaunt their social status as both "consumer and consumed."[38]

Midcentury promotional efforts at RMNP speak to the expectations and assumptions that imbued skiing. As part of the broader effort to promote skiing in the park, for example, photographers staged a photo shoot in 1940

Ski Hidden Valley poster, circa 1950. Courtesy of Barbara James Williams.

that included five women skiing. Although innocuous at first glance, the photo reveals many of the gender assumptions and pressures of the sport. For example, the women, all of whom appear to be having a grand time, are skiing in a group, not as individuals. The women's skimpy outfits, which are clearly not intended for skiing, also sexualize them in ways not seen with their male counterparts.

This photograph and those like it are especially telling when viewed against the midcentury promotional poster "Ski at Hidden Valley." First, the poster connects the act of skiing in RMNP to the park's fauna in obvious and interesting ways. But the poster does so much more. It appears to feature a single bull elk, with its chest hair jutting outward as an obvious sign of virile masculinity. The anthropomorphized animal also sports sunglasses that evoke stardom and the glamour of Hollywood. Whereas the photo of scantily clad, "giddy" women tells us that women are social—and not serious—skiers, the "Ski at Hidden Valley" poster reveals the assumption that male skiers were serious, confident, and powerful.

Although some people were decidedly against further expansion of a frivolous endeavor, the Aspen Skiing Corporation saw things differently. In January 1947, Aspen powered up its new Lift No. 1 before an ebullient crowd. Rather than dragging skiers of all skill levels mercilessly up the mountain, as rope tows and other devices did, Aspen's Lift No. 1 scooped riders comfortably into a seat as they floated effortlessly to the top of the mountain. More than a nifty piece of technology that made for a more comfortable day on the slopes, this lift—which was the world's longest and fastest of its kind—marked a key transition away from the small-town ski areas toward a corporate skiing experience increasingly characterized by more and better amenities. Anxious to keep pace with the growth of the sport, Hidden Valley supporters pressed on.

As demand for skiing increased, however, investors with deeper pockets were stepping into the industry. Berthoud Pass, for example, opened the world's first double chairlift in 1947, and Steamboat Springs benefited from $100,000 in city bonds to build an impressively long ski lift. Meanwhile, new ski areas, like Arapahoe Basin, were opening every year. In short order, ski destinations that offered only the tiresome and difficult-to-use rope tows and T-bars fell farther behind.[39]

Still, Hidden Valley had important supporters of its own who were hop-

Using a rope tow at Hidden Valley, 1958. Courtesy of Rocky Mountain National Park, ROMO MSF NEG 1481.

ing to transform it into the next skiing hotspot. Senator Edwin Carl John-son, a Colorado Democrat, championed Hidden Valley, penning letters to the secretary of the interior and other key officials. Much to the dismay of proponents, Secretary of the Interior J. A. Krug remained reticent about a full-scale ski resort at RMNP. Hidden Valley, he claimed, did not have ter-rain well suited for further development; it was too heavily forested and was already operating at capacity. Further widening of slopes and construction of facilities, argued Krug, would "seriously impair the high scenic values en-joyed by thousands of people traversing the Trail Ridge Road during the summer months." Rather than building still more at Hidden Valley, Krug informed Senator Johnson that Hidden Valley would stay as it was until fur-ther appropriations could be made to develop the Mill Creek site.[40] But if locals had learned anything about dealing with the NPS, it was that patience could bear fruit.

Regional pressure for the development of Hidden Valley continued to mount. The Estes Park Winter Sports Club, which had long championed skiing around Estes Park, wanted the NPS to allow installation of a high-capacity double chairlift of their own, to undertake further trail widening, and to build larger parking areas and a warming lodge.[41] The EPCC's Hidden Valley Development Committee also sought to raise $5,000 to promote increased winter use of the park.[42]

The Winter Sports Committee and the Estes Park Chamber of Commerce also funded a prospectus for development at Hidden Valley. To its authors, who were far more interested in proving the area's merits than actually studying if growth was feasible, Hidden Valley was an ideal location. Not only did it offer perfect snow, but nightly winds would—as if by magic—smooth the runs while skiers slept. Moreover, boasted the authors, the park lay within overnight driving distance of some 28 million people who brought an estimated $47 million into Colorado in 1952 alone.[43] Construction of a lodge and a double chairlift that ran the entire length of the mountain were both needed to capitalize upon the area's natural potential.

The authors of the prospectus were careful, however, to include counterpoints to those who felt that further development would impair the park's scenic beauty. "The area in question," they argued, "is not a so-called virgin area, but contains the Trail Ridge Road which can plainly be seen for miles in practically every direction, a burned area, and a blown-down area." To them, arguments that a ski resort would destroy a beautiful area untouched by human hands rang hollow. They also advocated installation of the most advanced lift towers, which when painted green were "indistinguishable" from trees at "relatively short distances."[44]

Had Hidden Valley been located on United States Forest Service land, rather than within a national park, things would have been much different. Whereas proponents of Hidden Valley had to fight vociferously to convince the NPS to cut a tree here or divert a stream there, other ski areas located on Forest Service lands were essentially free to do as they pleased. When Aspen's manager, Dick Durrance, for example, wanted to open a new run he felt no compunction to ask the USFS for permission. Aspen simply sharpened its saws and got to cutting. When other resorts decided the time was right to install a new lift, they installed one.[45] In this key way, resorts located on USFS lands were much more responsive to market forces and could make decisions based solely upon a business calculus. Hidden Valley, however, brought with it heavy cultural baggage regarding the meaning of national parks and a vigilant government agency that was less concerned with private economic development as compared to its institutional cousins. Concessionaires often got their development but it was seldom approved in a timely manner—and seldom lived up to the scope and scale developers had advocated.

The NPS's reticence to step aside and allow a private business to shape park policy makes good sense, if for no other reason than that not everyone was in favor of still more development at Hidden Valley. Like countless other visitors, Helen Dean had been coming to the park for fifteen years and was "disturbed to learn that the business men of Estes Park are asking to have a chair lift built in the Hidden Valley ski area." It was true, conceded Dean, that Trail Ridge Road was a scar upon the landscape, but it was needed to open the "beauty and grandeur of the high mountains to many persons who could not see them otherwise." But the installation of a chairlift would be an eyesore better suited for an "amusement park," not a "magnificent national park."[46]

Writing for *National Parks* magazine, Devereux Butcher agreed. According to Butcher, the prime reason for local support for ski-area development was a business slump caused by the conclusion of the Bureau of Reclamation's Colorado–Big Thompson project. The proposed facilities, he argued, amounted to an "unnecessary mechanical invasion of the park," the sole purpose of which was "to attract crowds for the sake of profit to business," which was "an obvious violation of park objectives." Allowing construction of a lift at Hidden Valley for profit "would set a dangerous precedent" and jeopardize the "magnificent heritage of primeval nature" in the park.[47] Like many writing before and after him, Butcher was either unaware of or ignored the area's rich human history prior to the 1950s. Hidden Valley was far from a human- and history-free landscape.

While debate over Hidden Valley was heating up, the NPS had been conducting yet another feasibility study. This time, landscape architect Harold Fowler investigated four alternative sites to Hidden Valley in 1952–1953, including Allenspark, Mill Creek, and Willow Park, and met with many boosters of skiing in the park. According to Fowler, Allenspark, which is located just outside the boundary of RMNP, included good intermediate terrain and excellent views, but building a parking lot to accommodate 600 cars would have cost an estimated $100,000. The location would also require extensive grading to create adequate space for a lodge, and it was subject to heavy winds that would scour the runs of their snow. Mill Creek, which the NPS had long considered as an alternative to Hidden Valley, was even less suitable. The site would require the construction of three miles of road and the improvement of many more miles to make the area accessible. By Fowler's estimate, the roadwork alone would cost upward of $500,000. Mill Creek, however, did have the great benefit of being out of the view of Trail Ridge Road. Finally, the Willow Park area, which lay at the head of Fall River Road adjacent to Fall River Pass, offered excellent skiing but presented significant wintertime access issues. Interestingly, Fowler found that Willow Park was "located in an area of high summer use and the installation of lifts and other constructed features" would be too intrusive. For some reason, he did not reach the same conclusion regarding Hidden Valley and the iconic road that encircled it.

With construction costs too high at Allenspark and Mill Creek, and with Willow Park too intrusive of a location, Hidden Valley remained the lone option.[48] Revealing the influence of the Estes Park Chamber of Commerce, Fowler also contended that winter temperatures and the topography of Hidden Valley meant that powder "wafted" into the area in amounts not seen across other parts of the park. Hidden Valley's frigid temperatures also kept the snow well frozen and thus reduced the amount lost to freeze-thaw cycles at other areas.[49] Like the EPCC, Fowler concluded that the winds at Hidden Valley, which many locals nicknamed Hurricane Hill, would kindly "blow the snow to fill in ruts and sitzmarks after the slopes have had heavy use."[50] The wind would also, opined the rapt Fowler, keep snow levels low at the parking lot, thereby obviating the need to plow it frequently.[51]

Although Fowler supported developing Hidden Valley, as a landscape architect he was sensitive to the "defacement of the landscape" that development would entail.[52] Because one of the central reasons that parks were created was to spare them the lumberman's axe, cutting trees in any national park was nearly always controversial. Attempting to put the matter into perspective—and perhaps offer a measure of justification for his position—Fowler argued that "millions of trees have been cut in our national parks in order that trails and roads be constructed and that lodges, cabins and the many various structures and developments needed for the convenience of the people could be realized." To Fowler, it was a "matter of weighing of values, the losses against the benefits. In one instance we would not approve of the cutting of a single tree because the reason for the cutting was not sufficiently justified. On the other hand, we might approve of the cutting of some thousands of trees because an overbalance of benefits would result."[53]

Here Fowler captured the ironies surrounding the park's management. Many have long assumed that "conservation" was born of the utilitarian desire to use resources in the most efficient way for the greatest purpose and that "preservation" was founded on a different ideal, perhaps even a loftier one. But time and again, as the NPS argued its way through a range of management decisions, the base justification—the root of the root of their decisionmaking—was deeply utilitarian. In this instance, the cutting of large swaths of trees was justified because of the countless benefits this would generate for park visitors, communities, concessionaires, and the park itself. Cutting trees for timber sales was, generally speaking, not allowed. But cutting trees to provide regional economic development and sport for visitors, according to Fowler, was acceptable. The end result, however, is much the same. The trees are felled, and the landscape bears witness to environmental attitudes regarding nature and national parks. Slippery slopes, indeed.

Fowler was also careful to include in his report methods of naturalizing the development so that it remained as hidden as possible. In addition to "naturalistic clearing," whereby trees would be selectively cut to leave some in place, Fowler also advocated "camouflaging" the ski lift itself by using tapered towers painted green and allowing an undergrowth beneath the lift. He also advised that any material that revealed the mechanical character of the development—including oil drums, excess cables, and the like—be stowed out of sight. In subtle but important ways, Fowler was advocating an activity while seeking all feasible measures to conceal the human hands behind it. If the development was properly concealed, the millions of visitors that traversed Trail Ridge Road every year would give little consideration to the cables, pulleys, and towers that were the heart of the ski area. Neither would they pay heed to the large sections of trees that had been cut to make room for carefree days on the slopes.

But not everyone within the NPS agreed with Fowler's assessment. The chief NPS naturalist, John Doerr, for example, reminded Director Conrad Wirth that installing a full chairlift at Hidden Valley and scaling up operations would very likely increase property values in and around the park. Because the NPS had been patiently buying out private inholdings, a resort development would make it more expensive to purchase the remaining ones.[54] Doerr also argued that Fowler had underestimated the adverse impact of high winds on skiing in Hidden Valley, just as he largely failed to consider the full range of environmental impacts of future development. Increased runoff and erosion, changes in forest composition, and disruptions to stream flows below the proposed ski area were all likely consequences, counseled Doerr.[55] Wirth should have given Doerr's concerns more consideration.

As park visitation soared in the postwar era and pressure to develop Hidden Valley mounted, NPS managers had significant data to consider. Rather than choosing between full development and no development at all, they instead chose a middle road. This decision, however, set them farther down a path that would bring still more development to the area—yet in a way that pleased none of the parties involved. Rather than allow installation of a "high speed" chairlift running from the bottom of the mountain to at least the Trail Ridge Road crossing—which local boosters and ski enthusiasts wanted—NPS Director Wirth agreed to allow further development of lower Hidden Valley with the installation of a new tow from the base of the mountain to Trail Ridge Road. He also gave his blessing to the construction of an impressive lodge at the base of the slopes. To accommodate the increase in skiers expected as a result, Wirth also permitted further widening of existing ski runs and the relaunching of shuttle services to the Trail Ridge Road crossing.[56] To allow skiers to cross over Trail Ridge Road the NPS would also install two massive temporary snow tunnels that would be removed at the end of each ski season. This plan, hoped Wirth, would quiet local pressure for development while minimizing the visual impact of development upon the landscape.

Even landscape architect Harold Fowler, who supported the plan to install a full-length lift from the bottom of the ski area, warned Director Wirth of the dangers of half-measures. Installation of a new rope tow to the Trail Ridge Road crossing, argued Fowler, would bring "considerable agitation for additional ski lift facilities to make the upper slopes available" in due time. The NPS could, he cautioned, take "a very firm stand against the extension of lift developments beyond the upper road crossing," but he feared that once the NPS supported further development with the lodge, extended runs, and more lifts the NPS would be "plagued" by more pressure for further development.[57] On this count, Fowler was right.

Meanwhile, environmental groups and their leaders praised Wirth for withstanding local agitation. David Brower of the Sierra Club, Fred Packard of the National Parks Association, J. W. Penfold of the Izaak Walton League,

Burning slash for the construction of Hidden Valley Ski Area, 1954. Courtesy of Rocky Mountain National Park, ROMO MSF NEG 4919.

as well as Olaus Murie and Howard Zahniser of the Wilderness Society expressed relief that Wirth had not allowed the installation of a ski lift from the bottom of the valley to the top.[58] None of them, however, expressed concern over the development that had been approved or the future development it might necessitate.

In summer 1954 the *Denver Post* proudly reported that the NPS was launching a $350,000 development program, which it hoped would draw 2,500 people per day to the park in winter and help grow the state's "tourist crop." In addition to new rope tows and T-bars lower on the ski area, the NPS allowed concession holder I. B. James to install a removable T-bar from the Trail Ridge Road crossing to the top of the Big Drift (near the very top of Tombstone Ridge), which would be dismantled prior to the summer driving season. Although the approval marked a major step forward in the development of the valley, not everyone was pleased. Specifically, Hidden Val-

Cutting trees and loading logs in construction of Hidden Valley Ski Area, 1954. Courtesy of Rocky Mountain National Park, ROMO MSF NEG 1457.

ley Committee Chairman and EPCC Secretary Fred Clathworthy called the plan a "half way" measure while insisting that public pressure would eventually "force chair lift construction for 'maximum development' at double the presently planned cost."[59]

Despite some disappointment that the NPS had not gone far enough, many were enthusiastic in supporting better lifts, larger runs, improved shuttle service, and a luxurious lodge. Between October 1954 and December 1955, contractors labored to transform lower Hidden Valley into a first-class ski area. The lodge, once complete, offered equipment rentals, food, and a cozy place to rest tired legs while watching others ski. Revealing the excitement for the new and improved Hidden Valley, some 700 people attended the opening ceremony of the lodge for the 1955–1956 season.[60]

But not everyone was enamored with the new ski area. Chester McQueary, from Granby, Colorado, had spent time camping in Rocky in 1958 and was disgusted by the hypocrisy he saw. During two different presentations, park rangers explained the importance of protecting the "natural scene." Boiling, McQueary pointed to Hidden Valley as an example of a sanctioned "rape" where the parking "scab" and "steel-aluminum tow towers symbolize modern man's progress over nature's trees." The development of Hidden Valley, fumed McQueary, "betrayed the inherent principles of the National Park System and denied future generations a heritage which many men had long worked to preserve." In his acerbic closing, McQueary wished a "plague upon [Wirth's] house."[61] Though no one wrote a stronger letter of opposition to Hidden Valley, many felt the same deep emotions that flowed from McQueary's pen.

Although the opening of the new and improved Hidden Valley was attended with a great deal of enthusiasm in 1955, the excitement was short-lived. As early as 1958 the NPS and the concessionaire that ran Hidden Valley were facing a slew of problems, many of which threatened the viability of the ski area. Most troublesome was the fact that the existing lifts were not adequate. Wind had driven so much snow around the lift towers that they were rendered useless for a good deal of the 1957–1958 season, and the lifts were also prone to mechanical failure. For families who had traveled considerable distance to enjoy trouble-free and modern skiing at Hidden Valley, lift closures were more than frustrating. To address the issue, the concessionaires advocated installation of newer, higher-capacity permanent lifts.[62]

The increases in use that the new lodge, lifts, and parking area made possible also caused problems. As Fowler had earlier predicted, the improvements of the 1955 season brought more people to Hidden Valley. As early as 1958, however, the larger crowds necessitated more clearing of trees around the lodge, at the beginner's slope, and between upper and lower Hidden Valley. The lodge itself, thought Fowler, was also overcrowded and in need of further expansion in the near future.[63] Likewise, more rope tows were also in order.

Beyond mechanical failures and overcrowding, the Hidden Valley winds that so many saw as a boon quickly turned into a major headache. In addition to causing skier discomfort, the winds scoured many of the slopes of snow and made much of the area—especially at lower Hidden Valley—"not entirely useable." To address the issue, the concessionaires asked for permission to install snowmaking machines. These machines, which sprayed compressed air and water, could be used at night to make a "good blanket" of snow for the next morning. Hidden Valley Creek, which had already been rerouted to accommodate the lodge and lifts, provided the water to make the

Hidden Valley Ski Area parking lot, 1958. Courtesy of Rocky Mountain National Park, ROMO MSF NEG 4035.

snow.[64] The snow fairies that Fowler and others had hoped would show up nightly to smooth the runs and clear the parking lot had yet to appear.

But larger problems loomed. According to historian Annie Coleman, the late 1950s and early 1960s brought the development of some of the state's most popular winter destinations including "Aspen Highlands, Buttermilk, Crested Butte, Breckenridge, Ski Broadmoor, and Cuchara Basin." By 1967 other popular areas opened including Vail, Purgatory, and Sunlight. Year by year, Hidden Valley's market share was dwindling.

The 1959–1960 season revealed the shifting business landscape as weekend winter use of Hidden Valley dropped by more than 18 percent. The long lift lines and biting cold also brought more cases of frostbite, reaching an astounding six cases in just one day in February 1960.[65] Disappointing many, there was no snow on lower Hidden Valley on opening day, which further concentrated visitors on snow-covered areas, which in turn increased the number of accidents. This near-perfect storm of poor conditions was reflected in the ski area's bottom line. Although Hidden Valley generated more than $7,000 in net revenue for the concessionaires—ten times more than it had during its first year of full operation—it cost more than $52,000 for the NPS to keep the area open and visitors safe.[66] Likely hoping to save money, the concessionaires sometimes operated the ski area with only a skeleton crew, which faced withering criticism from disgruntled patrons. According to park officials, many of the employees subsequently adopted a "don't give a damn attitude and were rather curt with visitors."[67]

While Hidden Valley struggled, however, other major resorts around the state were redoubling their efforts to attract cash-laden skiers. In part, their efforts centered upon hiring experts to handle advertising campaigns to promote the resorts. In 1961, for example, Vail hired its first director of marketing.[68] In a business where branding and messaging were linked tightly to success, Hidden Valley was losing control of both its brand and its messaging.

Losing Hidden Valley

By the early 1970s pressure was again mounting to install a full chairlift at Hidden Valley. Chairlifts, supporters argued, offered an easier ascent of the slopes, a faster turnaround time for skiers, and better distribution of skiers across the mountain. Finally, nearly three decades after Aspen fired up its Lift No. 1, and after nearly thirty years of campaigning and cajoling by ski enthusiasts, the NPS granted the Rocky Mountain Park Company permission to install a chairlift at Hidden Valley in 1971. The new lift, the NPS rationalized, would also eliminate the need to clear Trail Ridge Road, the plowing of which was expensive and harmful to the trees adjacent to it.

Beyond saving roadside trees from the harm of winter plowing and reducing skier accidents, the NPS's ultimate justification for allowing the chairlift bears scrutiny. At the core of this latest decision to expand Hidden Valley was the belief that because the "ski operation is already an accomplished fact, it [was] the conviction of the National Park Service that the chair lift will improve rather than degrade the environmental situation at Hidden Valley."[69] In other words, the chief justification for further development rested firmly upon the fact that the NPS had allowed the ski resort to be there at all. What the NPS apparently failed to comprehend, however, was the long and slippery slope that brought the ski area to Hidden Valley in the first place and the role of the NPS in that process. Desire for year-round park use, pressure from local and regional organizations, changing demands for outdoor recreation, proximity to Trail Ridge Road, lack of other viable locations within the park, and rising demand driven by increased advertising and expanding facilities had all pushed the NPS toward the development of Hidden Valley. Now, the very existence of the ski area became justification enough for further development.

To clear the way for the new chairlift the NPS cut a 28-foot swath of spruce and fir trees more than a mile long from lower Hidden Valley to Trail Ridge Road. Using helicopters to pour the concrete and set the lift towers, the contractors constructed the chairlift parallel to the Columbine run. Although the lift did not run from the bottom of the mountain to the top, as many had called for, the installation of a modern chairlift marked an important development in the history of Hidden Valley, and boosters hoped that it would make Hidden Valley a more popular destination.

But the crowds were slow to come. During the 1969–1970 season, before the chairlift was installed, some 105,993 people enjoyed the facilities during one or more of the 117 days that the ski area was open. That number dipped to 86,342 during the following year and to 73,914 during the first full season that the chairlift was in operation. Although visitor use did rebound somewhat during the 1972–1973 season, with more than 80,000 people playing at Hidden Valley, by 1973–1974 just 56,527 people used the area. It had been nearly a decade since use at the resort had been so low.[70]

Hidden Valley now boasted a fully equipped three-story lodge, one chairlift, two T-bars, two J-Bar Pomas, expanded runs, a longer season, and the capacity to move some 3,800 skiers per hour. In the face of near perennial improvements, why were fewer and fewer people skiing Hidden Valley? As it turns out, a constellation of factors was responsible for the decline. First, by the 1970s skiers in the West generally and in Colorado specifically had more choices. When the NPS first allowed the development of Hidden Valley in the 1950s there were just a handful of ski areas around the state. By 1973 the Front Range alone was dotted with ten ski areas, some of which, like Loveland and Eldora, had multiple chairlifts and far better terrain.

More problematic for family ski areas like Hidden Valley was the fact that increasing numbers of skiers sought experiences beyond the joys of skiing itself. With each passing decade, more and more skiers sought plush accommodations, reliable, fast, high-capacity lifts, and commodious, well-groomed runs. They also sought a commercialized experience that put them in proximity to movie stars and the chance to be seen close to them. Fewer and fewer of those willing to invest the time and money required to ski sought the decidedly family-friendly atmosphere of places like Hidden Valley, and instead chose to experience places like Aspen.

Still others turned away from Hidden Valley because of the continued unreliability of its lifts. Between January and April 1973, rangers counted no less than twenty-three days for which the lift and tows at Hidden Valley were inoperable for some or all of the day. In at least one case, failure of the chairlift necessitated a rope rescue of those stranded on the lift. For those who lived in Estes Park the closings were little more than a nuisance. But for those who traveled from far away and lodged at Estes Park, days wasted waiting for lifts to get fixed were a major problem, especially in the face of alluring opportunities at higher-end resorts.

Still more problematic was the fact that snowfall was often less than abundant. In 1973, for example, the popular Platter Hill was open for less than a month due to insufficient snow. The drought also meant that the Rocky Mountain Park Company had to use its snowmaking machines to supplement Mother Nature's deficiencies. But these efforts, too, often fell short. According to the Park Service, the staff at the ski area was not all well trained in how to use the snowmaking equipment, and often it was improperly set up. Although the snowmaking machines sometimes produced good usable snow, they also often created so-called blue ice on the slopes that posed further hazards to skiers. Compounding matters, the runs at Hidden Valley were comparatively narrow, and many of the slopes designated for beginners required the use of difficult T-bar and Poma lifts to drag (sometimes literally) rookies up the hill. Many novices chose to avoid a punishing pull to the top of the mountain and instead rode the chairlift to the top of lower Hidden Valley. Once there, however, many faced terrain well beyond their skill level.[71] All of these factors combined meant that the accident rate at Hidden Valley was an exceptionally high .72 percent as compared to a national average of .4 percent.

If all of the above were not enough to dissuade would-be thrillseekers, comprehensive scientific study demonstrated conclusively that Hidden Valley was a very windy place indeed. Contrary to the hopes of early ski enthusiasts, who alleged that the gale-force winds blew only at night, researchers discovered that wind values at upper Hidden Valley and Trail Ridge Road were ranked *"among the highest occurring at known weather stations around the world."*[72] Some of the measurements taken from sample sites showed a daily maximum wind of 90 miles per hour. At the base of Hidden Valley, February winds reached 64 miles per hour for 14 percent of the month and peak gusts of 77 miles per hour were recorded. Researchers concluded that the base of the ski area "experiences high winds which can exceed hurricane-force." In March 1974 winds in excess of 80 miles per hour forced closure of the lift. A data-collection site was also established at nearby Deer Ridge and recorded a gust of wind in excess of 130 miles per hour in March.[73]

A new set of challenges was also rapidly emerging. Well into the 1950s park managers believed that because skiing took place on snow, which melted with the arrival of spring, the environmental impact of the activity was nearly benign. The rise of ecology, however, intensified scrutiny on the possible consequences of operations at Hidden Valley. Sewage studies, for example, demonstrated that the septic tanks at Hidden Valley were not adequate and that federal and state standards for clean water were not being met. The seasonal nature of Hidden Valley, with its heaviest use coming during the winter months when stream flows were low, meant that water pollution from Hidden Valley's septic systems was even more acute.[74] The nature of skiing and slope management also meant that snow was being unnaturally distributed throughout the valley and thus reshaping vegetation patterns. Because the area seldom received good, consistent snow, the use of snowmaking equipment was common. But it, too, was impacting the hydrology of the basin by reducing the stream flow below the ski area and by distributing that water up the drainage.[75] All of these issues combined, discovered researchers, were having negative consequences upon the greenback trout recovery within Hidden Valley Creek.[76]

It is difficult to imagine a set of factors more damning for a ski resort than those that surrounded Hidden Valley in the early 1970s. Poor employee morale, mechanical failures, inability to respond rapidly to market forces, poor snow, an extremely windy location, and growing recognition of the environmental impacts of skiing upon the park all worked to reshape the NPS's position on the ski area. Although the NPS had been directly responsible for allowing the birth and development of commercial skiing at Hidden Valley over the previous decades—including the installation of a modern chairlift just four years prior—it was backpedaling by the middle of the 1970s.

Then, in 1975, the NPS announced that it would allow only "minor" improvements at Hidden Valley that would enhance skier safety and prohibit all other major expansions. Further, the NPS intensified efforts to reduce the visibility of the ski area, set carrying capacity quotas to reduce congestion and accidents, and reduce the federal subsidy that had become "disproportionate in relation to other ski areas and to the very localized source of users."[77] Once viable alternatives became available in the region, the NPS stated that the ski area should be phased out.[78] Many people agreed with the move. At a public meeting held on the matter, some fifty individuals and twenty-four organizations supported keeping Hidden Valley as a ski area; more than 400 citizens and twenty-one organizations favored phasing it out.[79]

After negotiations to enhance some of the runs at Hidden Valley failed, concessionaires Ted and Ike James, who had owned the concession since 1953, requested that the NPS buy out the company's equipment and release them from the contract. The NPS eventually capitulated and agreed to a sale price of $750,000 with the understanding that the concessionaire would remove the chairlift. Perhaps hoping to keep some allies in Estes Park, the NPS transferred management to the Estes Park Valley Recreation and Parks Department.[80] Under its management, which began in 1978, the now-renamed Ski Estes Park continued to struggle. With just 60 skiable acres and poor conditions, still more skiers sought downhill thrills at resorts with more runs and better snow. Making matters worse, by the late 1980s the NPS was no longer willing to pay for repairs and maintenance at Hidden Valley (by now officially named Ski Estes Park at Hidden Valley). Instead, it sought a new contract with the parks department, which would effectively make it responsible for such costs.[81] This was not welcome news for the department, which lost an astounding $450,159 between 1983 and 1989 at Hidden Valley.[82]

Amid this latest hemorrhaging of cash, and hoping to improve skier safety and access to beginner runs, the NPS gave a green light to the parks department to install no less than two new chairlifts.[83] Less than two decades prior, the NPS had dismantled the one chairlift, citing both its landscape scar and the windy conditions that made its operation unsafe. The winds still blew down Hidden Valley, and two lifts would surely leave more of a visual intrusion than just one.[84]

In another maddening reversal, however, the NPS concluded that the proposed lifts would obviate the shuttle buses that had run up Trail Ridge Road since the removal of the original chairlift. Part of the rationale for installing the chairlift in the 1970s, we must remember, rested upon the fact that with a chairlift running to the Trail Ridge Road crossing the NPS would no longer have to plow the road, which would be good for the budget and the trees. When the NPS decided that it wanted the chairlift removed in the 1970s, it cited the lift's unsightly landscape scar as a leading reason. Removing the lift, however, meant that the NPS would once again be forced to plow Trail Ridge Road, which it well knew was not good for the trees along the road. Now, yet again, the NPS gave permission to install the two lifts in part to escape the burden of plowing and because, they argued, a "chair lift is more acceptable environmentally since it allows little disturbance to the terrain and trees." Had the NPS taken more care to understand the rationale for previous decisions at Hidden Valley, it may have—certainly should have—reached a different conclusion.

To be fair, the NPS was alert to the importance—perceived or otherwise—of the ski area to the community of Estes Park. The majority of Chamber of Commerce businesses supported the ski area and believed that it enhanced bottom lines. Reflecting such support, the citizens of Estes Park launched the Take Stock in Ski Estes Park program, which raised $44,000 for the ski area in 1989 alone. The town of Estes Park also spent $10,000 in advertising.[85] But adding more chairlifts, as the James brothers (the owners of the old concession) had earlier learned, would not be enough to transform Hidden Valley into a profitable enterprise, especially in a competitive market where fashion, a booming nightlife, and the chance to ski next to a movie star were all powerful factors that prospective skiers considered before booking a vacation.

In the end, the parks department did not move forward with plans to install the two chairlifts. In February 1992 the NPS announced that it would be closing—once and for all—the ski area.[86] In a fitting development, Vail Associates picked through the bones and purchased the Upper T-bar, the Aspen T-bar, and two Poma lifts.[87] Meanwhile, the NPS began the arduous task of erasing the ski area from the landscape with the removal of the buildings, concrete, and other materials that once made it a winter playground. By 2004 the work was complete, and today little more than swaths of trees cut through the valley bear witness to its rich human history.

Conclusion

Hidden Valley is a fitting—if somewhat ironic—name for a place that generations of park officials and businessmen sought to make popular. But in many ways it remained hidden, difficult to see for what it was. When some looked up the valley they saw pristine nature, whereas others saw prosperity, play, and endless joy under the winter sun. Still others saw a deeply historical landscape awash in human activity. What is clear, however, is that how we envision the valley, how we imagine that it is and how it should be, has proven to be a powerful force.

In this case the National Park Service dedicated significant resources to making Hidden Valley known while seeking to keep its human history hidden. The agency promoted the area through brochures and supported it through decades of subsidies. But the NPS also undertook an impressive array of activities that obscured its role in transforming the valley into a ski area. Through the efforts of rangers like Jack Moomaw and landscape architects like Harold Fowler, they sought to naturalize development by hiding— or removing during the summer—the cables, pulleys, towers, and massive snow tunnels needed to transform the valley into a winter playground. Likewise, the NPS buried the snowmaking equipment that created the illusion of copious winter snow and removed acres of stumpage that spoke to an earlier history of logging. More recently, the removal of the chairlifts, lift towers, T-bars, and buildings after the official closure of the ski area in 1992 (the 1990–1991 season was its last) tells us still more about how we make places like Rocky. Rather than leave a carcass of machinery to serve as a reminder of the complicated interplay between nature and culture, the NPS is waiting for the trees and shrubs to obscure the hopes and dreams that delivered such changes in the first place. But that decision, too, reveals powerful beliefs about nature and history.

Our desires, behaviors, beliefs, and regulations have played a central role in making Rocky Mountain National Park. This process has not been simple, consistent, or tidy. The park's history is complicated and contradictory precisely because it is a product of fluid human culture interacting with unpredictable and uncontrollable nonhuman forces.

For nearly a century the NPS, its agency partners, visitors, and scientists have envisioned many different parks at Rocky. Responding to, revealing, and sometimes entrenching the cultures of ecology and tourism, the NPS has drawn a mad and shifting assortment of imaginary polygons across the landscape. Inside, outside, and between each subdivision, some acts, some species, and some processes are deemed acceptable while others are strictly forbidden. National Park Service officials have drawn boundaries that distinguish between roadside trees and those in the remote corners of the park. They have drawn protective borders around elk, deer, and bighorn sheep but not always around coyotes, martens, and mountain lions. In some reaches of Rocky the NPS has allowed fire and bark beetles to return, but in others it eliminates them. At various times, protective boundaries have been drawn around nonnative fish, then around native imposters, and now around none at all. Park officials have drawn boundaries to foster solitude and contemplation, to segregate horses from hikers, and to open the park to automobiles, too.

This system of imaginary lines—and the rationales and assumptions that lurk beneath it—is remarkably telling. At any one time the subdivisions reveal prevailing attitudes about nature, beauty, purity, science, and right and wrong, just as they speak to political and institutional realities. As the NPS has discovered, however, humans are not alone in deciding where exactly those boundaries should be drawn and to what ends. The nonhuman world has very often had little regard for the ways that we have attempted to carve the park into discrete units.

The most important boundary—the one so proudly decreed in 1915 that brought Rocky into being—has also been difficult to maintain. Elk, wildfires, bark beetles, invasive plants and animals, and climate change have drawn into question the integrity of this border time and again. And the challenges keep coming. A recent study indicates, for example, that the "deposition of anthropogenic nitrogen" has "increased substantially over the past half century" near RMNP. The uptick in nitrogen, which is the "result of increased agricultural, industrial, and dispersed suburban development" in Denver and along the Front Range, now poses an enormous risk to the park. Although nitrogen is a "common limiting resource for plant growth," too much nitrogen initiates ecological changes including "increases in primary" plant production, "changes in diversity of both native and exotic species . . . plant susceptibility to stress . . . and acidification of soils."[1] Significant changes to plant communities over a large area can and will impact other members of the natural world, even if such impacts are not yet well understood. Denver—the power and influence of which were absolutely integral to the creation of Rocky Mountain National Park—now threatens the very place it brought into being as a function of that very same power and prosperity. As towns, cities, counties, and states across the American West chase the panaceas of tourism and recreation, they would do well to remember this.

The lessons go far beyond Denver and Rocky Mountain National Park. In 2007, travel generated more than $187 billion in the American West.[2] Likewise, outdoor recreation, which includes "trail sports, biking, camping, snow sports, water sports, fishing, hunting, wildlife watching, motorcycle riding, and off-roading," brought in an astonishing $255 billion in 2011— some 40 percent of the national total.[3] In response to such figures Governor Christine Gregoire of Washington, as president of the Western Governors Association, proclaimed that outdoor recreation "creates sustainable jobs and incomes" and that it is integral to the future health and prosperity of the region.[4] As Rocky Mountain National Park demonstrates, however, we must look askance at this gospel of sustainability. If tourism and recreation are to be centerpieces of the American West for generations to come, we must embrace them with our eyes wide open, knowing full well their power to remake the very places they seek to sell.

But tourism and recreation have not acted alone in making Rocky Mountain National Park. Ecology, which lapped upon the park's outer banks for generations, brought changes of its own. Whereas a good deal of the culture of tourism was dedicated to making the park consonant with both sublime perfection and convenience, those immersed in the science and culture of ecology were much more interested in how various aspects of the park functioned. As historian Donald Worster reminds us, however, "before committing ourselves too firmly" to ecology's "tutelage," we owe it to ourselves to "know our teacher better."[5] Even our best teachers do not have all of the answers all of the time.

In their zeal to return the park to what they understood as its natural state, those who favored an ecological view set about tinkering with the plants, animals, fires, waters, soils, and insects within the park—often with less than desirable results. They may have had the very best of intentions, but evolving scientific techniques and institutional realities have continually challenged what exactly restoration implies, requires, and allows. We need look no further than greenback trout, elk, and fire to see this. Like most of us, the NPS has too often mistaken the science of the day—even sound science—as final truth. But scientific inquiry is not thus designed. Rather, good science, like good history, uses new methods and innovative questions to challenge persisting assumptions and beliefs. Its advancement toward a knowable truth usually comes in dribs and drabs and seldom weathers the crush of time fully intact. As we ponder places like Rocky, we should remember this, too.

None of this means that Rocky Mountain National Park is less beautiful, less worthy of our esteem and love, or less deserving of the very best care we can give it. It does, however, demand that we come to terms with the role of humans and our history in making this magnificent place.

INTRODUCTION

1. For more on the many built aspects of national parks, see Linda Flint McClelland, *Building the National Parks: Historic Landscape Design and Construction* (Baltimore: Johns Hopkins University Press, 1998); Ethan Carr, *Wilderness by Design: Landscape Architecture and the National Park Service* (Lincoln: University of Nebraska Press, 1998).

2. William Cronon, "The Trouble with Wilderness: Or Getting Back to the Wrong Nature," in Char Miller and Hal Rothman (eds.), *Out of the Woods: Essays in Environmental History* (Pittsburgh: University of Pittsburgh Press, 1997), 28–50; see also Alston Chase, *Playing God in Yellowstone: The Destruction of America's First National Park* (Boston: Atlantic Monthly Press, 1986), ch. 3. Although I disagree with so much of what Chase argues, I agree when he states that "natural areas were not made less natural by human presence" (374).

3. Historian Paul Sutter argues that "one of the most pressing intellectual problems environmentalists face today is the affinity between environmental sentiment and consumerism." "How," he asks, "have we constructed nature as consumers?" Paul Sutter, *Driven Wild: How the Fight against Automobiles Launched the Modern Wilderness Movement* (Seattle: University of Washington Press, 2002), 263. Much of *Making Rocky Mountain National Park* aims to answer this core question.

4. For more on the role of imagination in shaping history, see Elliot West, *Contested Plains: Indians, Goldseekers, and the Rush to Colorado* (Lawrence: University Press of Kansas, 1998).

5. Earl Pomeroy and Hal Rothman both demonstrated, each in their own way, the power of expectations to shape both the tourists and the toured upon. See Hal Rothman, *Devil's Bargains: Tourism in the Twentieth Century American West* (Lawrence: University Press of Kansas, 1998); Earl Pomeroy, *In Search of the Golden West: The Tourist in Western America* (New York: Alfred A. Knopf, 1957).

6. The $5.3 billion for Colorado in 2011 is based on "marketable trips," which are those that can be and are influenced by advertising and marketing. The total spent by all domestic visitors to Colorado is a much higher $10.76 billion. Longwoods International, "Colorado Travel Year 2011," June 2012, http://www.colorado.com/sites/colorado.com/files/Colorado LongwoodsReport2011_3.pdf (accessed November 11, 2012), 23–24, 11.

7. I employ "culture of ecology" to speak to the popularization of core

ecological concepts and perspectives as received by the general public. As the following chapters demonstrate, there was seldom agreement between tourism and ecology, just as there were important—and
fluid—divisions within each.

8. For more on the role of science and important concepts of nature itself, see James Pritchard, *Preserving Yellowstone's Natural Conditions:
Science and the Perception of Nature* (Lincoln: University of Nebraska
Press, 1999); and Richard West Sellars, *Preserving Nature in the National Parks: A History* (New Haven: Yale University Press, 1997).

9. Adam Rome, *The Bulldozer in the Countryside: Suburban Sprawl and the
Rise of American Environmentalism* (Cambridge: Cambridge University Press, 2001); see also Kenneth T. Jackson, *Crabgrass Frontier: The
Suburbanization of the United States* (Oxford: Oxford University Press,
1985), ch. 13, "The Baby Boom and the Age of the Subdivision."

10. For more on the differences between *place* and *space* as discussed in
this book, and the role of culture in constructing them, see Yi-Fu
Tuan, *Space and Place: The Perspective of Experience* (Minneapolis:
University of Minnesota Press, 1977).

11. Karl Hess Jr., *Rocky Times in Rocky Mountain National Park: An Unnatural History* (Niwot: University Press of Colorado, 1993).

CHAPTER 1. MAKING A NATIONAL PARK

1. Enos Mills, *Rocky Mountain National Park* (New York: Doubleday, Page
and Company, 1924), 92.

2. Donald C. Swain, "The Passage of the National Park Service Act of 1916,"
Wisconsin Magazine of History 50, no. 1 (Autumn 1966).

3. Theodore Catton, *National Park, City Playground: Mount Rainer in the
Twentieth Century* (Seattle: University of Washington Press, 2006).
Catton finds a strong connection in the region between urban areas of
Seattle and Tacoma and the growth of national parks in their hinter-
lands.

4. William Wyckoff, *Creating Colorado: The Making of a Western American
Landscape, 1860–1940* (New Haven: Yale University Press, 1999), esp.
ch. 3, "Mountain Geographies."

5. William Cronon, *Nature's Metropolis: Chicago and the Great West* (New
York: W. W. Norton, 1991).

6. Wyckoff, *Creating Colorado*, 106.

7. Ibid., 117–118.

8. Charles Denison, *The Influence of the Climate of Colorado on the Ner-
vous System* (Denver: Richards, 1874), in Carl Abbot, Stephen Leonard,
and David McComb, *Colorado: A History of the Centennial State* (Niwot: University Press of Colorado, 1992), 230–231.

9. Abbot, Leonard, and McComb, *Colorado,* 233.

10. Wyckoff, *Creating Colorado,* 84.

11. Marguerite S. Shaffer, *See America First: Tourism and National Identity, 1880–1940* (Washington, DC: Smithsonian Institution Press, 2001), 137.

12. Wyckoff, *Creating Colorado,* 85.

13. Enos Mills, "A Bit of Autobiography" (unpublished manuscript) Western History Collection 236, Denver Public Library, Box 1, ff "23," 7.

14. Alexander Drummond, *Enos Mills: Citizen of Nature* (Boulder: University Press of Colorado, 1995), 57.

15. Mills, "A Bit of Autobiography," 7.

16. Drummond, *Enos Mills,* 57.

17. Enos Mills, "A Chance Meeting with John Muir" (unpublished draft), Western History Collection 236, Denver Public Library, Box 1, ff "18," 3.

18. Drummond, *Enos Mills,* 59; Mills, "A Chance Meeting with John Muir," 3–4.

19. Drummond, *Enos Mills,* 124–129.

20. Jack London's *Call of the Wild* was published first in 1903, and on several occasions Mills drew upon its imagery in his writing.

21. "Itinerary of Enos A. Mills," Western History Collection 236, Denver Public Library, Box 1, ff "11." Judging from a multitude of newspaper accounts from several states, Mills spoke more often of the economic value of trees and timber to audiences made up predominantly of men. When speaking to groups of women, however, Mills chose instead to emphasize the "sentimental" importance of trees. Not only does his flexible message reveal a bit about what was important (or supposed to be important) to men and women, but it also demonstrates Mills's less than concrete connection to a single ideology.

22. Drummond, *Enos Mills,* 202.

23. Ibid., 226.

24. J. Horace McFarland to James Ballinger, 20 July 1910, NARG79, Entry 6, Box 159, ff "Estes," 1, 3.

25. J. Horace McFarland to Thorndike Doland, 19 December 1911, Pennsylvania Historical Museum Commission, State Museum Building, Harrisburg, Pennsylvania. Manuscript Group 85, J. Horace McFarland Papers, File 80, ff "National Parks-Enos Mills." On file at Special Collections, Rocky Mountain National Park. Hereafter referred to as MF Collection; J. Horace McFarland to James Ballinger, 20 July 1910, NARG79, Entry 6, Box 159, ff "Estes," 1, 3.

26. Thorndike Doland to J. Horace McFarland, 10 December 1910, MF Collection.

27. Edmond Sholtz to Walter Fisher, 17 January 1911, NARG79, Entry 6, Box 159, ff "Estes II."

28. Edmund Sholtz to President Taft, 17 January 1911, NARG79, Box 159, ff "Estes II."

29. Chester Hitchings to Walter Fisher, 11 January 1911, NARG79, Entry 6, Box 159, ff "Estes II."

30. "Resolution of the Board of Country Commissioners and Citizens of Grand County," 18 January 1911, NARG79, Entry 6, ff "Estes."

31. Boulder County Metal Mining Association to President Taft, 8 August 1911, NARG79, Entry 6, Box 159, ff "Estes."

32. H. Bitner to President Taft, 30 December 1911, NARG79, Entry 6, Box 159, ff "Estes II," 1–2.

33. R. W. Johnson to President Taft, 3 January 1912, NARG79, Entry 6, Box 159, ff "Estes II."

34. Frederick Ross to Walter Fisher, 1 November 1911, NARG79 Box 159, ff "Estes"; Robert Speer to Walter Fisher, 2 November 1911, NARG79, Box 159, ff "Estes"; Denver Chamber of Commerce to Walter Fisher, 3 November 1911, NARG79 Box 159, ff "Estes"; Denver Real Estate Exchange to Walter Fisher, 25 November 1911, NARG79, Box 159, ff "Estes"; Crescent Realty and Investment Co. to Walter Fisher, 25 November 1911, NARG79, Entry 6, Box 161, ff "Miscellaneous."

35. Denver Chamber of Commerce to Walter Fisher, 7 September 1911, NARG79, Box 159, ff "Estes."

36. Memorandum George A. Ward, 27 November 1911, NARG79, Box 159, ff "Estes," 2.

37. Denver Chamber of Commerce to Walter Fisher, 18 November 1911, NARG79, Box 159, ff "Estes," 2.

38. Chief Clerk, Department of the Interior to Commissioner of General Land Office, 28 November NARG79, Box 159, ff "Estes."

39. Simon Guggenheim to Walter Fisher, 6 January 1912, NARG79, Box 159, ff "Estes II."

40. James Grafton Rogers, "The Creation of Rocky Mountain Park," *Trail and Timberline* (June 1965): 99, 100.

41. Robert Marshall to Enos Mills, 7 August 1912, NARG79, Entry 6, Box 161, ff "Miscellaneous."

42. "Rocky Mountain National Park, Colorado," Report to Accompany S. 6309, 63rd Cong., 3rd sess., House Miscellaneous Document 1275, 21.

43. Ibid., 22.

44. Ibid., 22–23.

45. James Grafton Rogers to Chief Clerk, Department of Interior, 26 September 1911, NARG79, Entry 6, Box 159, ff "Estes II."

46. James Grafton Rogers to Frederick Ross, 17 February 1913, NARG79, Entry 6, Box 161, ff "Miscellaneous," 1; ibid., 2, 4.

47. James Grafton Rogers to Robert Marshall, 15 March 1913, NARG79, Entry 6, Box 161, ff "Miscellaneous."

48. James Grafton Rogers to Ross, 14 October 1913, NARG79, Box 160, Entry 6, ff "Legislation," 1–2.

49. James Grafton Rogers to Thomas Patterson, 2 October 1913, NARG79, Box 160, Entry 6, ff "Legislation."

50. Enos Mills to James Grafton Rogers, 3 May 1914, MF Collection, 2–3.

51. "Bulletin from the Front Range Settler's League," 7 December 1914, NARG79, Entry 6, Box 159, ff "Estes IV"; Charles Edwin Hewes to President Wilson, 7 December 1914, NARG79, Entry 6, Box 159, ff "Estes IV"; Charles Edwin Hewes to Lane, 7 December 1914, NARG79, Entry 6, Box 159, ff "Estes IV."

52. Mark Daniels to Edwin Gillette, 22 December 1914, NARG79, Entry 6, Box 159, ff "Estes IV."

53. "Rocky Mountain National Park, Colorado," Report to Accompany S. 6309, 63rd Cong., 3rd sess., House Miscellaneous Document 1275, 21.

54. Edward Taylor, "Rocky Mountain National Park, Colorado," *Congressional Record*, S. 6309, 63rd Cong., 3rd sess., 2644–2646.

CHAPTER 2. A VAST MOVING CARAVAN

1. David Louter, *Windshield Wilderness: Cars, Roads, and Nature in Washington's National Parks* (Seattle: University of Washington Press, 2006).

2. The development of "backcountry" as a concept will be addressed thoroughly in Chapter 3.

3. Ronald A. Foresta, *America's National Parks and Their Keepers* (Washington, DC: Resources for the Future, 1984), esp. ch. 2, "The First Fifty Years" at [do we need the at here? 9–57.

4. Peter Blodgett, "Selling the Scenery: Advertising and the National Parks, 1916–1933," in David Wrobel and Patrick Long (eds.), *Seeing and Being Seen: Tourism in the American West* (Lawrence: University Press of Kansas, 2001).

5. Union Pacific Railroad, "Colorado for the Tourist" (1911). Estes Park Museum, Box Railroad Advertisements and Souvenirs.

6. *Estes Park Trail*, 27 June 1913.

7. Ibid.

8. *Estes Park Trail*, 7 September 1912.

9. Rocky Mountain National Park Superintendent's Annual Report, 1915 and 1924, Rocky Mountain National Park Library. Hereafter cited as

Superintendent's Annual Report. The annual reports were compiled and bound in two volumes in the RMNP Library (1915–1930 and 1931–1953).

10. *New York Times*, 31 May 1925.

11. James Pickering, *America's Switzerland: Estes Park and Rocky Mountain National Park—The Growth Years* (Boulder: University Press of Colorado, 2005), 185.

12. Superintendent's Annual Report, 1918.

13. Pickering, *Switzerland*, 185.

14. Ibid.

15. U.S. Department of the Interior, *Rocky Mountain National Park, Colorado* (Washington, DC: U.S. Department of the Interior, 1927), 4. Estes Park Museum, Box General Advertisements, ff "RMNP Brochures Folder 1."

16. *Rules and Regulations Rocky Mountain National Park, Colorado* (Washington, DC: U.S. Department of the Interior, 1927), 12–16. Estes Park Museum, Box General Advertisements, ff "RMNP Brochures Folder 1."

17. Superintendent's Annual Report, 1915.

18. Superintendent's Annual Report, 1920.

19. Ibid.

20. Superintendent's Annual Report, 1923.

21. Lloyd K. Musselman, *Rocky Mountain National Park Administrative History, 1915–1965* (Washington, DC: U.S. Department of the Interior, National Park Service, 1971), at http://www.nps.gov/romo/historyculture /upload/chapter6.pdf (accessed September 1, 2007).

22. Superintendent's Annual Report, 1926.

23. Ibid., 1928.

24. Ibid., 1929.

25. Ibid., 1929 and 1931.

26. Ibid., 1929.

27. Ibid., 1932.

28. Linda Flint McClelland, *Building the National Parks: Historic Landscape Design and Construction* (Baltimore: Johns Hopkins University Press, 1998), 187.

29. Linda Flint McClelland, *Presenting Nature: The Historic Landscape Design of the National Park Service, 1916 to 1942* (Washington, D.C.: U.S. Government Printing Office, 1993), 115–137.

30. McClelland, *Building the National Parks*, 195–196.

31. Ibid., 197–198.

32. Ibid., 202–204.

33. Charles Eliot II, "Landscape Problems in Rocky Mountain National Park," NARG79 Box 400, ff "Rocky Mountain Administration and Personnel Reports," 3 July 1930, 12.

34. *Estes Park Trail*, 15 July 1932.

35. Superintendent's Annual Report, 1918.

36. Rocky Mountain National Park Superintendent's Monthly Report, September 1921, Rocky Mountain National Park Library. Hereafter cited as Superintendent's Monthly Report.

37. Superintendent's Annual Report, 1930.

38. Ibid.

39. Superintendent's Monthly Report, July 1933.

40. Ibid., August 1933.

41. Eliot, "Landscape Problems," 2–3.

42. Superintendent's Monthly Report, July 1932.

43. Ibid., September 1933.

44. Ibid., July 1942.

45. Superintendent's Annual Report, 1942.

46. Ibid., 1943.

47. Superintendent's Annual Report, 1931; Superintendent's Draft Annual Report, 1943.

48. Adam Rome, *The Bulldozer in the Countryside: Suburban Sprawl and the Rise of American Environmentalism* (Cambridge: Cambridge University Press, 2001).

49. Hal Rothman, *Devil's Bargains: Tourism in the Twentieth-Century American West* (Lawrence: University Press of Kansas, 1998).

50. Conrad Wirth, *Parks, Politics, and the People* (Norman: University of Oklahoma Press, 1980), 261.

51. Superintendent's Annual Report, 1951.

52. Bernard DeVoto, "Let's Close the National Parks," *Harper's Magazine* (October 1953): 49–52.

53. Mrs. Veit to Lyndon B. Johnson, 28 July 1957, National Archives, Kansas City, Record Group 79, Box A2, Book 1, September 1952–January 1960, ff "ROMO." Hereafter cited as NAKCRG79.

54. C. W. Buchholtz, *Rocky Mountain National Park: A History* (Boulder: Colorado Associated University Press, 1983), 202. Most recently, National Park Service historian Sarah Allaback has completed a study on the relationship between Mission 66 and shifting patterns in architecture in national parks. Especially helpful is her chapter regarding the construction of three new visitor centers within Rocky Mountain National Park. Although her study is rather complete, her interest lies less with RMNP and more with the broader trends within the NPS as related to Mission 66 architecture. Sarah Allaback, *Mission 66 Visitor Centers: The History of a Building Type* (Washington, D.C.: U.S. Department of the Interior, National Park Service, 2000).

55. Wirth, *Parks,* 239.

56. Ibid., 241.

57. Ibid., 258.

58. "Final Rocky Mountain National Park Mission 66 Prospectus, 1957," NAKCRG79, Box A98, 3-8-55 to 2-8-56, ff "Mission 66," 5–6; James Lloyd to Frank Cooper, 23 October 1956, NAKCRG79, Box A98, 3-8-55 to 2-8-56, ff "Mission 66."

59. "Draft Mission 66 Prospectus," 20 July 1955, NAKCRG79, Box A98, 3-8-55 to 2-8-56, ff "Mission 66."

60. "Bear Lake Traffic Study," 30 August 1956, National Archives Denver Record Group 79, Numerical Subject Files 1953–1965, Box 2, 8ns-079-97-437, ff "Travel Studies and Stats RMNP," 1–2. Hereafter cited as NADRG79.

61. Superintendent's Monthly Report, September 1957.

62. RMNP Monthly Progress Reports 1957–1963 in Superintendent's Monthly reports 1957–1963.

63. Memorandum, Acting Superintendent Rocky Mountain to Regional Director Midwest Region, 29 August 1963. NADRG79 Numerical Subject Files 1953–1965, Box 2, 8ns-079-97-437, ff "A9819."

64. James Lloyd to Conrad Wirth, 20 July 1955, NAKCRG79, Box A98, 3-8-55 to 2-8-56, ff "Mission 66."

65. Ibid.

66. Bill Ladd to Conrad Wirth, NAKCRG79 Box A2, Book 1, September 1952–January 1960, ff "ROMO," 1.

67. Ibid., 3.

68. Maren Thompson Bzdek and Janet Ore, "The Mission 66 Program at Rocky Mountain National Park: 1947–1973" (Colorado State University: Public Lands History Center, 2010), 17–18.

69. Wirth, *Parks*, 268–270.

70. Allaback, *Mission 66*, 2.

71. John Marr and Beatrice Willard, "Effects of Visitors on Natural Ecosystems in Rocky Mountain National Park, Final Report 1958–1959" (Institute of Arctic and Alpine Research, University of Colorado, 1959, mimeographed), 4.

72. Ibid., 5.

73. Ibid., 28.

74. Ibid., 43.

75. Ibid., 18.

76. John Marr and Beatrice Willard, "Effects of Visitors on Natural Ecosystems in Rocky Mountain National Park, Final Report 1960–1961" (Institute of Arctic and Alpine Research, University of Colorado, 1960, mimeographed), 4.

77. For a comprehensive look at the changing nature of environmental

thought in the postwar era, see Samuel P. Hays, *Beauty, Health, and Permanence: Environmental Politics in the United States, 1955–1985* (Cambridge: Cambridge University Press, 1989).

78. R. Burnell Held, Stanley Brickler, and Arthur T. Wilcox, "A Study to Develop Criteria for Determining the Carrying Capacity of Areas within the National Park System, Final Report" (Department of Recreation and Watershed Resources, Colorado State University, 15 November 1969, mimeographed).

79. Ibid., 23–24.

80. Ibid., 4–5.

81. Richard H. Quin, "Written Historical and Descriptive Data," Rocky Mountain National Park Roads, Historic American Engineering Record (National Park Service, U.S. Department of the Interior, 1993) http://lcweb2.loc.gov/pnp/habshaer/co/co0300/co0351/data/co0351data.pdf (accessed 4 April 2013), 67.

82. "Rocky Mountain National Park Transportation Study, Summary Report" (Parsons, Brinckerhoff, Quade, and Douglas, Denver, 2000), Figure 1-3.

83. *Estes Park Trail*, 19 June 1981.

84. *Estes Park Trail*, 5 December 1979.

85. Ibid.

86. *Estes Park Trail*, 5 February 1982.

87. Barbara J. Keller and Louis Bender, "Influence of Traffic and Road-Related Disturbance on Rocky Mountain Bighorn Sheep (*Ovis canadensis canadensis*) Use of the Sheep Lakes Mineral Site" (U.S. Geological Survey, New Mexico Cooperative Fish and Wildlife Research Unit, Las Cruces, New Mexico, March 2004), 2–3.

88. It should be remembered that the location of their study area coincides with the area where rangers placed salt blocks in 1918 to attract sheep and tourists.

89. Keller and Bender, "Influence of Traffic," 2–4.

90. "Rocky Mountain National Park Transportation Study," 1.

CHAPTER 3. HAPPY TRAILS

1. Isabella L. Bird, *A Lady's Life in the Rocky Mountains*, 2nd ed. (London: John Murray, 1879), 94.

2. C. W. Buchholtz, *Rocky Mountain National Park: A History* (Niwot: University Press of Colorado, 1983), 73.

3. Bird, *A Lady's Life*, 123.

4. Marjorie Hope Nicolson, *Mountain Gloom and Mountain Glory: The Development of the Aesthetics of the Infinite* (Seattle: University of Washington Press, 1997).

5. Bird, *A Lady's Life*, 97–98.

6. Ibid., 114, 120.

7. Buchholtz, *Rocky Mountain*, 73, 78.

8. Ibid., 73.

9. Lawrence R. Borne, *Dude Ranching: A Complete History* (Albuquerque: University of New Mexico Press, 1983), 4.

10. Ibid., 6.

11. Ibid., 18.

12. Ibid., 35.

13. *Elkhorn Lodge, Estes Park, Colorado* (Mrs. W. E. James and Sons, circa 1907), Estes Park Museum, ff "Hotels and Lodges, Elkhorn Lodge."

14. Rocky Mountain National Park Superintendent's Annual Report, 1915, Rocky Mountain National Park Library, Rocky Mountain National Park. Hereafter cited as Superintendent's Annual Report.

15. Ibid., 1918.

16. *Circular of Information regarding Rocky Mountain National Park*, NARG79, Central Classified Files 1907–1949, 07-32, Entry 7, Box 415, 6.

17. Ibid., 9.

18. Ibid., 21.

19. Superintendent's Annual Report, 1922.

20. Ruth Alexander, *People and Nature on the Mountaintop: A Resource and Impact Study of Longs Peak in Rocky Mountain National Park* (Center for Public History and Archeology, Colorado State University, 2010), 14–16.

21. Ibid., 11, 17.

22. "Five Year Development Program," 29 April 1925, NARG79, Central Classified Files 1907–1949, 07-32, Entry 7, Box 400, ff "Five Year Development Program."

23. *Circular of Information regarding Rocky*, 33.

24. Superintendent's Annual Report, 1922.

25. Ibid., 1923.

26. Ibid., 1923–1930.

27. Ibid., 1932.

28. Arthur Draper to Superintendent Thos. J. Allen, 18 July 1936, NARG79 Superintendent's Annual Narrative Reports 1980–2001, Box 45, Entry P17, ff "Rocky Mountain National Park."

29. Superintendent Thos. J. Allen to Arthur Draper, 22 July 1936, NARG79 Superintendent's Annual Report, 1980–2001, Box 45, Entry P17, ff "Rocky Mountain National Park."

30. "Information Bulletin Rocky Mountain National Park" (U.S. Department of the Interior, National Park Service, 9 November 1940), NARG79 Superintendent's Annual Report 1980–2001, Box 45, Entry P17, ff "Rocky Mountain National Park."

31. ROMO Superintendent Memoranda to Director, 23 July 1941, NARG79 Superintendent's Annual Report, 1980–2001, Box 45, Entry P17, ff "Rocky Mountain National Park."

32. "Report of Mountain Climbing Safety Activities in Rocky Mountain National Park, July 1941," NARG79 Superintendent's Annual Report, 1980–2001, Box 45, Entry P17, ff "Rocky Mountain National Park."

33. Superintendent's Annual Report, 1948.

34. Ibid., 1950.

35. J. V. K. Wagar, "Visitor Concepts of National Park Policies and Conservation Needs" (Colorado State College, no date), NARG79 Central Classified Files 1933–1949, Box 1573, ff "Inspirational Activities."

36. Louis Weinberg to Newton Drury, 15 October 1945, NARG79 Central Classified Files 1933–1949, Box 1572, ff "ROMO Accidents 945 case No. 36 Accident report."

37. Superintendent's Annual Report, 1945.

38. Ibid., 1953.

39. Robert Kahn to Superintendent Canfield, 19 July 1953, NARG79, Box 395, ff "A 3619 ROMO pt 1."

40. "A Report to the Superintendent for A Back Country Management Plan in Rocky Mountain National Park" (U.S. Department of the Interior, 1965), Rocky Mountain National Park Library, i–iii.

41. Ibid., 4–8.

42. Ibid., 8, 12, 14.

43. Ibid., 19–21, 38.

44. Ibid., 48, 52, 55.

45. "Hearing on Proposed Wilderness in Rocky Mountain National Park," 26 January 1974, Rocky Mountain National Park Library, 8.

46. For a thorough exploration of the impacts of wilderness on the management of Longs Peak, see Ruth Alexander, "The Diamond, the Cable Route, and Wilderness Values on Longs Peak in the 1960s," in Alexander, *People and Nature*.

47. Alexander, *People and Nature*, 50–51, 58.

48. Ibid., 58, 60.

49. Ibid., 67; Joe Arnold, "Performance Evaluation of Backcountry Solar Toilets" (Rocky Mountain National Park, 8 January 2010), at http://www.americanalpineclub.org/uploads/mce_uploads/Files/PDF/Solar_Toilet_Report.pdf (accessed 10 October 2012), 4.

50. *Estes Park Trail*, 28 April 1972.

51. Arnold, "Performance Evaluation," 3; Alexander, *People and Nature*, 67.

52. "Hearing on Proposed Wilderness," 22.

53. Ibid., 26.

54. Thomas Bulat to Secretary Hickel, Department of the Interior, 8 Sep-

tember 1970, NARG79 Administration Files 1949–1971, Box 2645, Entry P11, ff "A3615 ROMO Part 1."

55. Theodore Thompson to Thomas Bulat, 15 October 1970, NARG79 Administration Files 1949–1971, Box 2645, Entry P11, ff "A3615 ROMO Part 1."

56. "Hearing on Proposed Wilderness," 29–33.

57. "Rocky Mountain National Park Final Master Plan" (U.S. Department of the Interior, National Park Service, January 1976,) 11.

58. Ibid., 19.

59. *Estes Park Trail-Gazette*, 26 May 1972.

60. "Final Master Plan," 12.

61. Ibid. For more on the role of freedom in conceptions of wilderness, see Sutter, *Driven Wild*, ch. 6, "The Freedom of Wilderness: Bob Marshall," 194–238.

62. "Final Master Plan," 24.

63. "Task Directive: Trail System Analysis Rocky Mountain National Park" (National Park Service, Denver Service Center, 17 April 1979), 3.

64. Libbie Landreth, "A Comparative Analysis of Backpackers Using Designated Sites and Crosscountry Zones in Rocky Mountain National Park" (Master's thesis, University of Wyoming, 1979), 2.

65. "Commercial Horse Use Management Plan and Environmental Assessment, Rocky Mountain National Park, Colorado" (National Park Service, Denver Service Center, 1994), 33–34.

66. *Estes Park Trail-Gazette*, 4 July 1980.

67. Ibid., 25 March 1981.

68. Mary Benniger, "Trails as Conduits of Movement for Plant Species in Coniferous Forests of Rocky Mountain National Park, Colorado" (Master's thesis, Miami University [Oxford, OH], 1989), ii.

69. Ibid., 1, 19.

70. "Horse Management Plan," i.

71. Ibid., 32, 45.

72. *Estes Park Trail-Gazette*, 23 February 1994.

73. "Wilderness Experience in Rocky Mountain National Park," Report to RMNP (National Park Service, January 2004), at http://www.fort.usgs.gov/Products/Publications/21181/21181.pdf (accessed June 1, 2012), 45–46.

CHAPTER 4. OUR FRIENDS THE TREES

1. Christopher Hussey, *The Picturesque: Studies in a Point of View*, 2nd ed. (London: Frank Cass, 1967), 83; Ethan Carr, *Wilderness by Design: Landscape Architecture and the National Park Service* (Lincoln: University of Nebraska Press, 1998), 11–12.

2. Francis K. Pohl, *Framing America: A Social History of American Art* (New York: Thames & Hudson, 2002), 235.

3. Angela Miller, *The Empire of the Eye: Landscape Representation and American Cultural Politics, 1825–1875* (Ithaca: Cornell University Press, 1993), 11–13.

4. Ibid., 28.

5. Ibid., 29–30.

6. Conjuring images of destruction and imbalance through trees and stumps was no fleeting phenomenon. Nearly a century and a half after Cole finished his brilliant series, another master, Dr. Seuss, also drew upon the power of trees to move audiences through the pages of *The Lorax*. In his world of the Once-ler and his frivolous Thneeds, we witness a tale of greed and destruction as told through the Truffula Trees, and the Humming-Fish, Swomee-Swans, and Bar-ba-loots that depended upon them.

7. Carr, *Wilderness by Design*, 11.

8. Ibid., 23.

9. Enos Mills, "Our Friends the Trees," Western History Collection 236, Denver Public Library, Box 1, Envelope 3, date unknown, 2. Western History Collection hereafter cited as WHC.

10. Ibid., 4–5, 7.

11. Enos Mills and WGM Stone, Brochure, "Forests and Trees: An Arbor Day Souvenir" (Denver: Denver Chamber of Commerce and Board of Trade, 1905), WHC 236, Box 2, ff "39," 3.

12. Charles Eliot, *Garden and Forest*, 26 August 1896, in Linda Flint McClelland, *Building the National Parks: Historic Landscape Design and Construction* (Baltimore: Johns Hopkins University Press, 1998), 49.

13. McClelland, *Building the National Parks*, 50–51.

14. "Report on an Examination of the Area Proposed Rocky Mountain of the (Estes) National Park, Colorado" (National Park Service, 9 January 1913), WHC 236, Box 2, M1403, ff "42," 5.

15. Union Pacific Railroad Company, Brochure, "Where the Rockies Reign Supreme" (1913), Estes Park Museum, Box MSH07 RR Souvenirs, 18.

16. Christine Macy and Sarah Bonnemaison, *Architecture and Nature: Creating the American Landscape* (London: Routledge, 2003), 97.

17. Ibid., 71.

18. "Bark Beetle Management Plan Environmental Assessment" (U.S. Department of the Interior, National Park Service, 2005), at http://www.nps.gov/romo/parkmgmt/upload/pine_beetle_ea_07–05.pdf5 (accessed 1 June 2012), 5–6.

19. Heather J. Lynch, Roy A. Renkin, Robert L. Crabtree, and Paul R. Moorcroft, "The Influence of Previous Mountain Pine Beetle (*Dendroctonus*

ponderosae) Activity on the 1988 Yellowstone Fires," *Ecosystems* 9, no. 8 (December 2006): 1325.

20. Hal K. Rothman, "A Test of Adversity and Strength: Wildland Fire in the National Park System" (U.S. Department of the Interior, National Park Service), 31; Rocky Mountain National Park Superintendent's Annual Report, Rocky Mountain National Park Library, 1916. Hereafter cited as Superintendent's Annual Report.

21. Superintendent's Annual Report, 1916.

22. Rothman, "A Test of Adversity," 35, 40.

23. Annual Report of the Secretary of the Interior, 1918, 1918–1975, in Mc-Clelland, *Building the National Parks*, 134.

24. Annual Report of the Secretary of the Interior, 1919, 941, in McClelland, *Building the National Parks*, 138.

25. Rothman, "A Test of Adversity," 46.

26. Donald H. Robinson, *Through the Years in Glacier National Park: An Administrative History* (n.l.: Glacier Natural History Association, 1960), at http://www.nps.gov/history/history/online_books/glac/index.htm (accessed 20 March 2012).

27. Rothman, "A Test of Adversity," 54.

28. Superintendent's Annual Reports, 1927, 1928, 1930.

29. *Rocky Mountain National Park: Mountain Pine Beetle* (National Park Service, 9 August 2000), at http://www.nps.gov/romo/planyourvisit/upload/mountain_pine_beetle_2007.pdf (accessed 6 June 2012), 1–2.

30. Ibid., 2.

31. F. E. Clements, "The Life History of Lodgepole Burn Forests," *United States Forest Service Bulletin* 79 (1910).

32. Donald Worster, *Nature's Economy: A History of Ecological Ideas*, 2nd ed. (Cambridge: Cambridge University Press, 1994), 209.

33. Clements, "The Life History," 8–9.

34. Ibid., 11–12, 23–24.

35. Ibid., 54.

36. Rothman, "A Test of Adversity," 48–49.

37. J. D. Coffman, "1930 Report on Fire Protection Requirements of Rocky Mountain National Park," NARG79 Central Classified Files 1907–1949, Box 414, Entry P10, 2.

38. Ibid., 3–4.

39. Superintendent's Annual Report, 1932.

40. Superintendent's Monthly Report, September 1932.

41. Rothman, "A Test of Adversity," 63–64.

42. Superintendent's Annual Report, 1933.

43. Ibid., 1941.

44. Ibid., 1942.

45. Ibid., 1943.
46. Ibid., 1945. For more on the role of chemicals, including DDT, in the postwar world, see Edmund Russell, *War and Nature: Fighting Humans and Insects with Chemicals from World War I to* Silent Spring (Cambridge: Cambridge University Press, 2001), chs. 8–10.
47. Superintendent's Annual Report, 1946.
48. Ibid., 1950.
49. Ibid., 1950, 1951.
50. Eldon Knecht to Phil Weaver, 31 August 1956, NARG79 Correspondence Subject Files 1928–1959, Box 179, Entry P84, ff "Suppression."
51. Rothman, "A Test of Adversity," 89.
52. Ibid., 91–94.
53. Harold Weaver, "Fire and Management Problems in Ponderosa Pine Forests" (Proceedings of the Annual Tall Timbers Fire Ecology Conference, 1964), http://nps01.origin.cdn.level3.net/seki/naturescience/up load/hw_tt64.pdf (accessed 20 March 2012), 2.
54. Ibid., 7.
55. Richard West Sellars, *Preserving Nature in the National Parks: A History* (New Haven: Yale University Press, 1997), 200–201.
56. A. S. Leopold, S. A. Cain, C. M. Cottam, I. N. Gabrielson, T. L. Kimball, "Wildlife Management in the National Parks" (Washington, D.C.: National Park Service, U.S. Government Printing Office, 1963), 5.
57. Ibid.
58. Ibid.
59. Sellars, *Preserving Nature*, 244. As Sellars points out, the embrace of the document did not always—or often—reflect the full implementation of its recommendation and core philosophies.
60. Rothman, "A Test of Adversity," 109.
61. B. M. Kilgore, "Fire Management in the National Parks: An Overview" (Proceedings of the Tall Timbers Fire Ecology Conference, 1976), 45.
62. Rothman, "A Test of Adversity," 130.
63. Kilgore, "Fire Management," 48.
64. "Let 'Em Burn," *Time* 104, no. 18 (28 October 1974), 67.
65. "Final Master Plan, Rocky Mountain National Park, 1976" (National Park Service, 1976), 14. RMNP first promulgated a fire management policy in 1973 and revised it in 1974 and again in 1975.
66. Ibid.
67. "Rocky Mountain National Park and Shadow Mountain Recreation Area Wildland Fire Management Plan, Part I—Fire Control" (National Park Service, 1977), Denver Service Center, 1.
68. Sellars, *Preserving Nature*, 244.
69. "Rocky Mountain National Park and Shadow Mountain," 1–2.

70. Richard D. Laven, "Natural Fire Management in Rocky Mountain National Park: A Case Study of the Ouzel Fire," n.d. (circa 1978), Denver Service Center, 38.

71. Ibid., 41.

72. Rothman, "A Test of Adversity," 171–172.

73. *Estes Park Trail-Gazette*, 15 July 1988.

74. Jason S. Sibold, Thomas T. Veblen, and Mauro E. González, "Spatial and Temporal Variation in Historic Fire Regimes in Subalpine Forests across the Colorado Front Range in Rocky Mountain National Park, Colorado, USA," *Journal of Biogeography* 32 (2006), 644–645.

75. Arne Buechling and William Baker, "A Fire History from Tree Rings in a High-Elevation Forest of Rocky Mountain National Park," *Canadian Journal of Forest Research* 34 (2004), 1259.

76. William L. Baker, Thomas T. Veblen, and Rosemary L. Sherriff, "Fire, Fuels, and Restoration of Ponderosa Pine–Douglas Fir Forests in the Rocky Mountains, USA," *Journal of Biogeography* 34 (2007), 251.

77. *United States Forest Service Bark Beetle Fact Sheet, 2011*, at http://www.fs.usda.gov/main/barkbeetle/home (accessed 30 March 2012), 2.

78. Ibid.

79. Herbert C. Frost, "The Impacts of Climate Change on National Parks in Colorado and Related Management Activities" (Senate Subcommittee on National Parks, 24 August 2009), at http://www.gpo.gov/fdsys/pkg/CHRG-111shrg52524/html/CHRG-111shrg52524.htm (accessed 1 October 2012), 2.

80. "Bark Beetle Management Plan," 17. The NPS earlier used a diluted carbaryl solution to protect the "high capital investment" that the NPS had made in the "high value" trees planted in the Aspenglen Campground after the Lawn Lake flood. The NPS also used Banvel, Round-Up, and Telar to treat small portions of the park for the invasive Canada thistle and leafy spurge. *Estes Park Trail-Gazette*, 5 August 1987.

81. "Bark Beetle Management Plan," 20.

82. "Protection of High Value Trees and Hazard Mitigation Projects Continue in 2010 at Rocky Mountain National Park," at http://www.nps.gov/romo/parknews/pr_beetle_mitigation_2010.htm (accessed 16 April 2012.)

83. Bayer Crop Science, *SEVIN brand XLR PLUS Carbaryl Insecticide Fact Sheet*, at http://www.entomology.umn.edu/cues/cwlb/labels/SevinXLRplus.pdf. (accessed 9 April 2012), 2.

CHAPTER 5. GROWING ELK

1. "Elk and Vegetation Management Plan, Rocky Mountain National Park, Colorado" (Washington, D.C.: U.S. Government Printing Office, 2007), v.

2. Bart W. O'Gara and Robert G. Dundas, "Distribution: Past and Present," in Dale E. Toweill and Jack Ward Thomas (eds.), *North American Elk: Ecology and Management* (Washington, D.C.: Smithsonian Institution Press, 2002), 68.

3. John G. Crook, "Nutrition and Food," in Toweill and Thomas (eds.), *North American Elk*, 260.

4. Robert J. Hudson, and Jerry C. Haigh, with the assistance of Anthony B. Bubenik, "Physical and Physiological Adaptations," in Toweill and Thomas (eds.), *North American Elk*, 200.

5. Crook, "Nutrition and Food," 277, 281.

6. "Elk and Vegetation Management Plan, Rocky Mountain National Park, Colorado" (Washington, D.C.: U.S. Government Printing Office, 2007), 1.

7. Valerius Geist, "Adaptive Behavior Strategies," in Toweill and Thomas (eds.), *North American Elk*, 418.

8. Ibid., 420.

9. Hudson, "Physical and Physiological Adaptations," 241.

10. Ibid., 242, 246.

11. *Colorado for the Tourist* (Union Pacific Railroad: 1911), Estes Park Museum, Box MSH07 RR Souvenirs, 32.

12. *Colorado Mountain Playgrounds* (Union Pacific Railroad: 1924), Estes Park Museum, Box MSH07 RR Souvenirs, 8–10.

13. James H. Pickering, *This Blue Hollow: Estes Park—The Early Years, 1859–1915* (Boulder: University Press of Colorado, 1999), 94–95.

14. "Elkhorn Lodge Estes Park Colorado" (circa 1918), Estes Park Museum, ff "Hotels and Lodges, Elkhorn Lodge," 13.

15. "Elk and Vegetation Management Plan, Rocky Mountain National Park, Colorado" (Washington, D.C.: U.S. Government Printing Office, 2007), 14.

16. *Estes Park Trail*, 25 July 1914; Superintendent's Annual Report, 1915.

17. Superintendent's Monthly Report, October 1917.

18. Ibid., November 1917.

19. Superintendent's Annual Report, 1918.

20. Superintendent's Monthly Report, April 1918.

21. "Elk and Vegetation Management Plan," 1.

22. Superintendent's Annual Report, 1915; for more on the NPS and predators, see Richard West Sellars, *Preserving Nature in the National Parks* (New Haven: Yale University Press, 1997), 69–75.

23. Superintendent's Annual Report, 1917; Superintendent's Monthly Report, February 1917.

24. Ibid., April 1917.

25. Ibid., September 1919.

26. Ibid., December 1919; April 1920.

27. Ibid., December 1920.

28. Ibid., January 1922.

29. Ibid., February 1922.

30. Ibid., October 1922.

31. Ibid., December 1926.

32. Superintendent's Annual Report, 1926.

33. Superintendent's Monthly Report, March 1927.

34. R. Gerald Wright, *Wildlife Research and Management in the National Parks* (Chicago: University of Illinois Press, 1992), 13.

35. Sellars, *Preserving Nature,* 87.

36. Ibid., 91.

37. Ibid., 96.

38. George M. Wright, Joseph S. Dixon, and Ben H. Thompson, *Fauna of the National Parks of the United States: A Preliminary Survey of Faunal Relations in the National Parks, Contributions of Wildlife Survey, Fauna Series No. 1* (Washington, D.C.:. U.S. Government Printing Office, 1933), 1.

39. Ibid., 107–108.

40. Ibid., 41.

41. Sellars, *Preserving Nature,* 98–99.

42. Superintendent's Annual Report, 1932; Neal Guse, Ben Rice, Lee Carr, and Richard Denney, "Rocky Mountain Cooperative Elk Studies: Preliminary Report 1962–1963," 1 April 1964, NADRG79, Numerical Subject files 1953–1965, Box 14 8ns-079-97-437, ff "Wildlife Jan. 63-Dec. 64 Elk," 14.

43. Superintendent's Monthly Report, November 1932.

44. Superintendent's Annual Report, 1935.

45. Ibid., 1937.

46. Ibid., 1938.

47. Guse, et al., "Rocky Mountain Cooperative Elk Studies," 33.

48. Fred Mallery Packard, "Wildlife and Aspen in Rocky Mountain National Park, Colorado," *Ecology* 23 (October 1942): 478–482.

49. Ibid., 481.

50. Ibid., 478.

51. Ibid., 480.

52. "Elk and Vegetation Management Plan," 15.

53. RMNP Annual Report, 1945.

54. "Elk and Vegetation Management Plan," 15.

55. Fred Mallery Packard, "Study of the Deer and Elk Herds of Rocky Mountain National Park, Colorado," *Journal of Mammalogy* 1 (February 1947): 4–12.

56. Ibid., 11.

57. Ibid.

58. Ibid., 12.

59. Neal Guse Jr., "Effective Management Program Requirements for Eastern Rocky Mountain Deer and Elk Herds," n.d., NADRG79, Numerical Subject Files 1953–1965, Box 14 8NS-8NS-079-97-437, ff "Wildlife Elk, 1 of 2," 3.

60. Ibid.

61. Superintendent's Annual Report, 1950.

62. Ibid., 1951.

63. Ibid., 1952.

64. C. N. Feast to Cal Queal, Denver, 13 January 1962, NADRG 79, Numerical Subject Files 1953–1965, Box 14, 8NS-079-97-437, ff "Wildlife Elk 1 of 2".

65. Stanley Browman to Superintendent RMNP, 14 December 1954, NADRG79, Numerical Subject Files 1953–1965, Box 14 8ns-079-97-437, ff "Wildlife Elk 2 of 2."

66. Mrs. RJ Thornburg to Fred Packard, 13 March 1952, NADRG 79, Numerical Subject Files 1953–1965, Box 14 8ns-079-97-437, ff "Wildlife Elk 2 of 2."

67. Guse, "Effective Management Program," 3.

68. "Long Range Management Plan for the Eastern Rocky Mountain Elk and Deer," 2 October 1961, NADRG79, Numerical Subject Files 1953–1965, Box 14 8ns-079-97-437, ff "Wildlife Elk 2 of 2."

69. James Cole to Superintendent of RMNP, n.d., NADRG79, Numerical Subject Files 1953–1965, Box 15 8ns-079-97-437, ff "Wildlife Mgt. 57–62."

70. Press Release, 19 October 1961, NADRG79, Numerical Subject Files 1953–1965, Box 14 8ns-079-97-437, ff "Wildlife Elk 2 of 2."

71. It is interesting to note that allowing the population dynamics of the elk themselves to serve as the sole means of regulating their numbers, known as natural regulation and referred to here as "cruel," would soon become the centerpiece of elk management in Yellowstone National Park.

72. "Press Release."

73. Dewey Brown to Stewart Udall, 12 January 1962, NADRG79 Numerical Subject Files 1953–1965, Box 14 8NS-079-97-437, ff "Wildlife Elk 1 of 2."

74. Arthur Carhart to Conrad Wirth, 3 March 1961, NADRG79, Numerical Subject Files 1953–1965, Box 14 8NS-8NS-079-97-437, ff "Wildlife Elk, 2 of 2," 3.

75. Ibid., 4.

76. *Denver Post*, 21 January 1962, NADRG79, Numerical Subject Files 1953–1965, Box 14 8NS-8NS-079-97-437, ff "Wildlife Elk, 1 of 2."

77. Ibid.

78. Regional Director to Superintendent of RMNP, 17 January 1962, NAD-RG79, Numerical Subject Files 1953–1965, Box 14 8NS-8NS-079-97-437, ff "Wildlife Elk, 1 of 2."

79. *Rocky Mountain News*, 3 February 1962.

80. Guse, "Effective Management Program," 6, 8.

81. Ibid.; Guse, et al., "Rocky Mountain Cooperative Elk Studies," 41.

82. Guse, "Effective Management Program," 18.

83. Guse, et al., "Rocky Mountain Cooperative Elk Studies," 28.

84. Ibid., 28.

85. Ibid., 41.

86. Ibid., 16.

87. Linda C. Zeignefuss, Francis J. Singer, and David Bowden, "Vegetation Responses Following the Release of Elk from Artificial Controls within Rocky Mountain National Park, 1968–92," 21 March 1997, Rocky Mountain National Park Library, 2.

88. Hess, *Rocky Times*, 24.

89. Zeignefuss, et al., "Vegetation Responses," 2.

90. "Elk and Vegetation Management Plan," 8.

91. Ibid., 2.

92. Ibid.

93. Ibid., 1.

94. Ibid., 7, 9.

95. "Elk Management Plan Rocky Mountain National Park, 1960–1961," 6.

96. William L. Baker, Jennifer A. Munroe, and Amy E. Hessl, "The Effects of Elk on Aspen in the Winter Range in Rocky Mountain National Park," *Ecography* 20 (1997), 155.

97. "Elk and Vegetation Management Plan," 10.

98. Ibid.

99. "Elk Management Plan Rocky Mountain National Park, 1960–1961," 7.

100. "Elk and Vegetation Management Plan," 11.

101. Ibid.

102. Zeignefuss, et al., "Vegetation Responses," 14.

103. Ibid., 4.

104. "Elk and Vegetation Management Plan," i, 50.

105. *Denver Post*, 12 December 2007, "Birth Control to be Tried on Colorado Elk," at http://www.denverpost.com/news/ci_7830310 (accessed 24 November 2012).

CHAPTER 6. FISHING FOR TOURISTS

1. The author wishes to express his sincere thanks to Rocky Mountain National Park fisheries biologist Chris Kennedy for generously shar-

ing his private research collection and expertise on the fish of Colorado.

2. "Greenback Trout Recovery Plan" (Denver: U.S. Fish and Wildlife Service, 1998), 1.

3. Patrick C. Trotter, *Cutthroat: Native Trout of the West* (Boulder: Colorado Associated University Press, 1987), 11–12.

4. Ibid., 12.

5. "Greenback Trout Recovery Plan," 11.

6. Ibid., 10.

7. Robert Behnke, *Trout and Salmon of North America* (New York: The Free Press, 2002), 4.

8. Ibid.

9. Trotter, *Cutthroat*, 165.

10. *Rocky Mountain News*, 20 August 1868.

11. Ibid., 25 February 1874.

12. *Rocky Mountain News Weekly*, 22 July 1874.

13. C. F. Orvis and A. N. Cheney (eds.), *Fishing with the Fly: Sketches by Lovers of the Art, With Illustrations of Standard Flies* (Troy, NY: H. B. Nims, 1885), 145–155.

14. Frank S. Byers, *Sports Afield* 3 (August 1889), 282.

15. Joseph Taylor III, *Making Salmon: An Environmental History of the Northwest Fisheries Crisis* (Seattle: University of Washington Press, 1999), 69.

16. Margaret Beattie Bogue, "To Save the Fish: Canada, the United States, the Great Lakes, and the Joint Commission of 1892," *Journal of American History* 79 (March 1993), 1439.

17. Taylor, *Making Salmon*, 75.

18. Ibid., 76–77. It is worth noting that while the United States turned increasingly toward fish culture to address the problem of overfishing, Canada was more willing to embrace more stringent regulation.

19. Wilson Sisty, "Biennial Report of the Fish Commissioner of the State of Colorado for the Two Years 1879–80" (Denver: Tribune Publishing Company, 1880), 34.

20. John Pierce, "Report of the State Fish Commissioner of Colorado for 1886" (Denver: Collier and Cleveland Lithographic Company, 1886), 5. Colorado also benefited from the construction of a federal fish hatchery in 1889.

21. E. B. Gorton, "Trout Fishing in Estes Park," *Sports Afield* 9 (June 1892): 33–34.

22. Timothy R. Cummings, "Brook Trout Competition with Greenback Cutthroat Trout in Hidden Valley Creek Colorado" (Master's thesis, Colorado State University, 1987), iix–ix.

23. J. S. Swan, "Biennial Report of the State Forest, Game and Fish Com-

missioner of the State of Colorado for the Years 1897 and 1898" (Denver: Smith-Brooks Printing Company, 1898), 25.

24. Ibid., 33.

25. *Outdoor Life*, January 1905, 88, in Chris Kennedy Collection, Rocky Mountain National Park. Hereafter cited as CKC.

26. *Longmont Ledger*, 23 June 1895.

27. Roger Bergquist, *Historical Estes Park: Pictorial Edition* (Estes Park, CO: Estes Park Trail, 1968), 35.

28. *The Mountaineer*, 11 June 1907; *Mountaineer*, August 6, 1907; *Mountaineer*, 13 August 1907; *Mountaineer*, 27 August 1908; *Longmont Ledger*, 7 May 1907.

29. *Estes Park Trail*, 24 August 1912.

30. Ibid.

31. J. S. Swan, "Biennial Report of the State Forest, Game and Fish Commissioner of the State of Colorado for the Years 1897 and 1898" (Denver: Smith-Brooks Printing Company, 1898), 27.

32. "Greenback Trout Recovery Plan," 13.

33. Nick Karas, *Brook Trout: A Thorough Look at North America's Great Native Trout—Its History, Biology, and Angling Possibilities* (Guilford, CT: Lyons Press, 1997), chs. 11–18.

34. James A. Shinn, "Biennial Report of the State Game and Fish Commissioner of the State of Colorado for the Years 1911–12" (Denver: Smith-Brooks Printing Company, 1912), 18.

35. James Pritchard, *Preserving Yellowstone's Natural Conditions: Science and the Perception of Nature* (Lincoln: University of Nebraska Press, 1999), 79; Richard West Sellars, *Preserving Nature in the National Parks: A History* (New Haven: Yale University Press, 1997), 23. Yellowstone was first stocked in 1881.

36. Pritchard, *Preserving Yellowstone's Natural Conditions*, 79–83.

37. Roger Toll to Director of the National Park Service, 29 September 1922, NARG79 Central Files 1907–1939, E6, Box 159 Rocky Mountain Employment General to Estes (1913–1915), ff "fish hatchery."

38. Arno B. Cammerer to Henry O'Malley, 3 October 1922, NARG79 Central Files 1907–1939, E6, Box 159 Rocky Mountain Employment General to Estes (1913–1915), ff "fish hatchery."

39. *Estes Park Trail*, 8 August 1930.

40. Superintendent's Annual Report, 1932.

41. Of the estimated 16,000 historically fishless mountain lakes in the western United States, upward of 95 percent of the "larger, deeper lakes now contain nonnative trout." Roland Knapp, Paul Corn, and Daniel Schindler, "The Introduction of Nonnative Fish into Wilder-

ness Lakes: Good Intentions, Conflicting Mandates, and Unintended Consequences," *Ecosystems* 4 (June 2001): 275.

42. Ibid.

43. Ibid., 276.

44. David Pilliod and Charles Peterson, "Local and Landscape Effects of Introduced Trout on Amphibians in Historically Fishless Watersheds," *Ecosystems* 4 (June 2001): 322.

45. Ibid., 323. For more examples of the impact of stocking historically fishless water, see A. S. McNaught, et al., "Restoration of the Food Web of an Alpine Lake Following Fish Stocking," *Limnology and Oceanography* 44 (1999), 127–136.

46. Susan Adams, Christopher Frissell, and Bruce Reiman, "Geography of Invasion in Mountain Streams: Consequences of Headwater Lake Fish Introductions," *Ecosystems* 4 (June 2001): 296.

47. Ibid., 302.

48. *Estes Park Trail*, 30 September 1935.

49. Melvin Potts, Field Notes, 15 May 1936, as cited in CKC, 18.

50. George M. Wright, Joseph S. Dixon, and Ben H. Thompson, "Fauna of the National Parks of the United States: A Preliminary Survey of Faunal Relations in the National Parks, Contributions of Wildlife Survey" (Washington, D.C.: U.S. Government Printing Office, 1933), 1.

51. Ibid., 63.

52. Lisa Mighetto, *Wild Animals and American Environmental Ethics* (Tucson: University of Arizona Press, 1991).

53. Ibid., 56.

54. Wright, et al., "Fauna No. 1," 63–64.

55. "Information Bulletin, Rocky Mountain National Park," 26 May 1936, as cited in CKC.

56. Roger Toll to Director of the National Park Service, 10 December 1923, NARG79, Box 159, E6 PI 166, Central Files 1907–1939 ff "Fish Hatchery."

57. "Information Bulletin."

58. Ibid.

59. *Estes Park Trail*, 13 May 1938.

60. *Estes Park Trail*, 2 September 1938.

61. Superintendent's Annual Report, 1940–1941. Some 900,000 fingerlings were planted in the park in 1940 and 254,160 more in 1941.

62. David H. Madsen, "Report of David H. Madsen," 20 February 1941, RMNP Resource Management Files, RMNP Archives, 1–2. CKC.

63. Ibid., 2–3.

64. Superintendent's Annual Report, 1943.

65. Stillman Wright, "A Report on Some Fishery Problems in Rocky Mountain National Park, 1944," RMNP Resource Management Files, RMNP Archives, 1–2, CKC.

66. Superintendent's Annual Report, 1949, 1950, and 1952.

67. "Report on 1957 Studies on the Green Back Trout in Rocky Mountain National Park," CKC ff "1959 Rocky Mountain National Park Report," 1.

68. Ibid.

69. Oliver Cope, "Report on 1959 Fishery Studies by the Bureau of Sport Fisheries and Wildlife in Rocky Mountain National Park," 15 October 1959, NADRG79, Numerical Subject Files 1953–1965, Box 13, 8NS-079-97-437, ff "Wildlife Fish, 1953–1962."

70. Ibid., 1.

71. Ibid., 7.

72. Ibid., 10.

73. Ibid., 11.

74. Ibid., 4.

75. Ibid.

76. "Supplement to Report 10A5 1959 Annual Fish Planting Report, Rocky Mountain National Park," NADRG79, Numerical Subject Files 1953–65, Box 13, 8NS-079-97-437, ff "Wildlife Fish, 1961–1962."

77. O. L. Wallis, "An Evaluation of the Fishery Resources of Rocky Mountain National Park and Needs for Interpretation, Research, and Management," NADRG79, Numerical Subject Files 1953–1965, Box 13, 8NS-079-97-437, ff "Wildlife Fish," 3.

78. Robert Azevedo and O. L. Wallis, "Inter-Agency Lake Surveys and Trout Investigations Rocky Mountain National Park, 1961," 15 February 1961, NADRG79, Numerical Subject Files 1953–1965, Box 13, 8NS-079-97-437, ff "Wildlife Fish, 1961–1962," 10.

79. Ibid., 11.

80. Orthello L. Wallis, "The Challenge of Fishing for Fun" (National Convention of Trout, Unlimited, Allenberry, PA, 7 September 1963), NADRG79, Numerical Subject Files 1952–1965, Box 15 8ns-079-97-437, ff "Fish."

81. Ibid.

82. Ibid.

83. Greenback Trout Recovery Team, "Greenback Trout Recovery Plan" (Denver: U.S. Fish and Wildlife Service, 1998, mimeographed), 1.

84. Ibid., 59.

85. *Estes Park Trail*, 29 December 1989.

86. "Greenback Trout Recovery Plan," 45–50.

87. Ibid., 17.

88. Ibid., 62.

89. Jessica Metcalf, "Conservation Genetics of the Greenback Cutthroat Trout (*Oncorhynchus clarkii stomias*)" (Ph.D. diss., University of Colorado, 2007).

90. Josie Garthwaite, "Rare Trout Survives in Just One Stream, DNA Reveals," *New York Times*, at http://green.blogs.nytimes.com/2012/09/25/rare -trout-survives-in-just-one-stream-dna-reveals/ (accessed 11 November 2012).

91. Front Range Anglers, http://frontrangeanglers.com/rocky-mountain -national-park-fishing (accessed 11 November 2012).

CHAPTER 7. SLIPPERY SLOPES

1. Annie Gilbert Coleman, *Ski Style: Sport and Culture in the Rockies* (Lawrence: University Press of Kansas, 2004), 16.

2. Ibid., 17–19.

3. Ibid., 23–26.

4. Ibid., 34, 36.

5. Superintendent's Annual Report, 1917.

6. Ibid., 1919.

7. Ibid., 1923.

8. Ibid., 1926.

9. "Work Program Design—Environmental Inventory and Assessment Document For Hidden Valley Winter Sports Area" (National Park Service, 1973), Denver Service Center, ROMO_121_D1.

10. *Rocky Mountain News*, 31 October 1915.

11. *Longmont Ledger*, 5 November 1915.

12. "Work Program Design."

13. "Resolution of the Loveland Chamber of Commerce" (1932), RARG79 Central Classified Files 1933–1949, Box 1574, ff "Winter Sports."

14. *Circular of General Information regarding Rocky Mountain National Park, Colorado* (U.S. Department of the Interior, 1932), Estes Park Museum, Box Estes Park Souvenirs and Pamphlets.

15. Coleman, *Ski Style*, 87, 85.

16. Jack C. Moomaw, *Recollections of a Rocky Mountain Ranger* (YMCA of the Rockies, 1994), 165–167.

17. Edmund Rogers to Director A. B. Cammerer, 17 January 1935, NARAG79 Central Classified Files 1933–1949, Box 1574, ff "Winter Sports."

18. Ibid.

19. Charles H. Page and John G. Turnbull, "Badger Pass Ski Area Yosemite National Park, California, Determination of Eligibility," 13 August 2009, at http://www.nps.gov/yose/historyculture/upload/Badger-Pass -low-res.pdf (accessed 6 June 2012), 24.

20. Ibid., 27.

21. Ibid., 29.

22. A. B. Cammerer to Superintendent Rogers, 28 October 1935, NARG79 Central Classified Files 1933–1949, Box 1574, ff "Winter Sports."

23. Editorial, *Estes Park Trail*, 20 March 1936, in Katherine Howes Barth and Ann Alexander Leggett, *Finding Hidden Valley: A Recollective History of a Colorado Ski Area* (Boulder: White Sands Lake Press, 2006).

24. Superintendent Allen to NPS Director, 30 March 1937, NARG79, Central Classified Files 1933–1949, Box 1574, ff "Winter Sports."

25. *Estes Park Trail*, 26 March 1937.

26. *Estes Park Trail*, 11 February 1938, in Barth and Leggett, *Finding Hidden Valley*, 32–33.

27. Barth and Leggett, *Finding Hidden Valley*, 35.

28. Roe Emery to Paul Hauk and Charles Hardin, n.d., Estes Park Museum, ff "Hidden Valley Ski Area."

29. NPS Press Release (U.S. Department of the Interior Information Service), 7 December 1941, NARG79 Central Classified Files 1933–1949, Box 1574, ff "Winter Sports," 1941.

30. Lloyd K. Musselman, *Rocky Mountain National Park: Administrative History, 1915–1965* (U.S. Department of the Interior, 1971), at http://www.nps.gov/history/history/online_books/romo/adhi.htm (accessed 6 October 2008), ch. xi.

31. Barth and Leggett, *Finding Hidden Valley*, 41.

32. Lawrence Merriam to Superintendent of Rocky, 14 December 1945, RARG79 Central Classified Files 1933–1949, Box 1574, ff "Winter Sports."

33. "Report of winter use in ROMO, 1946" (National Park Service), RARG-79 Central Classified Files 1933–1949, Box 1574, ff "Winter Sports."

34. David Canfield to Region Two Director, 9 May 1946, with excerpts from Mill Creek Report, RARG79 Central Classified Files 1933–1949, Box 1574, ff "Winter Sports."

35. "Report of winter use in ROMO," 1946.

36. Memorandum from the Superintendent of Rocky Mountain National Park, 1 August 1947, NARG79 Central Classified Files 1933–1949, Box 1574, ff "Winter Sports."

37. Robert C. Ruark, "Mr. Ruark Finds Skiing Is Just a Disease," *Rocky Mountain News*, 10 February 1947.

38. Coleman, *Ski Style*, 60–63.

39. Ibid., 118, 121, 122.

40. Secretary of the Interior (J. A. Krug) to Senator Johnson (Colorado), 18 February 1949, NARG79 Central Classified Files 1933–1949, Box 1574, ff "Winter Sports."

41. "About the 21st Annual Summer Ski Jump," n.d., Estes Park Museum, Box Estes Park Winter Sports Club, ff "Org. History."

42. "Bulletin no. 14, Estes Park Chamber of Commerce, 7 August 1953," NARG79 Administrative Files, 1949–1971 L3427 to LL3427, Box 1933 Entry P11, ff "L3427, Part I Recreational Activities (Winter Sports) From September 1949–December 1953."

43. George Peck Jr. and Fred Clatworthy, "Prospectus for Development of a Ski Area at Hidden Valley, Estes Park, Colorado, Commensurate with Other Ski Areas in Colorado and in Other National Parks," November 1952, NARG79 Administrative Files 1949–1971, Box 1935, Entry 11, ff "L3427 Rocky Mountain Hidden Valley," 2–7.

44. Ibid., 8.

45. Coleman, *Ski Style*, 140.

46. Helen Dean to Superintendent David Canfield, 8 September 1953, NARG79 Administrative Files, 1949–1971 L3427 to LL3427, Box 1933, Entry P11, ff L3427 Part I "Recreational Activities (Winter Sports) From September 1949–December 1953."

47. Devereux Butcher, Draft, "A Chair Lift for Rocky Mountain National Park?" *National Parks Magazine*, NARG79 Administrative Files, 1949–1971 L3427 to LL3427, Box 1933, Entry P11, ff "L3427 Part I Recreational Activities (Winter Sports) From September 1949–December 1953."

48. Harold Fowler, "A Report on the Potentialities of Hidden Valley as a Winter Use Area, Rocky Mountain National Park" (National Park Service, March 1953), Denver Numerical Subject Files, 1952–1965, Box 11, 8NS-079-97-437, ff "L3427 1960–1964," 8–12.

49. Ibid., 16.

50. Ibid., 18; Philip Baker to Conrad Wirth, 6 March 1953, NARG79 Administrative Files, 1949–1971 L3427 to LL3427, Box 1933, Entry P11, ff "L3427 Part I Recreational Activities (Winter Sports) From September 1949–December 1953."

51. Fowler, "A Report on the Potentialities," 21.

52. Ibid., 25.

53. Ibid., 26.

54. John Doerr to Director Conrad Wirth, 19 June 1953, NARG79 Administrative Files, 1949–1971 L3427 to LL3427, Box 1933, Entry P11, ff "L3427 Part I Recreational Activities (Winter Sports) From September 1949–December 1953."

55. John Doerr to Director Conrad Wirth, 25 May 1953, NARG79 Administrative Files, 1949–1971 L3427 to LL3427, Box 1933, Entry P11, ff "L3427 Part I Recreational Activities (Winter Sports) From September 1949–December 1953."

56. Conrad Wirth to Director, Region Two, 14 October 1953, NARG79 Administrative Files, 1949–1971 L3427 to LL3427, Box 1933, Entry P11, ff "L3427 Part I Recreational Activities (Winter Sports) From September

1949–December 1953"; Conrad Wirth to Howard Baker, 4 December 1953, NARG79 Administrative Files, 1949–1971 L3427 to LL3427, Box 1933, Entry P11, ff "L3427 Part I Recreational Activities (Winter Sports) From September 1949–December 1953."

57. Harold Fowler to Conrad Wirth, "CONFIDENTIAL," 8 October 1953, NARG79 Administrative Files, 1949–1971 L3427 to LL3427, Box 1933, Entry P11, ff "L3427 Part I Recreational Activities (Winter Sports) From September 1949–December 1953."

58. Conrad Wirth to David Brower, 18 December 1953, NARG79 Administrative Files, 1949–1971 L3427 to LL3427, Box 1933, Entry P11, ff "L3427 Part I Recreational Activities (Winter Sports) From September 1949–December 1953."

59. *Denver Post*, 29 January 1954; *Denver Post*, 16 July 1954, in Barth and Leggett, *Finding Hidden Valley*, 71.

60. Barth and Leggett, *Finding Hidden Valley*, 93.

61. Chester F. McQueary to Conrad Wirth, 28 July 1958, NADRG79, Denver Numerical Subject Files, 1953–1965, Box 24, 8NS-079-437, ff "Complaints 54–60."

62. Harold G. Fowler, "Report on Meeting at Rocky Mountain National Park regarding the Future Development of Hidden Valley (National Park Service)," NADRG79, Denver Numerical Subject Files, 1952–1965, Box 11, 8NS-079-97-437, ff "L3427 1960–1964," 1.

63. Ibid., 2–4.

64. Ibid., 4–5.

65. "Operational Report Hidden Valley Winter Use Area, 1959–1960 Season" (National Park Service), Rocky Mountain National Park Archives, Temporary Box 54, 2.

66. Ibid., 13.

67. Ibid., 20.

68. Coleman, *Ski Style*, 151.

69. Letter, Assistant NPS Director Lawrence Hadley to Senator John Tower, 11 November 1971, NARG79 Administration Files, 1949–1971, Box 2645, Entry P11 ff "A3615 ROMO pt. 1."

70. "Environmental Inventory and Assessment, Hidden Valley Winter Sports Area, Rocky Mountain National Park, Colorado" (U.S. Department of the Interior, National Park Service, 1973).

71. Ibid.

72. Ibid. (emphasis in original).

73. Ibid.

74. "Sewage System, East Side, Rocky Mountain National Park, Environmental Assessment" (U.S. Department of the Interior, 1974), 2.

75. Ibid., 13.

76. Ibid., 2.
77. "Final Environmental Statement, Proposed Master Plan Rocky Mountain National Park, Colorado" (National Park Service, 1975), 14–15.
78. Ibid., 43.
79. Ibid., 91.
80. Barth and Leggett, *Finding Hidden Valley*, 185–189.
81. "Economic Feasibility Study: Concessions Operations—Ski Estes Park. Hidden Valley, Rocky Mountain National Park, Estes Park, Colorado" (U.S. Department of the Interior, Denver Service Center, Professional Support Division, Concessions Branch, 1989), 3.
82. Ibid., 6.
83. Ibid., 4.
84. Ibid., 3, 14.
85. Ibid., 14–15.
86. Barth and Leggett, *Finding Hidden Valley*, 193.
87. Ibid., 196.

CONCLUSION

1. William D. Bowman, Julia R. Gartner, Keri Holland, and Magdalena Widermann, "Nitrogen Critical Loads for Alpine Vegetation and Terrestrial Ecosystem Response: Are We There Yet?" *Ecological Applications* 16 (2006): 1183.
2. "The Impact of Travel on State Economies 2009" (U.S. Travel Association, Research Report), at http://commerce.idaho.gov/assets/content/docs/Research/Impact%20of%20Travel%20on%20State%20Economies%2009.pdf (accessed 21 November 2012), 72–73, 80 (travel defined as "activities associated with all overnight trips away from home in paid accommodations, and day and overnight trips to places 50 miles or more, one way, from the traveler's origin").
3. "A Snapshot of the Economic Impact of Outdoor Recreation" (Southwick Associates, Inc., 2012), at http://www.outdoorindustry.org/images/researchfiles/SnapshotEconomicImpact.pdf?160 (accessed 21 November 2012), 3.
4. Ibid., 1.
5. Donald Worster, *Nature's Economy: A History of Ecological Ideas*, 2nd ed. (Oxford: Oxford University Press, 1994), ix–x.

SELECTED BIBLIOGRAPHY

COLLECTIONS AND ARCHIVES
Chris Kennedy Collection
Denver Public Library, Western History Collection
Estes Park Museum
Estes Park Public Library
National Archives II
National Archives Central Plains Region, Kansas City, MO
National Archives Rocky Mountain Region, Denver, CO
National Park Service, Denver Service Center
Rocky Mountain National Park Archive
Rocky Mountain National Park Library

SELECTED SOURCES
Abbot, Carl. *How Cities Won the West: Four Centuries of Urban Change in Western North America.* Albuquerque: University of New Mexico Press, 2008.
Abbot, Carl, Stephen Leonard, and David McComb. *Colorado: A History of the Centennial State.* Niwot, CO: University Press of Colorado, 1992.
Adams, Susan, Christopher Frissell, and Bruce Reiman. "Geography of Invasion in Mountain Streams: Consequences of Headwater Lake Fish Introductions." *Ecosystems* 4, no. 4 (2001): 296–307.
Allaback, Sarah. *Mission 66 Visitor Centers: The History of a Building Type.* Washington, DC: Department of the Interior, National Park Service, 2000.
Allen, John B. *From Skisport to Skiing: One Hundred Years of an American Sport, 1840–1940.* Amherst: University of Massachusetts Press, 1993.
Baker, William. *Fire Ecology in Rocky Mountain Landscapes.* Washington, DC: Island Press, 2009.
Baker, William L., Jennifer A. Munroe, and Amy E. Hessl. "The Effects of Elk on Aspen in the Winter Range in Rocky Mountain National Park." *Ecography* 20 (1997): 155–165.
Barringer, Mark Daniel. *Selling Yellowstone: Capitalism and the Construction of Nature.* Lawrence: University Press of Kansas, 2002.
Barth, Katherine Howes, and Ann Alexander Leggett. *Finding Hidden Valley: A Recollective History of a Colorado Ski Area.* Boulder: White Sands Lake Press, 2006.
Behnke, Robert. *Trout and Salmon of North America.* New York: The Free Press, 2002.
Black, Michael. "Tragic Remedies: A Century of Failed Fishery Policy on California's Sacramento River." *Pacific Historical Review* 64, no. 1 (1995): 37–70.
Bogue, Margaret Beattie. "To Save the Fish: Canada, the United States, the Great Lakes, and the Joint Commission of 1892." *Journal of American History* 79, no. 4 (1993): 1429–1454.

Borne, Lawrence R. *Dude Ranching: A Complete History.* Albuquerque: University of New Mexico Press, 1983.

Bowman, William D., Julia R. Gartner, Keri Holland, and Magdalena Widermann. "Nitrogen Critical Loads for Alpine Vegetation and Terrestrial Ecosystem Response: Are We There Yet?" *Ecological Applications* 16, no. 3 (2006): 1183–1193.

Buchholtz, C. W. *Rocky Mountain National Park: A History.* Boulder: Associated University Press of Colorado, 1983.

Buechling, Arne, and William Baker. "A Fire History from Tree Rings in a High-Elevation Forest of Rocky Mountain National Park," *Canadian Journal of Forest Research* 34, no. 6 (2004): 1259–1273.

Carr, Ethan. *Mission 66: Modernism and the National Park Dilemma.* Amherst: University of Massachusetts Press, 2007.

———. *Wilderness by Design: Landscape Architecture and the National Park Service.* Lincoln: University of Nebraska Press, 1998.

Catton, Theodore. *National Park, City Playground: Mount Rainer in the Twentieth Century.* Seattle: University of Washington Press, 2006.

Chase, Alston. *Playing God in Yellowstone: The Destruction of America's First National Park.* Boston: Atlantic Monthly Press, 1986.

Clifford, Hal. *Downhill Slide: Why the Corporate Ski Industry Is Bad for Skiing.* San Francisco: Sierra Club Books, 2002.

Coleman, Annie Gilbert. *Ski Style: Sport and Culture in the Rockies.* Lawrence: University Press of Kansas, 2004.

———. "The Unbearable Whiteness of Skiing." *Pacific Historical Review* 65, no. 4 (1996): 583–614.

Cronin, Keri. *Manufacturing National Park Nature: Photography, Ecology, and the Wilderness Industry of Jasper.* Vancouver: UBC [University of British Columbia] Press, 2001.

Cronon, William. *Nature's Metropolis: Chicago and the Great West.* New York: W. W. Norton, 1991.

Drummond, Alexander. *Enos Mills: Citizen of Nature.* Boulder: University Press of Colorado, 1995.

Dunlap, Thomas R. *Saving America's Wildlife.* Princeton: Princeton University Press, 1988.

———. "Wildlife, Science, and the National Parks, 1920–1940." *Pacific Historical Review* 59, no. 2 (1990): 187–202.

Etulain, Richard W., and Ferenc Morton Szasz, eds. *The American West in 2000.* Albuquerque: University of New Mexico Press, 2003.

Flader, Susan L. *Thinking Like a Mountain: Aldo Leopold and the Evolution of an Ecological Attitude toward Deer, Wolves, and Forests.* Columbia: University of Missouri Press, 1974.

Foresta, Ronald A. *America's National Parks and Their Keepers.* Washington, DC: Resources for the Future, 1984.

Fry, John. *The Story of Modern Skiing.* Hanover: University Press of New England, 2006.

Hadley, K., and Thomas Veblen. "Stand Response to Western Spruce Budworm and Douglas-Fir Bark Beetle Outbreaks, Colorado Front Range." *Canadian Journal of Forest Resources* 23, no. 3 (1993): 479–491.

Hays, Samuel P. *Beauty, Health, and Permanence: Environmental Politics in the United States, 1955–1985.* Cambridge: Cambridge University Press, 1989.

———. *Conservation and the Gospel of Efficiency: The Progressive Conservation Movement, 1890–1920.* Pittsburgh: University of Pittsburgh Press, 1999.

Hess, Karl. *Rocky Times in Rocky Mountain National Park: An Unnatural History.* Niwot: University Press of Colorado, 1993.

Hunter, Colin, and Howard Green. *Tourism and the Environment: A Sustainable Relationship?* London: Routledge, 1995.

Hussey, Christopher. *The Picturesque: Studies in a Point of View.* 2nd ed. London: Frank Cass, 1967.

Hyde, Anne Farrar. *An American Vision: Far Western Landscape and National Culture, 1820–1920.* New York: New York University Press, 1990.

Jackson, Kenneth T. *Crabgrass Frontier: The Suburbanization of the United States.* Oxford: Oxford University Press, 1985.

Jacoby, Karl. *Crimes against Nature: Squatters, Poachers, Thieves, and the Hidden History of American Conservation.* Berkley: University of California Press, 2001.

Jakle, John A. *The Tourist: Travel in Twentieth-Century North America.* Lincoln: University of Nebraska Press, 1985.

Karas, Nick. *Brook Trout: A Thorough Look at North America's Great Native Trout—Its History, Biology, and Angling Possibilities.* Guilford, CT: Lyons Press, 1997.

Klingle, Matthew W. "Spaces of Consumption in Environmental History." *History and Theory* 42, no. 2 (2003): 94–110.

Knapp, Roland, Paul Corn, and Daniel Schindler. "The Introduction of Nonnative Fish into Wilderness Lakes: Good Intentions, Conflicting Mandates, and Unintended Consequences." *Ecosystems* 4, no. 4 (2001): 275–278.

Langston, Nancy. *Where Land and Water Meet: A Western Landscape Transformed.* Seattle: University of Washington Press, 2003.

Liddle, Michael. *Recreation Ecology: The Ecological Impact of Outdoor Recreation and Ecotourism.* London: Chapman and Hall, 1997.

Louter, David. *Windshield Wilderness: Cars, Roads, and Nature in Washington's National Parks.* Seattle: University of Washington Press, 2006.

Lowry, William R. *Repairing Paradise: The Restoration of Nature in America's National Parks.* Washington, DC: Brookings Institute Press, 2007.

———. *The Capacity For Wonder: Preserving National Parks.* Washington, DC: Brookings Institution, 1994.

Lynch, Heather J., Roy A. Renkin, Robert L. Crabtree, and Paul R. Moorcroft. "The Influence of Previous Mountain Pine Beetle (*Dendroctonus ponderosae*) Activity on the 1988 Yellowstone Fires." *Ecosystems* 9, no. 8 (December 2006): 1318–1327.

Macy, Christine, and Sarah Bonnemaison. *Architecture and Nature: Creating the American Landscape*. London: Routledge, 2003.

Magoc, Chris. *Yellowstone: The Creation and Selling of an American Landscape*. Albuquerque: University of New Mexico Press, 1999.

Maher, Neil. *Nature's New Deal: The Civilian Conservation Corps and the Roots of the American Environmental Movement*. Oxford: Oxford University Press, 2008.

McClelland, Linda Flint. *Building the National Parks: Historic Landscape Design and Construction*. Baltimore: Johns Hopkins University Press, 1998.

———. *Presenting Nature: The Historic Landscape Design of the National Park Service, 1916 to 1942*. Washington, DC: U.S. Government Printing Office, 1993.

McNaught, A. S., et al. "Restoration of the Food Web of an Alpine Lake following Fish Stocking." *Limnology and Oceanography* 44, no. 1 (1999): 127–136.

Metcalf, Jessica, S. Stowell, Chris Kennedy, and K. B. Rogers. "Historical Stocking Data and 19th Century DNA Reveal Human-Induced Changes to Native Diversity and Distribution of Cutthroat Trout." *Molecular Ecology* 21, no. 21 (2012): 1–14.

Mighetto, Lisa. *Wild Animals and American Environmental Ethics*. Tucson: University of Arizona Press, 1991.

Miller, Angela. *The Empire of the Eye: Landscape Representation and American Cultural Politics, 1825–1875*. Ithaca: Cornell University Press, 1993.

Miller, Char, and Hal Rothman, eds. *Out of the Woods: Essays in Environmental History*. Pittsburgh: University of Pittsburgh Press, 1997.

Moomaw, Jack C. *Recollections of a Rocky Mountain Ranger*. Estes Park, CO: YMCA of the Rockies, 1994.

Nash, Roderick. *Wilderness and the American Mind*. 3rd ed. New Haven: Yale University Press, 1982.

———. "The American Cult of the Primitive." *American Quarterly* 18, no. 3 (1966): 726–735.

———. "The American Invention of National Parks." *American Quarterly* 22, no. 3 (1970): 726–735.

Nicolson, Marjorie Hope. *Mountain Gloom and Mountain Glory: The Development of the Aesthetics of the Infinite*. Seattle: University of Washington Press, 1997.

O'Brien, Bob R. *Our National Parks and the Search for Sustainability*. Austin: University of Texas Press, 1999.

Packard, Fred Mallery. "Study of the Deer and Elk Herds of Rocky Mountain National Park, Colorado." *Journal of Mammalogy* 28, no. 1 (1947): 4–12.

———. "Wildlife and Aspen in Rocky Mountain National Park, Colorado." *Ecology* 23, no. 4 (1942): 478–482.

Pederson, Henry. *Those Castles of Wood: The Story of the Early Lodges of Rocky Mountain National Park and Pioneer Days of Estes Park, Colorado*. Estes Park, CO: Published by the Author, 1993.

Pickering, James. *America's Switzerland: Estes Park and Rocky Mountain National Park— the Growth Years*. Boulder: University Press of Colorado, 2005.

————. *This Blue Hollow: Estes Park—The Early Years, 1859–1915.* Boulder: University Press of Colorado, 1999.

Pilliod, David, and Charles Peterson. "Local and Landscape Effects of Introduced Trout on Amphibians in Historically Fishless Watersheds." *Ecosystems* 4, no. 4 (2001): 322–333.

Pohl, Francis K. *Framing America: A Social History of American Art.* New York: Thames & Hudson, 2002.

Pomeroy, Earl. *In Search of the Golden West: The Tourist in Western America.* New York: Alfred A. Knopf, 1957.

Pritchard, James. *Preserving Yellowstone's Natural Conditions: Science and the Perception of Nature.* Lincoln: University of Nebraska Press, 1999.

Pyne, Stephen. *Fire in America: A Cultural History of Wildland and Rural Fire.* Seattle: University of Washington Press, 1997.

————. "Fire Policy and Fire Research in the U.S. Forest Service." *Journal of Forest History* 25, no. 2 (1981): 64–77.

————. *World Fire: The Culture of Fire on Earth.* Seattle: University of Washington Press, 1997.

Reed, Nathaniel P., and Dennis Drabelle. *The United States Fish and Wildlife Service.* Boulder: Westview Press, 1984.

Reiger, John F. *American Sportsmen and the Origins of Conservation.* Rev. ed. Norman: University of Oklahoma Press, 1986.

Righter, Robert. *The Battle over Hetch Hetchy: America's Most Controversial Dam and the Birth of Modern Conservation.* Oxford: Oxford University Press, 2005.

————. *Crucible for Conservation: The Creation of Grand Teton National Park.* Boulder: Colorado Associated University Press, 1982.

————. "National Monuments to National Parks: The Use of the Antiquities Act of 1906." *Western Historical Quarterly* 20, no. 3 (1989): 281–301.

Robinson, Donald H. *Through the Years in Glacier National Park: An Administrative History.* West Glacier, MT: Glacier Natural History Association, 1960.

Rome, Adam. *The Bulldozer in the Countryside: Suburban Sprawl and the Rise of American Environmentalism.* Cambridge: Cambridge University Press, 2001.

Rothman, Hal. *America's National Monuments: The Politics of Preservation.* Lawrence: University Press of Kansas, 1989.

————. *Blazing Heritage: A History of Wildland Fire in the National Parks.* Oxford: Oxford University Press, 2007.

————, ed. *The Culture of Tourism, the Tourism of Culture: Selling the Past to the Present in the American Southwest.* Albuquerque: University of New Mexico Press, 2003.

————. *Devil's Bargains: Tourism in the Twentieth-Century American West.* Lawrence: University Press of Kansas, 1998.

————. "'A Regular Ding-Dong Fight': Agency Culture and Evolution in the NPS-USFS Dispute, 1916–1937." *Western Historical Quarterly* 20, no. 2 (1989): 141–161.

————, ed. *Reopening the American West.* Tucson: University of Arizona Press, 1998.

————. "Selling the Meaning of Place: Entrepreneurship, Tourism, and Community

Transformation in the Twentieth-Century American West." *Pacific Historical Review* 65, no. 4 (1996): 525–557.

———. "A Test of Adversity and Strength: Wildland Fire in the National Park System." Department of the Interior, National Park Service, n.d.

Runte, Alfred. *National Parks: The American Experience.* 2nd ed. Lincoln: University of Nebraska Press, 1979.

———. *Yosemite: Embattled Wilderness.* Lincoln: University of Nebraska Press, 1990.

Russell, Edmund. *War and Nature: Fighting Humans and Insects with Chemicals from World War I to* Silent Spring. Cambridge: Cambridge University Press, 2001.

Schein, Richard. "The Place of Landscape: A Conceptual Framework for Interpreting an American Scene." *Annals of the Association of American Geographers* 87, no. 4 (1997): 660–680.

Schullery, Paul. *Searching for Yellowstone: Ecology and Wonder in the Last Wilderness.* Boston: Houghton Mifflin, 1997.

Sellars, Richard West. *Preserving Nature in the National Parks.* New Haven: Yale University Press, 1997.

Shackel, Paul, ed. *Myth, Memory, and the Making of the American Landscape.* Gainsville: University Press of Florida, 2001.

Shaffer, Marguerite S. "'See America First': Re-Envisioning Nation and Region though Western Tourism." *Pacific Historical Review* 65, no. 4 (1996): 559–581.

———. *See America First: Tourism and National Identity, 1880–1940.* Washington, DC: Smithsonian Institution Press, 2001.

Sibold, Jason S., Thomas Veblen, and Mauro E. González. "Spatial and Temporal Variation in Historic Fire Regimes in Subalpine Forests across the Colorado Front Range in Rocky Mountain National Park, Colorado, USA." *Journal of Biogeography* 32 (2006): 644–645.

Sutter, Paul. *Driven Wild: How the Fight against Automobiles Launched the Modern Wilderness Movement.* Seattle: University of Washington Press, 2002.

Swain, Donald C. "The Passage of the National Park Service Act of 1916." *Wisconsin Magazine of History* 50, no. 1 (Autumn 1966): 4–17.

Taylor, Joseph III. *Making Salmon: An Environmental History of the Northwest Fisheries Crisis.* Seattle: University of Washington Press, 1999.

Toweill, E., and Jack Ward Thomas, eds. *North American Elk: Ecology and Management.* Washington, DC: Smithsonian Institution Press, 2002.

Trotter, Patrick C. *Cutthroat: Native Trout of the West.* Boulder: Colorado Associated University Press, 1987.

Tuan, Yi-Fu. *Space and Place: The Perspective of Experience.* Minneapolis: University of Minnesota Press, 1977.

Washabaugh, William, and Catherine Washabaugh. *Deep Trout: Angling in American Popular Culture.* New York: Berg, 2000.

West, Elliot. *Contested Plains: Indians, Goldseekers, and the Rush to Colorado.* Lawrence: University Press of Kansas, 1998.

Wirth, Conrad. *Parks, Politics, and the People.* Norman: University of Oklahoma Press, 1980.

Worster, Donald. *Nature's Economy: A History of Ecological Ideas.* 2nd ed. Cambridge: Cambridge University Press, 1994.

Wright, Gerald R. *Wildlife Research and Management in the National Parks.* Chicago: University of Illinois Press, 1992.

Wright, Leonard M. Jr., ed. *The Field and Stream Treasury of Trout Fishing.* New York: Lyons Press, 1986.

Wrobel, David, and Patrick Long, eds. *Seeing and Being Seen: Tourism in the American West.* Lawrence: University Press of Kansas, 2001.

Wyckoff, William. *Creating Colorado: The Making of a Western American Landscape, 1860–1940.* New Haven: Yale University Press, 1999.

Young, Emily. "State Intervention and Abuse of the Commons: Fisheries Development in Baja California Sur, Mexico." *Annals of the Association of American Geographers* 91, no. 2 (2001): 283–306.

Young, Terence. "Modern Urban Parks." *Geographical Review* 85, no. 4 (1995): 535–551.

INDEX

002375960